THEY PREYED UPON THEIR FELLOW MEN

Thief and highwayman, killer and cutthroat, here are the true stories of the world's most vicious criminals. Not for greed alone, but driven by an inhuman need for wanton savagery, their deeds haunt the pages of history.

Here are: the fabulous genius of crime who created a one-man empire of brigandage and blackmail . . .

the midwife whose warped mind devised horrible tortures to flay her helpless victims . . .

the "Bluebeard," wooing and killing lonely women, whose address book held the names of 283 potential victims . . .

the ghoulish partners whose business was delivering fresh corpses C.O.D. to anatomy students . . .

Through these pages stalk fifteen fiends who made the unspeakable their way of life. Gathered from authentic police and eye-witness records, you will find the full account of their dreadful lives displayed here.

Here are the true lives of—

SCOUNDRELS, FIENDS
and HUMAN MONSTERS

by
CLIFF HOWE

WILDSIDE PRESS

SCOUNDRELS, FIENDS AND HUMAN MONSTERS

FOREWORD

Ever since Cain first struck down his brother in anger, the lawless and the criminal have plagued mankind. But the fifteen whose stories are told here were more than outlaw or criminal; they were fiends who pillaged in the guise of men. Cruelty to them was a lust, murder a hunger, and they reveled in brutality and torture. For them, though many seemed motivated by greed, money was actually a by-product of their depradations and atrocities. Their real thirst was to bait and outsmart the law-abiding, to draw blood from their fellow man, to plunge into orgies of savagery and barbarity.

There was a demonic drive behind their depradations. The organizational genius that enabled Jonathan Wild to build an empire of crime would have made him a Titan in any field, had he chosen to stay within the law. And the tortures that the noble Gilles de Rais devised for his victims smacked of a pact with the Devil, which was indeed the charge leveled against him. Not gain so much as warped impulses actuated these masters of villainy.

Nor were these violators limited to the more belligerent of the sexes. As some primitive tribes turned over malefactors and prisoners of war to their womenfolk for cruelest reprisal, so did many women of higher cultures show themselves surpassing men in savagery. Though Elizabeth Brownrigg committed but a single murder, her everyday brutality shocked and sickened a nation. And

Marie de Brinvilliers, highborn and gentle, a marquise of the blood, could shun violence, but with gentle grace she spread her poisons about, smiling as she doled out her lethal doses. If Cain showed the way, his sister quickly learned that humans could be monsters too.

Psychopath and scoundrel, each thirsted, it almost seems, to make a name in infamy. And the unanswered questions remains. The question of why Landru, small and retiring, the notorious "Bluebeard," chose to woo and then to willfully destroy the women who received him in love. And why a Sawney Beane, tasting of the crime adjudged the worst among mankind, should bring up his progeny in the same inhuman practice. Could they indeed find no other way of survival? The life of each man who toils says yes. The blood of their every victim spells yes.

What, then, were these fifteen? Men or monsters? Fiends or misshapen fanatics, steeped in hatred of their fellow man? Psychiatrists today have probed deeply into the reasons why men behaved as these did, but in their day society knew them as scourges who balked at no atrocity.

Quick and horrible retribution on society's part held no fears for these poisoners and butchers. The forces of law have found no certain way to forestall all the descendants of Cain. They still move among us.

—*Cliff Howe*

I

GILLES DE RAIS

GILLES DE RAIS, one of the strangest personalities in history, was an aristocrat, a soldier, an epicure in perverted sensation; a man of genius and immense wealth, and of furious twisted lusts. He sinned more recklessly and cruelly than perhaps any Roman emperor of the Decadence, or any Italian nobleman of the Renaissance, and he did so with all his imagination and with almost superhuman energy.

Students of abnormal psychology know that a man who lives only for pleasure often reaches a point where normal satisfactions can no longer thrill or excite him. Gratification can be achieved only when those pleasures are preceded or followed by whippings, wounds, or the shedding of blood.

The case of Gilles de Rais would perhaps not have made history were it not for two outstanding facts. The first is that his life had episodes so horrible that they place him in the category of those monsters who loved cruelty, mutilation and murder above everything else. The second fact is that his trial constitutes the most notable trial for sorcery recorded during the late Middle Ages.

Gilles de Rais, born in 1404 in Brittany of a noble family, was the son of the mighty Baron de Rais, a powerful

7

nobleman of wealth, and Marie de Craon, daughter of the lord of the district, whom he married in 1404. As heir to the barony of Rais, he automatically was entitled to the headship of the baronage of Brittany—heir to great wealth and great estates.

Gilles de Rais began to practice many kinds of vices while still a boy. At the age of fourteen, he is described as being tall and graceful, with a lithe body that concealed great physical strength. Even at this age he was a precocious and vital personality.

Gilles' father died when he was nine years old, and on the remarriage of his mother, he and his younger brother René were entrusted to the care of their maternal grandfather, Jean de Craon, who was excessively indulgent and devoted to the children. Unfortunately, Gilles was now cut off from all womanly influence. René, the younger brother, was the grandfather's favorite, and Gilles drifted into the habit of solitude. He found his friends and companions among servants, grooms and pimps. From them he quickly learned adult interests and pleasures.

His grandfather, Jean de Craon, was too old to undertake the proper disciplining of Gilles, whose temperament made him unusually self-centered and intractable. In mind and in body, Gilles was far in advance of his years. He showed a phenomenal proficiency in everything he undertook and was given to habits of dark brooding and reflection. Conscious of his unusual talents, he early developed a haughty pride and arrogance that would brook no restraint.

It was a critical moment for Gilles when he took up the *Life of the Roman Emperors*. Their cruelties and obscenities exercised a strong fascination for him. This was the man he would be—a king, a tyrant, ruling by fear rather than by affection, bending everyone to his will. The rapture he found in these daydreams would leave him breathless. They became an obsession. Many years later, he admitted the deadly effect which this episode had upon him. "The said book was ornamented by pictures in which were seen the manner of life of the pagan emperors, and I read in the printed history how Caligula and other Caesars sported with children, and took singular pleasure in martyring them, upon which I desired to imitate the said Caesars."

At sixteen, Gilles formed a friendship with his cousin Roger de Bricqueville, a youth of his own age, who had a disastrous influence over him. The two lads were the victims of a "king and slave" delusion. At first Gilles was the king, but by degrees de Bricqueville was able to reverse the order of authority by trading upon Gilles' susceptibility.

Previous to this unusual friendship, Gilles, at the age of thirteen, had been promised by his grandfather to Joan, daughter of Foulques Peynel, Lord of Hambuie and Bricquebec; but the contract was voided by her death. In 1418, the next year, his grandfather made a second contract of marriage for him, this time with Beatrice de Rohan, eldest daughter of Alain de Porhoet, signed with great ceremony in the presence of an illustrious throng of Breton nobles. But this contract, too, came to an end with the death of the young lady.

Still, his doting grandfather was not discouraged. He immediately proceeded with his arrangements for a third contract, this time with Catherine de Thouars, daughter of Miles de Thouars, and the young lady brought him a vast fortune. Though Gilles was dismayed by the suddenness of the marriage, there were considerations in its favor. It would mean release for him from the nominal guardianship of his grandfather, and control of his own great wealth. Also, he anticipated no difficulty in subjugating his wife and, if necessary, disposing of her. Doubtless, the novelty of the experience intrigued him.

In November, 1420, when he was sixteen, the marriage, which was to prove a crucial test of Gilles' antipathy towards women, was celebrated. When the excitement of the event had cooled down. Gilles was faced with an anticlimax in the shape of a sixteen-year-old wife for whom he had no affection. He was bored and irritated, and took no pains to conceal his feelings. Catherine seems to have been a colorless sort of person and quite unfit to deal with the enigmatic character of her husband. It was a union as incongruous as the mating of a lion and a lamb, and Gilles tired of his bride and married life almost before it began.

After a brief honeymoon, he refused to cohabit with his wife altogether. After twelve weeks of married misery, he was overjoyed at the opportunity presented to leave his wife gracefully to go away on a diplomatic mission. So Catherine retired to the Chateau of Pouzages in company with Jean de Craon. When a girl-child, Marie, was born to the youthful couple, Gilles showed as little interest in her as in the mother.

It appears that Gilles de Rais was happy only amongst men and he realized, probably for the first time, that women were powerless to attract him. Normal sexual relationship had only resulted in confirming his unnatural repugnance towards women. Gilles was a homosexual—a sexual invert. Just when he discovered that he was also a sadist—a condition in which the sex instinct is gratified and stimulated by infliction of pain or cruelty on others—is not revealed.

France at that time was torn by fighting between various factions in the Hundred Years' War. Gilles de Rais had an aptitude for soldiering and he joined the army at the age of sixteen. His courage was tremendous, and a certain magnetic quality gave him leadership over men. This is what we should expect from a sadist. His supremacy fantasy was, no doubt, largely increased by his success in warfare. It was said that he could take his soldiers into perils from which they would have flinched had they been led by another man. Moreover, he displayed great strategic talents.

Later he was to attach himself to the army of Charles VII, where he won great distinction in his resistance to the English. Indeed, so admirably did Gilles comport himself that we find him a Marshal of France at the age of twenty-five.

The hard fighter is rarely a man devoted to the arts. But Gilles de Rais, ever a paradox, would come home from a hard campaign to enjoy the solace of pictures, books and music. His library was one of the most extensive in France. He surrounded himself with sculpture, with illumined missals, with exquisitely wrought carvings. Himself an excellent musician, he welcomed minstrels from many places. Music sometimes had so strong an effect on him that he would weep and develop a kind of emotional hysteria. He encouraged actors at a time when actors were despised, and his castles were frequently converted into theaters.

One would have said of Gilles de Rais at that time that here was the ideal *grand seigneur* of his period— gallant, wise, tolerant, cultured, a lover of beautiful things; the kind of man who would enjoy a long, full life and die at last in the odor of sanctity and safety. But in his brain, or soul, or spirit—call it what you will —there was a diabolical elemental force. That force took hold of him when he had reached the age of twenty-eight.

On the occasion of his marriage, he had produced at Angers a morality play, consisting of a series of *tableaux vivants* copied from tapestries in the Cathedral of Notre Dame. His interest in things theatrical had only been whetted, and now several companies of players were brought specially from Paris to follow in his train. Gilles wrote many satires himself and frequently played in them. His flamboyant egotism was gratified by the stir which his presence everywhere aroused, and the sumptuousness of the entertainments he gave had become the talk of France. Gilles' most striking triumph was at Champtocé, where the dauphin had come as the guest of honor. The dauphin was greatly impressed by the grandeur of Champtocé, as he was by its youthful, handsome lord.

Gilles was in his element at these spectacular functions. An eyewitness of the time describes him as "a real hero of majestic appearance, seductive face, graceful, petulant, with a lively and playful spirit."

If Gilles enjoyed all this splendor, poor Catherine and his grandfather were at their wits' ends. They had come from their seclusion for the sake of appearance to meet the dauphin, but it was clear to Jean de Craon that the marriage was doomed. There was no possibility of reconciliation. What he had feared might happen when he relinquished his stewardship over Gilles did happen. Gilles' sudden accession, upon his marriage, to great wealth had completely upset his balance. To the flood of sycophants who surrounded him, he dispensed money and gifts without stint or excuse. Even the dauphin borrowed freely to replenish the royal exchequer.

Gilles had reached a stage when his inchoate feelings demanded something more than luxury and aesthetic display. It was the beginning of a protracted spell of viciousness in which everything else was forgotten. Most of his associates were men of his own station, but his insatiable cravings soon weakened his pride of rank. A young man named Henri Griart, who acted as librarian, became his close companion. And de Bricqueville aided and abetted Gilles in his orgies, knowing this to be the surest way to consolidate his own position with Gilles.

Gilles' spells of debauchery were followed by fits of melancholy. In these moods, he would fly into violent rages and no one would venture near him while they lasted. His ego had a Jekyll and Hyde variability, now urging him to depravity, now propelling him on to self-fulfillment through the use of his undoubted gifts. Ideas were as dangerous to him as explosives in the hands of a child, and the passive life meant a mind constantly turning over the possibilities of new sins, the exploring of fresh obscenities. With action, his morbidity had a tendency to disappear, and at such times he would astonish the world by performing great deeds of valor and unexpected acts that revealed his penetrating intellect.

Fortunately for Gilles, the political situation developed on lines favorable to his career. His grandfather had brought about the meeting at Champtocé with the dauphin in the hope that Gilles might be tempted to abandon his vicious life and take his proper place in the councils of the nation. His move in that respect was successful. Gilles was sick of himself and his friends, and it pleased him to be mixing again with men of his own social and intellectual caliber.

When the dauphin returned to Paris, Gilles accompanied him. For nearly a year he remained at Court, taking advantage of every opening to impress himself on the dauphin and his circle. Georges la Tremoille, the power behind the weak ruler of France, was especially impressed by Gilles and attributed his indifference to the gallantries and amenities of the Court to the young seigneur's high and serious purpose. This was, of course, an overgenerous estimate, since Gilles had no interest in the frail and fair ladies who sought his favor and his riches. For the time, ambition swamped everything else. He was satisfied when the dauphin offered him the important military command of the border country between Maine and Anjou. The Anglo-Burgundians were harrying all this country.

Gilles returned at once to Champtocé and raised fresh companies from the ranks of his adherents. When he took the field, he quickly proved his generalship. He

became the dread of the English. He fought with a dash
that amazed everyone, and was noted for his ferocity on
the battlefield. He was the first to take the fortress of
Lude, and engaged Blackburn, the English commander,
in hand-to-hand combat. Blackburn went down with Gilles' sword in his throat.

War does not turn men into angels, and the effect of
an orgy of killing upon those who are emotively unstable
may be brutalizing. As his later life proved, Gilles had
all the instincts of the sadist to whom cruelty is a necessary part of sexual gratification. From his first experience in abnormality, Gilles had, on his own confession,
desired to kill and mutilate.

It was at Chinon on February 23, 1429, that Gilles met
the eighteen-year-old Joan of Arc for the first time. She
had arrivied to interview the dauphin. Gilles stood out
as her friend and champion, and insisted in his belief in
her divine mission to save France. The impact made by
Joan on such a man as Gilles de Rais is a mystery. It
might be argued that his impressionable and volatile
temperament quickly caught any contagion of enthusiasm or novelty, or that his superstitious nature was affected by Joan's talk of Voices and other mystical mani-
festations. Also, his religious sense was quickened by her
sanctity. When the dauphin finally entrusted the command of the armies to the Maid of Orleans, Gilles, at
her request, was made her protector on the field. Gilles'
co-operation with Joan throughout the hostilities set the
seal upon his career and greatly strengthened his power.

The dauphin was crowned and Gilles was made a
Marshal of France. The king also authorized "Gilles de
Rais, Marshal of France, in recognition of his glorious
service, to show in his coat of arms a bordering of fleur
de lys." Immediately after the Coronation, resisting the
king's invitation to remain at Court, Gilles rejoined the
army of the Maid at Senlis. Then, for some unknown
reason, the king ordered Gilles to rejoin him, and so it

was that at the hour of Joan's capture, Gilles was not by her side.

But the king's ingratitude and duplicity rankled, and soon Gilles found an opportunity to leave his sovereign. One cannot imagine the tempestuous Gilles submitting tamely to the injustice perpetrated against Joan of Arc. In November he reappeared suddenly in the vicinity of Louviers, some sixteen miles from Rouen, with two armed companies and a plan for rescuing Joan from her captors. The English got wind of the plot and threatened to throw her into the Seine rather than relinquish their prize. For six months Gilles and his two cavalry leaders vainly dashed their forces against the English in the hope of saving Joan.

On June first, news arrived of her martyrdom. It is impossible to overestimate the crushing and destructive effect of this blow on Gilles de Rais. The constant presence of the Maid of Orleans and the atmosphere of spirituality which always surrounded her was an incentive to decent living which even Gilles could not resist. It was a new and ennobled Gilles who rode by her side and shared her fortunes. But his ambition went up in smoke in the flames that destroyed the Maid.

Now warfare, honor and ambition had lost their appeal, and life no longer held savor. Gilles' newborn idealism had perished and the satyr and murderer lay in waiting to fill the gap.

Gilles arrived at Champtocé in December, 1432, recalled by the death of his grandfather, Jean de Craon. Roger de Bricqueville still ocupied the post of majordomo, but Gilles had discovered a new favorite, Gilles de Sillé, who accompanied him to Champtocé. They had met at Lagny, and recognizing in de Sillé the traits he looked for in his companions, Gilles induced him to leave the army. This friendship marked a turning point for Gilles de Rais. When he permanently abandoned his career, his normal life ceased to function. He was a man thrown back upon himself and cut adrift from his moorings. The old egomania was again dominant and there was nothing to hinder its action. From Gilles himself we learn that his days and nights, during this period, were spent "drinking and rejoicing" with de Sillé.

In the church of St. Hilaire de Poitiers, of which Gilles, by virtue of his fiefs was a lay canon, there was a boy whose wonderful singing had earned for him the name of le Rossignol. This youth was to prove the first link in the chain of circumstances which opened the era of horror in the life of Gilles de Rais. The boy's physical perfection matched his voice. He was a Greek type and blond, with a finely shaped head covered with close, curling hair. All Gilles' perverted love of beauty was awakened by le Rossignol. To tempt the boy, Gilles settled upon him the princely gift of the Rivière estate, which brought in a substantial revenue, and gave his parents three hundred crowns. Nobody suspected Gilles' real motives in going to such extravagant length except a corrupt cleric called Eustace Blauchet.

The report of Gilles' generosity to the choirboy spread far and wide, drawing many other youths who came from long distances hoping to find a place in the Lord de Rais' choir. In their train followed young beggars. Le Rossignol had proved a decoy for others, and the import of this was not lost on Gilles de Rais. All the principal members of his household were despatched to his various castles, and upon Roger de Bricqueville devolved the task of interviewing and selecting the prospective victims.

Encouraged by the presence and active participation of de Bricqueville and de Sillé, Gilles' sadistic tendencies were now getting the upper hand, and his satiated lusts were driving him to more intensive forms of brutality. His sadism did not restrict itself to those acts of violence, such as flagellation, which content the ordinary sadist; Gilles could only be satisfied by the infliction of intense suffering and the spilling of blood.

There had come back to his mind the phrase from Suetonius of how some of the Caesars "sported with children and took singular pleasure in martyring them." The idea obsessed him and he seriously considered making his first experiment with le Rossignol, but the boy's voice held too much fascination for him and he decided to look elsewhere for a victim. Neither de Bricqueville nor de Sillé guessed what was passing in Gilles' mind, but even if they had known, their own sordid depravity was equal to that of Gilles.

Although the names of many of those whom Gilles de Rais murdered were made known during his trial, there is no record as to the identity of his first victim. In his savage blood-hunger, he determined that the youth to be sacrificed should be strong and vigorous, so there should be enough resistance to whet his desire, but he had underestimated his power of control. Unnatural excitement had weakened his moral and mental faculties, and brutal horseplay succeeded the usual orgies. Gilles dealt the first blow and de Sillé, hardly conscious of impending tragedy, followed his example. Flogging and beating by two drunken perverts, who tried to outdo each other, culminated in Gilles' stabbing and afterwards strangling his victim. The bodies of the victims were thrown into a dry well where they were safe from observation.

A suite of apartments formerly used as a fencing hall and situated in a remote part of the chateau was set apart for the "sport of the Caesars." There is the story told that when the sudden desire took hold of him, Gilles would go to the room where the entrapped child was chained and set free the boy or girl with kind words and encouraging smiles. Having thus won the confidence of the child, he would begin to fondle it, bestowing upon it the kisses which the innocent little creature returned. He would then feed the child sweetmeats, watching with voluptuous eyes the pleasure in the eyes of the child, which in a few minutes would change to agony.

When the preliminary farce had been played long enough, he would suddenly assume a voice of great sternness. He would wrench the clothes from the terrified little creature and mercilessly flog the naked flesh until blood came. Then, with the blood-stirring fumes of lust in his brain, he would fall upon the child and commit a nameless outrage.

But that was not the end. Having regaled himself for some time with the screams of pain, with the slow writhings of the victim, he would then with a sharp knife proceed to perform horrible and obscene mutilations. After that the mood of the moment decided whether the victim was left to bleed to death or to be dispatched with a final stab.

At a later stage, it was calculated that perhaps no less than two hundred children had been thus murdered by Gilles de Rais.

It may seem incredible that it was possible for him to exterminate so many children without any news of his crimes reaching the outside world. The reason was that his position as a feudal chief, almost akin to a petty monarch, made his acts practically immune from question. Added to this, the condition of the country, torn by war, made discovery improbable. The widespread poverty had scattered the population. For a child to vanish in a land infested by the enemy, as well as by French brigands, would excite neither interest nor surprise.

After the fortieth murder, Gilles moved to Machecoul. But there was no pause in the sanguinary acts with which he had befouled Champtocé. Here, the same number of murders were committed. For some unaccountable reason there was always an interval after the fortieth murder—the number of victims apparently necessary for the gorging of the monster's blood-lust.

It is one of the characteristic phenomena of his life that Gilles seems to have been, until the end, quite unable to recognize the enormity of his guilt. Egotism was the chief source of his criminality.

Now, after a year of vice and bloodshed, his twisted mind formulated the idea of commemorating his victims in some pious manner. The more thought he gave to the idea, the stronger became its appeal. There was a deep and unconscious irony in the plan, which was to create a Foundation dedicated to the Holy Innocents, to be erected at Machecoul. He could thus insure his soul against the damnation he had so richly earned, and at the same time raise a memorial to his own piety. This was megalomania *in excelsis.*

After the riot of murder, he felt the need for relaxation. His theatrical sense longed again for the limelight, bade him strut and posture and artificially revive the glories of his heroic days. To the playgoing public of today, accustomed to the wonderful productions of the modern theatre, it will come as a surprise to learn that Gilles de Rais was a forerunner of this movement. Indeed, it is debatable whether the stage today could give us anything approaching in cost or display the lavish productions mounted by Gilles. A company of actors was attached to his household in the same manner as his clergy and military staff. Incidentally, Gilles was made bankrupt by his passion for the stage.

It might seem incredible that anyone possessing the great wealth reputed to belong to Gilles could come to suffer financial embarrassment. But the fabled wealth of a Midas could not have withstood the strain of Gilles' reckless spending. A lover of classic times, Gilles desired to imitate the insensate extravagances and wastefulness of the Caesars. A troop of more than two hundred horsemen would accompany him on all his journeys. He dressed more magnificently than the king. He squandered sums equivalent to several thousands of pounds on a single banquet. The chief factor in his ruin was undoubtedly the avarice and dishonesty of his followers and hangers-on.

The absence of a plentiful supply of ready money was intolerable to Gilles, and he commenced borrowing with a vengeance. More than one of his castles was mortgaged. His haughty pride was outraged at the indignity of being pressed for funds.

Catherine, his wife, made an attempt to see him with regard to the future of their daughter, Marie. Evidently she hoped that the subject itself might help bring him to his senses. But as on previous occasions he treated her with indifference, and he instructed de Bricqueville to find a husband for his daughter.

Nobody knew what Gilles' next move would be. He cut himself off finally from his family and entrenched himself at Tiffauges. Here he would be able to concentrate upon the problem of rehabilitating himself. He strained his intelligence now to discover a way out of his difficulties. It was not without significance that Gilles said to one of his friends, "God could refuse nothing to a Laval (a de Rais), but if He did, there is always the devil."

Gilles had come to Tiffauges to evolve the plan that was simmering in his brain—an idea as fantastic as all his thoughts, which at one stroke would give him the power of a demigod. The idea was black magic and alchemy. Incongruous as it may sound to modern ears, it must be remembered that alchemy and occultism were subjects of vital import in Gilles' time.

Gilles had always been attracted by the hidden and the mysterious. Saturated as he was with superstition and unbalanced by his sexual excesses and bloody crimes, the forbidden path of the black arts made an instant appeal to him. None had a better right than he to invoke the diabolic powers, which he believed to be all-potent.

Very soon he became the dupe of charlatans and wizards from various places. They came to him with their stories of the Philosopher's Stone, each one protesting that he alone possessed the long-sought magic that would change base metals into gold. Gilles, seized with a desire for infinite riches and for supreme power over mankind, greedily swallowed their lies. One by one, however, they were dismissed when their claims failed to achieve results.

But an Italian, Francesco Prelati, a loathsome scoundrel, contrived to retain Gilles' confidence. It is conceivable that he did possess some kind of esoteric talent; it is possible that he practiced hypnotism at a time when hypnotism did not bear that name and was regarded as a magic process. Gilles was ready to pay him huge sums in return for the alleged teaching of magic—for the three gifts of knowledge, wealth and power. He was convinced that Prelati possessed supernatural powers of a very high order and he regarded him as a valued representative of the devil.

There is the possibility that Gilles would have gone his way undisturbed and would have died without paying the penalty of his crimes, but for the intervention of the Church. His alchemic activities had long been known, but these activities were not regarded by the Inquisition as distinctly illegal. But there were several other possible indictments, and the Church, through the Bishop of Nantes, chancellor to Duke Jean, hastened to avail itself of those charges.

There was another purpose in addition to the motive of punishing a sorcerer. The bishop had associated himself with Duke Jean, his master, in negotiating for the enormously rich estates of Gilles de Rais. It was suddenly borne in upon their greedy consciousness that if Gilles were arraigned and condemned, those estates would automatically be confiscated and become the property of the duke and his chancellor. Urged on by this ambition, they set to work.

It was necessary that the duke and his chancellor should have some cause for the arrest of Gilles. This was furnished by Gilles himself. He was provoked into a quarrel that ended in a brawl in the church, and he led his troops of soldiers into a sacred house. He had committed the crime of sacrilege. The duke and his ally then proceeded to build upon it by further accusing Gilles of sorcery and of prolonged and systematic child-murder and outrage. The latter charge was regarded as trivial compared with the indictment of dealing with the devil.

The order was given for Gilles' immediate arrest, and two months later, Gilles was tried in the Civil Court on a charge of abduction. But this trial was merely a prelude to the more important proceedings that were to follow. In the meantime, evidence was being gathered for the more serious indictment.

The charge of abduction failed. Perhaps witnesses were not available to swear that they had actually seen Gilles seize and carry off children. He was acquitted.

But on September 13, 1440, to his great astonishment, Gilles received a mandate signed by the Bishop of Nantes, commanding him to appear before his tribunal in six days' time. He was then to answer indictments of child murder, heresy and sorcery. Panic seized his accomplices, servants and agents who had aided him in his crimes. His "entourage" were immediately arrested and chained and taken under guard to Nantes.

When brought before the bishop and the other members of the tribunal on October 13, Gilles suddenly burst into a rage. "I do not acknowledge you as my judges. And I vow that I would rather be executed this instant than be forced to undergo the humiliation of being judged by you!"

The court proceeded with the indictment. That he had practiced alchemy, he admitted, but nothing in that practice was held to be illegal. But he passionately denied all the other charges. His enemies had invented these stories to ruin him, he declared. After a long hearing, the proceedings were adjourned for forty-eight hours so that the prisoner might prepare his defense.

The agents and secretaries and servants of Gilles de Rais, having been subjected to the rack and other devices of the Inquisition, offered full confessions, probably embellishing the bare facts with ornamentations invented to appease their tormentors. These confessions were held to prove that Gilles had committed child murders. But thus far the sorcery charges had not been clearly demonstrated. Gilles, well aware of this fact, resolved to plead guilty to the former charge, but to deny the committal of what in those times would be regarded as the more heinous crime. To kill a multitude of children was a small offense compared with the crime of devil traffic.

Again the trial was adjourned. During the interval, the charlatan accomplice of Gilles, the notorious Francesco Prelati, had been subjected to the question by torture. He had then admitted his dealings with the Evil One and had given details of the co-operation of Gilles.

On October 20, Gilles was again brought before the tribunal. Again he denied his guilt. The evidence of Prelati would have been sufficient to convict him, but the Inquisition authorities prided themselves on the moral satisfaction they secured from a personal confession—the man himself must speak the words that would send him to the fire. The Inquisitor announced that Gilles would be subjected to the torture if he refused to confirm the evidence of his associate.

Gilles seemed unmoved by the announcement and was taken back to his cell. Everybody believed that he would undergo the torments bravely and perhaps refuse to speak, but when the hour came and Gilles was taken down to the room where the rack awaited him, the resolve of this torturer of children suddenly collapsed. "For Jesus' dear sake, give me a short respite. Give me time to think of this matter and perhaps you shall be satisfied." The Inquisition authorities were patient. They gave him until two o'clock in the afternoon to consider what to do. When the time had expired, he calmly offered a full confession. He admitted the murders, the heresies, the sorceries.

After that confession, a change took place in Gilles. All his insolence faded. He was now humble, so humble that he addressed a petition to his judges that his crimes and confession be made public throughout France for all the people to know. "My humiliation," he said, "will perhaps be the means of winning for me forgiveness hereafter."

Judge Pierre de l'Hôpital announced the sentence: All the castles, houses, lands and mines of the prisoner Gilles de Rais were to be immediately confiscated, and he himself, with his associates, was to be first hanged and then burned whilst he was still alive.

Gilles received the sentence with great calmness. He then turned towards the fathers and mothers of certain of his child victims and begged for their forgiveness, and with bowed head went from the place.

The vanity of the criminal asserted itself at that awful moment of his career, for presently he returned with the request that it would gratify him very much if the bishop and every member of the clergy would walk with him in his procession to the burning place. This request was granted.

Every person in Nantes, with the exception of the old and bedridden, came out on the morning of the execution to look upon the man whose deeds were already beginning to assume the mystery and the glamour of a legend.

Throughout his life, even when he was engaged in murder and sorcery, this man was intensely religious in the narrow sense, observing all the ceremonies of his faith with great precision.

The funeral of Gilles de Rais was a magnificent ceremony. There seemed to these people nothing incongruous in giving a very splendid funeral to a mass murderer and sorcerer.

However, the mild attitude of the people of Brittany towards Gilles de Rais at the time of his death and for some time afterwards was gradually exchanged for a kind of legendary terror. For many years after his execution, peasants who happened to be in the neighborhood of his former abodes would at once cross themselves and send up prayers for protection from the Devil.

The Bluebeard myth has in some unexplained way become associated with the name of Gilles de Rais. In Brittany there was a legend that the reddish beard of Gilles was changed by Satan into a beard of brilliant blue. His name was used for many centuries as a bogey by nurses anxious to quell rebellious children.

Gilles de Rais was perhaps the most deliberately cruel intellectual criminal of his age and epoch.

II

THOMAS DUN

THE PLEASANT, if dull little town of Dunstable, in the South of England, derived its name, according to the story, from a man who was one of the most diabolical scoundrels that ever infested town or country. The career of Thomas Dun, though savage enough, is marked also by a courage that seems almost psychopathic in its intensity.

Dun was born in a village near the Elstrow of John Bunyan sometime around the turn of the thirteenth century. His parents were respectable folk, from a long line of honest peasantry, but Thomas was a thief from the very beginning. A local gossip said of the child that he was so given to stealing that everything stuck to his hands "like birdlime."

Long before he was a man, Dun discovered that he had, besides the capacity to appropriate objects, another remarkable gift. He could distort his face into many shapes. He could do what he chose with brow, cheeks, and mouth. His eyes, moreover, could be sunk or projected.

In the beginning Dun used this gift only for practical jokes. Later, though, he found it very useful when he went out to commit his outrageous crimes. He could manipulate his body as well as his face, he learned then. Sometimes he appeared as a one-armed or a one-legged man, sometimes as a hunchback, or again as a dwarf, for, by means of certain tricks, he could give the impression of very small stature. Aided by this incredible capacity to mold his physical appearance at will, he was able for a long time to evade detection.

Dun's first deliberate murder was committed on the road to Bedford. Dun, hiding behind a hedge, saw a large wagon filled with corn and drawn by two well-nourished, handsome horses. Instantly Dun scented a good prize and made his plans. He crawled into the wagon, crept up behind the wagoner and coolly stabbed him to death. This done, he stopped the horses, flung down the body, and having stripped the corpse of its clothing, put on the clothing himself. He next dug a shallow grave for the dead wagoner, laid him in the trench and hastily covered him with brambles.

Later, Dun drove the wagon into Bedford, disposed of the load of corn at a good price, and finally sold the van and the horses. Then he went home, careful not to drink on the way. Indeed, throughout his career, Dun was careful to avoid drink and the ordinary vices of the criminal. To these abstinences, perhaps, he owed his long freedom.

Dun hated the life of the lone wolf. It was that hatred that shortly prompted him to raise a group of thieves to accompany him on his plundering. Though he seemed to fear nothing on earth, he was afraid of his own society. His gang soon discovered a remote underground hiding place, and here would meet—eating, drinking, fighting and bragging about their hauls.

"They committed," says the crime chronicle, "a thousand villainies." The road between Towcester and St. Albans was their chief hunting ground. After a time, so great was the fear set up by the gang that the king proclaimed Dun an outlaw and ordered a small town to be built on that road so that the distance between Towcester and St. Albans might be protected by an intervening community. And so it came about that the town of Dunstable was raised and Dun was its name-giver.

Dun's thieves and cutthroats were specialists. Each man had his "trade." One devoted himself to making false keys, another to making tools for breaking into houses, a third cultivated a talent for the filing of iron bars. Their preparations for thieving, however, did not fill all their time, and they frequently got into fights among themselves, sometimes almost killing each other. Dun, recognizing that some kind of order must be set up, actually instituted a sort of legislature among his ruffians. He imposed rules and regulations, and heavily fined any cutthroat who tried to practice in private life his profession as outlaw.

Dun exacted obedience, firstly, by his reputation for physical courage and, secondly, by his ability to strike terror into his gang by putting on horrible faces. It is possible that his thieves, in that simple time, credited him with demoniacal powers.

Those were lawless as well as simple times, but not so lawless but that the authorities tried to catch and hang, mutilate or roast criminals who disturbed the peace.

For a time, the fear inspired by Dun made him comparatively free from pursuit. But now there arose a strong man in the county of Bedfordshire—the Sheriff of Bedford. He vowed that he had no fear of Dun—that whether he was or was not aided by the devil, he would arrest the man and hang him on the highest tree in the county.

A large attack was organized. The sheriff's men, in their liveries of office, penetrated the woods and managed to come upon the gang, taking them, as they imagined, by surprise. But Dun, by means of spies and scouts, had been warned of the campaign against him. A man of genius in his own field, he was rarely unprepared for the unexpected.

The two groups engaged in battle and the sheriff's force was defeated. Soon it was in full flight, but not before Dun's men had managed to take eleven prisoners. Dun ordered these men promptly hanged. After the hanging, he had his men strip the bodies of the liveries so that a plan he had in mind might be put into effect.

Dun himself put on a livery. Accompanied by six of his brigands, also liveried, he went at night to a certain castle in the district, where great treasure was said to be hidden in a huge chest.

Then Dun played a trick that writers have used a hundred times. Posing as officers of the law, Dun, with great dignity, informed the head steward that he had reason to suspect that certain of "that infamous outlaw's men—I mean Thomas Dun—are hidden in the castle, for

the purpose of robbery." The steward, terrified, begged
the supposed officers to make a thorough search. Dun
made a great pretense of doing this. Meantime, the steward, anxious to avoid danger, locked himself in his room.

Soon Dun returned and, having prevailed on the old
man to open the door, told him that he had reason to
believe that the robbers had hidden themselves in the
treasure room. The steward, suspecting nothing—over-
whelmed, perhaps, by the livery of office that Dun and
his thieves were wearing—at once turned over the key.
Dun coolly went back, helped himself to the treasure,
and then left the castle with his men, having gained a
large booty without striking a single blow.

Dun was especially pleased with the success of this
venture. He was still more satisfied with what followed,
for the incident served to "score off" the sheriff, whom
he hated. For, as it turned out, four or five of the sheriff's men actually were hanged as the looters who had
made off with the booty. From the steward's vague and
garbled descriptions, the owner of the castle accused
these men who, dumfounded by the sudden and inexplic-
able charge, could not defend themselves with any conviction. The hanging followed within a few days. The
sheriff was, of course, horrified and swore immediate
vengeance on Dun.

But that was easier said than done. At all times and
at all points, Dun eluded capture. The sheriff's men
would arrange to capture him at a certain crossroads, but
on arrival they would find nothing but a caricature of
their leader pinned to a tree, with jeering and obscene
insults written by a member of the gang who had learned
how to write.

Dun had now become so great a terror of certain of the
highways that those roads were practically abandoned by
travelers, many of whom preferred to lose valuable business to having their throats cut and their goods stolen.
For some time, Dun went on robbing and murdering,

but at length he began to realize that the area was not yielding him sufficient harvest. He was too well known. He must change his place of operations.

Dun and his men now moved north. The gang had now reached the formidable number of fifty. Dun's savagery was increasing with the passage of years. He spared neither man, woman nor child. He would slit a throat as he would hum a tune, doing both very skillfully and with great good humor.

Evidently, except for a few cronies, Dun hated everybody. It must have been a cheerless sort of life that he led upon those dark roads, with very little to interest him, for he was no tippler, no glutton. And so he flung himself deeper into his savage plundering, the only release he could find for his hate and his restlessness.

In the course of time Thomas Dun became a sort of enveloping horror on the roads of Yorkshire—like a pestilence, an evil phantom, a recurring ghastly dream. Weakminded persons fell into mad delusions, actually believing that they had encountered the robber-murderer who had engraved upon their bodies some mark by which in the future he would recognize them and take their lives. Children, seeing a harmless, unknown man on the road after nightfall, would run screaming to their homes. Crimes of which this murderous villain was doubtless innocent were set down at his door. The countryside was obsessed, and when men and women spoke of the Devil, they thought of him in the shape of Dun.

At length, organized action was tried to bring him down. Half-hearted attempts to seize the ruffian had of course been made time after time, but no strongly organized force had been assembled. Eventually the Sheriff of York organized a considerable party for the purpose of attacking Dun, augmented by many citizens and villagers.

Dun, fearing nothing because of the great terror he inspired, had actually been living in a small house on the outskirts of a wood not far from York. It may seem strange to see a criminal coolly reposing at home, close to his victims but untouched by the law; but in order to get the proper perspective on this, one must remember that England at the time was a country possessed by foreign invaders who were frequently engaged in repelling attacks of native Saxons. Now picture Dun as a Norman baron, in his castle, enjoying a certain immunity from injury by reason of the fear that he inspired. That was the situation with Dun. In his little house he was lord of his castle because he had contrived to create an atmosphere of overwhelming terror.

But the end was near. Dun, finding his stronghold besieged, fought back with his usual courage. He forced his way through the mass of people surrounding his home and mounted his horse, striking right and left with the long dagger. His gang had deserted him and he had to rely on his own hands and weapons.

Dun showed no fear, but kept thrusting at the throats of the attackers. Soon the crowd forced him from his horse, but he had hardly touched the ground when, with a swift movement, he managed to remount. Drawing his sword now, he cut his way through the mass of one hundred and fifty people who, armed with clubs, bludgeons, pitchforks and other weapons, tried to hold him back. Putting spurs to his horse, Dun left the road and, galloping through a corn field, outdistanced his pursuers.

Dun was so indifferent to danger that he actually dismounted after a time and lay down to rest by a hedge. He was on the point of dozing when the attacking party, now swelled to several hundred people, discovered his presence. How he again managed to get away, thus surrounded, has not been told. But by some ruse he succeeded in doing this, and then ran towards the river. Thrusting his dagger in his teeth, he leaped into the stream and swam to a small island. Boats were launched and a dozen men rowed towards the island on which Dun landed, but he was ready for them.

Before they could ground their boats, he was thrusting at them with his dagger. His remarkable strength and agility enabled him to prevent them from landing. Other boats were then pushed off, but before they could touch the island, Dun was once again swimming towards a spot which he thought would be sufficiently thicketed to afford him a chance to escape. But for once his reckoning was wrong. A large number of the attacking party, figuring that he might make for that spot, had hidden themselves behind the trees. He landed and was taken by surprise. Before he could strike a blow, the monster had been knocked over the head with oars and stunned.

They bound Dun with ropes, which were soon exchanged for the strongest chains. He was taken before a magistrate and after a brief examination was sent under a powerful guard to Bedford, it being held by the authorities that he should be dealt with in the district where he had committed his first crimes.

So back to Bedford went Dun, knowing he was going there to die, but nevertheless continuing to maintain a stoical attitude and amusing his captors by coarse cynicisms.

There was no formal trial of Dun. He was an outlaw and the rights of citizenship did not exist for him. The sole problem that worried the authorities was the question of how to make his death as horrible as possible so that he might serve as a deterrent to other potential criminals.

Eventually, they decided that justice would be satisfied and a spectacular purpose served by a piecemeal execution. And so about two weeks after his arrest, Dun was solemnly taken to the marketplace at Bedford, where a huge crowd had assembled to see him die.

Unmoved, but nevertheless still very aggressive, Dun, having mounted the platform, told the two executioners that if they dared to lay a hand on him, he would kill them both. On their ignoring his words and trying to bind him, Dun caught their heads, knocked them together and would have brained the fellows had not others intervened and overpowered him.

That was the last struggle of Dun. The horrible sentence was then carefully carried out. First of all, the executioners, with jagged knives, cut off the arms below the elbows, and afterwards the upper arms of the writhing wretch. Slowly and with cruel deliberation, the torturers cut away his feet below the ankles, and then the legs were sawed off at the knees. The thighs were excised five inches from the trunk. Finally, the head was severed, and what remained of the body burned to ashes. The dismembered limbs and head were taken away and hung on posts in various parts of the county.

Dun, in all probability, was not more than thirty-five or forty when he came to this horrible end. It is conceivable that he packed into each year of his life more crimes than the average modern criminal packs into a lifetime. For years after his passing, he was a legend and a "bogey," used by nurses to terrify their charges into obedience.

Dun's ghost was said to haunt certain roads which he had terrorized during his life, and more than one superstitious traveler who had escaped the attentions of Dun while the latter was alive, came home with hair-raising stories of an encounter with the phantom, the apparition perhaps being an ingenious thief who had borrowed the guise of Dun in order to prey more successfully on fools and cowards.

III

SAWNEY BEANE

The story of Sawney Beane is so barbaric and inhuman that if it were not buttressed by unquestionable historical evidence, it would be rejected as altogether incredible and fictitious.

Out of the age-long record of cannibalism, a practice outlawed by all except a few most primitive societies, probably the strangest case is that of a man who for twenty-five years fed on human flesh, not because he was dimly working out some superstitious belief or tribal custom, but simply because he found himself in circumstances whereby his survival was most easily secured by means of robbery, murder and cannibalism.

Sawney Beane was born in the County of East Lothian, about eight miles east of Edinburgh, sometime in the last quarter of the sixteenth century. His father was a hedger and ditcher, and brought up his son in the same laborious employment.

The young Sawney Beane grew up with a strong loathing for any kind of physical exertion. He complained bitterly that a youth of his abilities should be asked to toil in the fields. Sometimes he would stay in bed all day, and would drive off with curses and blows those who tried to force him into the fields.

Idle and vicious as Sawney Beane was, he naturally looked for a companion of similar stripe, and one day he abandoned the village in company with a young woman, equally idle and profligate, for whom he had conceived

34

a passion. They fled to the deserts of Galloway, intending
to live by the seaside. A storm arose and drove them to
take shelter in what appeared to them a mere cave on
the rocky coast of Galloway. During the night they discovered that the cave was in reality a cavern of huge
length and dimensions. It extended nearly a mile under
the sea.

Beane and his companion made this cavern their home,
but it was, literally, "the habitation of horrid cruelty."
Here they began their depredations.

History, unfortunately, has not disclosed exactly how
this youth of twenty or twenty-two first happened on
robbery, murder and the horrible sequel of cannibalism.
But it is easy to reconstruct the situation to some extent.

Picture the scene for a moment. A wilderness of shore
and rock with the sea lashing an iron-bound coast. A
place where no man passes save a traveler bound for
the harbor, where he may embark for Ireland. A half-
savage young peasant—a girl beside him for whom, as
well as for himself, he must find food and drink. In his
heart and brain a rebelliousness, a lawlessness which
the wild spirit of unrest in Scotland of that period did
much to breed and foster and bring to a murderous climax.

The thoughts of the man must inevitably have turned
to robbery as the one means of livelihood. There was
nothing else, unless he worked—and, as we know, he
hated toil. From contemplating robbery, his thoughts
must have traveled to murder as the natural sequel—the
natural sequel because the robber of past centuries had
no incentive to spare his victim. If a thief was captured, he was promptly tried and hanged. Nothing more
could be done to a murderer. It was therefore a mere
instinct of self-preservation that frequently converted a
good-natured stealer of goods into a killer of men.

Now, imagine Sawney Beane having gone out from his
hiding place one night and having robbed and killed a

traveler. His first impulse would be to drag the man into the darkness of the cavern while he considered what he should do with the corpse. It is a night of storm. The larder contains no food. Hunger begins to gnaw the man and his companion. Already they have made some attempt to dissect the body of their victim, in order that the dismembered parts might be thrown into the sea. They decided that this method would doubtless prove the safest means of avoiding detection.

Their hunger becomes more intense. They search the dark corners of that strange home for food. Nothing! Slowly the madness of the hunger-pain seizes their vitals. Food! Food! They must have food! Nothing else matters. They stare at each other harshly. There is no kissing now—no twining of arms and limbs. Lust or love, or whatever drove these two to this place, is swamped in the still more fundamental passion of hunger.

Beane resolves to eat the human flesh that lies a few feet distant. This shall be the first and the last time. Hunger shall be satisfied—for this night only—by an impromptu feast. Tomorrow he will leave his cavern and go out to seek legitimate food. Tonight the wolf eating his vitals shall have other stuff to gnaw. He tells his woman what is in his mind; or perhaps a gesture, a look, a cry, reveals his purpose. She understands. She also compromises. Tonight they will do this, but never again.

They rush to the corner where the severed limbs lie covered with sacking. They heap them on the fire. The strong smell reassures them, whets their longings. Before the horrible meal is half-roasted, they are squatting on their haunches, tearing, gnawing, devouring. They laugh, they shout, as hunger finds relief. Their joy is the joy of the atavistic man crunching his prey.

They slept—long and deep—after their debauch. When morning came, they began to recognize dimly that they had found a solution of their problem. No longer need they starve when travelers are scarce. One robbery, one slaughter, and the larder will be filled for days and weeks.

All this is to some extent conjecture, but it is conceivable that something of the kind must have happened. How otherwise is one to explain the problem of this Scottish peasant of normal parentage, of civilized, if rough, mode of life, passing from the satisfaction of his appetites by legitimate foods to this primeval savagery? Some emergency, stark and horrible, must have arisen.

After they had murdered any man, woman or child, they carried their prey to their den, quartered it, salted the limbs and dried them for food. In this manner they lived, carrying on their depredations and murder, until they had eight sons and six daughters, eighteen grandsons and fourteen granddaughters—all the offspring of incest. What must have been the life of this family? Nothing in recorded history is comparable.

But though they soon became numerous, so many people fell into their hands that they often had an excess of provisions and would, at a distance from their cavern, throw legs and arms of dried human bodies into the sea at night. These were often cast up by the tide and found by the country people to the amazement and dismay of all the surrounding inhabitants. Nor could anyone discover what had befallen the many friends, relatives and neighbors who had unfortunately fallen into the hands of these merciless cannibals.

In proportion as Sawney Beane's family increased, everyone who was physically capable was assigned a part in these horrid assassinations. They would sometimes attack four or six men on foot, but never more than two on horseback. To prevent the possibility of escape, they would lie in ambush in every direction, so that if their victims escaped the first attackers, they might be assailed with renewed fury by another party, and eventually murdered. By this means they always secured their prey and prevented detection. Beane recognized the truth of the saying that dead men can give no evidence.

At last, however, the vast number who were slain aroused the inhabitants of the country, and all the woods and hiding places were carefully searched. And often they passed by the mouth of the horrible cavern, but it never occurred to them once even to suspect that any human being lived there. It was a section where people rarely penetrated for business or for any other purpose, since it was a wilderness of rock and water.

In this state of uncertainty and suspense concerning the authors of these frequent massacres, several innocent travelers and innkeepers were taken up on suspicion, because the persons who were missing had been seen last in their company, or had resided at their houses. Panic was the result of this well-meant but misguided justice. The greater part of the innkeepers in those parts decided to abandon their means of livelihood; some fled, to the great inconvenience of those who traveled through that district. The whole nation was at a loss to account for the numerous unheard-of villainies and cruelties that were carried out without leaving any clue.

What sort of life was lived by this strange set of people? That the children and grandchildren were virtually in a state of savagery, one can hardly doubt. Moral instruction was not to be expected from a cannibalistic father and mother. The probability is that the entire family alternated between debauches of feeding and debauches of drinking. Drink was probably the chief objective of the many robberies committed by Beane and his accomplices, for what other ambition could have possessed him? Life in a cavernous tunnel does not present many opportunities for the enjoyment of the commodities that money can buy. But there were many drinking-places and it must have been an easy thing for one of the family to procure the liquor and convey it to the cavern without arousing the least suspicion. Tavern-keepers of those days were frequently in a life-long condition of partial or complete fuddlement. They had just sufficient intelligence to discern the coins placed in their hands. They did not ask questions.

Sometimes, perhaps, the debauches were enlivened with snatches of song, reminiscences of the Lothian days of Beane and his woman. One can imagine this anthropophagist and his mate, roaring drunken melodies as they sat over the remains of their feasts on human flesh. It is conceivable, moreover, that life was rendered bare of monotony by frequent quarrels and internecine bloodshed. It was an existence partly gnomelike. For illumination there may have been candles—sinister candles wrought from human fat.

Thus for a period of twenty-five years these cannibals continued their blood-feasts. At last, however, an incident occurred that changed the course of their existence.

One evening, a man and his wife were riding home upon the same horse from a fair which had been held in the neighborhood and, being attacked, the husband put up a vigorous resistance. His wife, however, was dragged from behind him, her throat cut and her entrails instantly taken out. One of the cutthroats began sucking her streaming blood.

Struck with grief and horror, the husband redoubled his efforts to escape and even trod some of the assassins down under his horse's hooves. Fortunately for him— and for the inhabitants of that part of the country—in the meantime twenty or more persons in a company came riding home from the fair. Upon their approach, both men and women, Beane and his bloody crew fled into a thick wood and scurried to their infernal den.

This man, the first to escape from their hands, told the company what had happened. He showed them the mangled body of his wife, the bloodthirsty wretches not having had time to carry it along with them. They were all struck with horror, and took the man with them to

Glasgow and reported the whole episode to the chief magistrate of the city. He immediately wrote to the king, informing him of the matter.

In a few days his Majesty in person, accompanied by four hundred men, began to search the countryside for these incredible savages. The man whose wife had been murdered before his eyes, went as their guide, followed by a great number of bloodhounds, so that no possible hiding place might be overlooked.

They searched the woods and examined the seashore, but though they passed by the entrance to the cavern, they had no suspicion that any creature lived in that dark and dismal abode.

Fortunately, however, some of the bloodhounds entered the cave and raised a violent clamor, an indication that they were about to seize their prey. The king and his men then returned, but still could not see how any human being could live in a place of utter darkness, access to which was difficult and narrow. But, as the bloodhounds increased their howling and refused to return, it occurred to all that the cave ought to be explored to its darkest corner. Accordingly, a sufficient number of torches was provided, the hounds were permitted to pursue their course, and a large body of men penetrated through all the intricacies of the cavern and at length arrived at the private stronghold of the Beanes.

They were followed by all the band who were shocked to behold an unbelievable sight. Legs, arms, thighs, hands and feet of men, women and children were suspended in rows like dried beef. Some limbs and other parts were soaked in pickle. A great mass of money, both gold and silver, watches, rings, pistols, clothes, linens and woolens, and an immense quantity of other articles were either thrown together in heaps or suspended upon the sides of the cave.

The cavern reeked with a stench so overwhelming that several of the troop fainted. In a corner of the cave, garbage was heaped many feet high. Oozy mud and filth lay deep upon the ground. Strong liquor spilt during many orgies added its decaying fumes. Young children with matted hair, fierce eyes, a-crawl with insects, lay on the cold ground. The whole cruel, brutal, inhuman family was seized. The human flesh was buried in the sand of the seashore. The immense booty was carried away, and the King marched to Edinburgh with the prisoners.

This new and wretched spectacle attracted the attention of the inhabitants who flocked from all quarters to see, as they passed along, so bloody and unnatural a family, which had increased in twenty-five years to twenty-seven males and twenty-one females.

Arrived in the capital, they were all confined in the Tolbooth under a strong guard.

There was no question of trial. Indeed, at that period of Scottish history, these formalities were frequently overlooked. A conference was held and it was decided that a mass execution should take place within twenty-four hours. Moreover, the execution was to be on a grand scale—a scale that should awaken a sense of justice done among the terror-stricken inhabitants.

For twenty-five years Sawney Beane had robbed and murdered. To hang him and his progeny in crime would be a childish and trifling thing. Something more spectacular, something that would appeal to the demand for retribution, was obviously required.

The men were taken first. A preliminary of the punishment can only be inferred. It took the form of an excision of certain vital organs which were cast into a fire before the eyes of the agonized wretches. This initial operation having been performed with cruel slowness, their hands, arms and legs were then sawed off with blunt saws, the executioners prolonging the process to an inordinate degree. After this, they were left to bleed to death, the curses and jeers of the mob that had come to see them die accompanying their passage from life.

The wretched mother of the whole crew, the women and the young children were compelled to witness the horror. When at last the men had ceased to breathe, the females, with their young in their arms, were bound to iron stakes and burned at slow fires.

They did not display any signs of repentance or regret, but continued with their last breath to pour forth the most dreadful curses and oaths upon all around.

In view of the fact that with the exception of Beane and his woman, the culprits were on a level with savages in their knowledge of right and wrong, it is conceivable that not one of them realized for a single moment the horror and evil of their actions.

No correct estimate could be formed of the number of people who became victims of Sawney Beane and his family, but the chronicler suggests that probably a thousand men, women and children met their deaths at the hands of this monstrous criminal gang.

It is more than possible that the love of human flesh became a passion with Beane and his woman. In the beginning, as mentioned before, the act of cannibalism may have been a mere emergency measure, but the taste, once acquired, doubtless secured a hold on both of them. The children, born into a state of cannibalism, would naturally eat human remains as a matter of course. Beane and his family doubtless enjoyed the rude health of savage tribes.

It has been suggested by some that this hideous criminal and his woman were in reality semi-savage chieftains who robbed and killed after the fashion of those lawless and tempestuous times. The suggestion is absurd, although an engraving of Beane, presenting him in Scottish plaid, tartan and sporran—with amiable features and courageous mien—might help sustain the theory. The plain truth is that, though life then was rough and lawless, there is no example anywhere of such savage atavism, such a complete throwback to the most distant days of prehistory.

But it would be an oversimplification to consider Sawney Beane a man who killed—and ate his human victims—merely because he was lazy and took the life of least resistance in order to stay alive. No, the motives behind these dark and dreadful depravities lie deeper, something in his buried hungers—or submerged rebellions—that made Sawney Beane of the sixteenth century close kin to primordial man emerging from the miasmic mists of time.

But those motives, secret to him as to us, lie buried in the dark of an unnamed grave.

IV

MOLL CUTPURSE

Two ESSENTIAL facts distinguish "Moll Cutpurse," thief, highwayman and procuress, from many hundreds of criminal women: she dressed in men's clothes—and she died in her bed. A third point of distinction is that she lived to the age of seventy-three, a remarkable age for a person whose life is given up to crime. The majority of criminals are short-lived.

In 1589, in London, Mary Frith, afterwards to become famous in the pages of the Newgate Calendar as "Moll Cutpurse," was born of a shoemaker father and a mother who was probably the most excellent woman that ever gave birth to a monster of wickedness. Students of heredity would find Mary Frith a hard case.

There was nothing to account for Mary's swift and sudden departure from normal behavior. The father worked hard at his bench, loved a quiet chat about politics. The mother educated the child—or at least tried to educate her, but Mary, hating any kind of restraint from the age of three, refused to learn. She would bite, spit, and perform a trick that afterwards became one of her most notorious habits: she would twist her face into contortions so horrible that people said she was inhabited by the devil. Her chief delight was to hang about the doorways of taverns, leering at men when she was little more than twelve years old.

Domestic or feminine chores, such as sewing, she loathed. One chronicler has written: "A sampler was to her as grievous as a shroud." She loved a street fight, and long before she was twenty could hold her own even with a lusty youth of her own age.

Mary was repulsively ugly, and she decided that she would never attract men, but must aggressively compel them to yield her a certain solace. Abandoning her girl's clothes, she bought, at a secondhand dealer's, a complete suit of men's clothing, and from that time to the end of her life Mary wore breeches and coat. She walked like a man, with long swinging strides, swore heavily and invented new oaths. It was said of her that she could outswear and outdrink any coal heaver in the city.

This eccentric young woman had a relative whose interests and morals were altogether different from hers—an uncle clergyman. A family council was held and the parson suggested that Mary should be sent abroad. New England, the Puritan Colony, was proposed, but Mary, having agreed to the suggestion, suddenly changed her mind, just as the ship was sailing from Gravesend, and swam ashore immediately after it had put out to sea.

She returned to London and went home. Her friends then found her a position as a domestic servant, but Mary, having refused to abandon her masculine dress, had to look for something else.

Mary now plunged into a life of wickedness. She frequented the houses of ill fame and the taverns. She was received with great delight, her quaint behavior and her rough language delighting the inhabitants of the district.

It has been said that every person possesses a talent of some kind, but that the majority of men and women die without knowing it. Mary soon hit upon her essential talent. It lay in the direction of a wonderful skill for cutting out the pockets from the coattails of rich citizens. Her long thin hands had the artfulness of the conjurer. She boasted that she could beat any male pickpocket of long experience. It was this genius for the slicing of pockets that brought her the title of "Moll Cutpurse." She reveled in her gift and said that it served her better than beauty would have served her.

"Good looks often bring a girl a shameful brat," she is reported to have said. "But cutting purses will cause no woman sorrow."

Although Moll had no illusions regarding her appearance, she did not intend to go through life without any love affairs. She devised her own method of securing embraces. Having hit upon a man whom she liked, she would by sheer force compel him to make love to her. The unfortunate youth was battered into subjection and would eventually surrender to avoid further beatings. Moreover, she would sometimes use bribes as well as blows, and reward a satisfactory lover with shillings or guineas, according to the state of her purse.

Believers in atavism would say that Moll had reverted to type—that the primordial cave ancestor was bobbing up in this grimy, raucous-toned creature who dressed as a man and was more brutal than most of her male friends.

Unlike the ordinary thief, Moll was no extravagant spender. She hoarded her earnings and frequently added to her income by fortune-telling and other charlatan tricks. Her methods had the simplicity of genius. If the client was satisfied and paid uncomplainingly, all was well; if not, Moll, by sheer bullying and terrorizing, forced the dupe to pay. So terrifying were her face and manner that the wretched servant girls and apprentices, who were her chief clients, frequently became so cowed that they would yield to the most extortionate demands. She varied her predictions according to the possibilities of payment. If a client seemed likely to yield a good harvest, Moll would predict a rich marriage, with all the appropriate trappings. If, on the other hand, there seemed small chance of liberal payment, then a horrible future was solemnly prophesied to the innocent seeker of what lay in store.

Moll joined a society of petty thieves whose operations were confined within narrow limits. They would waylay children in the street and, having knocked them into the gutter, would steal from them money entrusted to the youngsters for errands. They would break open shop-tills, pick pockets, and generally undertake petty crimes that called for little skill and involved small risk.

Moll did not invariably escape. More than once she was arrested and convicted, and by some remarkable luck got off cheaply enough. Several times she was branded on the hands, but this process she could sometimes escape by bribing the officiating person, so that the branding process became little more than a perfunctory business.

It was impossible however, for a woman of Moll's talents to remain content with street thieving. She aimed at bigger goals. The roads in those stormy days were infested with highwaymen, and presently Moll decided to join those adventurous souls.

Moll's boldness—her contempt of danger and of death

—and her fine horsemanship enabled her to make a success of the highwayman business and soon she was able to gratify her political bias by "holding up" no less a personage than General Fairfax, whom she robbed of a very considerable sum. (Moll was a good loyalist, devoted to the cause of King Charles I. She hated the Roundheads.) Fairfax, of course, put up a good fight, but apparently he was no match for Moll, who not only wounded him in the arm, but killed two of his horses.

Had any other man but Fairfax been thus molested and outraged, there is no doubt that the culprit on being caught would have been summarily hanged. But Fairfax was more amused than infuriated. It seemed to him a very extraordinary piece of work for a woman to accomplish, and this admiration on his part proved of excellent service to Moll Cutpurse when, at a later time, she was found guilty and sentenced to death. For the general, having learned that Moll was a woman of means, proposed that she settle the affair for a considerable amount of money. Moll handed over two thousand pounds and was immediately released.

Funds were urgently needed by the rebels and they were not disposed to question too closely the source of their supplies. It is possible, however, that even had the bribe not been available, General Fairfax would have been generous enough to see to it that Moll's life was spared.

After this adventure, Moll, desiring a rest from the arduous life on the highway, set up a public-house in Fleet Street, London. It was while she was hostess of this tavern that she hit upon the notion of receiving and selling stolen goods. Moll soon became known to half the thieves, footpads and bullies of the town as a safe and reliable tradeswoman who would not only give a good price, but would never "peach" on a friend. A monster of deceit and cruelty, she was nevertheless loyal to her mob as she was loyal to her king.

Moll invented new kinds of robberies. She encouraged thieves to steal the books of merchants and tradesmen, knowing that the owners would be willing to buy back at a good price these records of their transactions. The houses of rich people and of noblemen were searched for compromising letters, and a good business in blackmail was carried on by Moll and her friends.

All this was bad enough, but what put her in the gallery of monstrous villains was the side line she practiced as a procuress. To her tavern in Fleet Street there would come rich men who desired young, innocent girls. Moll would go out into the streets, waylay young women seeking positions, especially girls who had come to London after running away from home.

Having brought these girls to her home, Moll would cajole or terrify them into submission. More than that, through a peephole in the wall she would sometimes gloat over their sufferings, enjoying a sort of vicarious delight when she beheld brutalities. Girls who offered strong resistance were flogged by Moll into giving in. It has been suggested that Moll, cheated by her ugliness and masculinity of the admiration of men, was delighted to see her sex suffer, and loved to gloat over its humiliation.

Because of her political attitudes—hating the Rump Parliament and anxious to victimize and harass the Revenue—Moll encouraged forgers and smugglers, and helped them in every way she could against the government.

Money came to Moll from many sources. She maintained a regiment of thieves of both sexes. She herself frequently went out on purse-cutting expeditions. Money earned by her trade of procuring swelled her savings. She loved crime for its own sake—she would never have been happy in any other occupation. She would smoke a clay pipe, swear, drink and tell a lewd story with any man in Drury Lane or St. Gile's!

For a long time Moll Cutpurse did not come into contact with the law. When at length the law saw fit to
come down upon her, it did so in a manner similar to
the present maneuvers of our law enforcers who convict killers for evading income tax laws. For, having shut
its eyes to her forgeries, street robberies and other crimes,
it solemnly arrested her on the charge of "indecently
and publicly wearing male attire."

Moll enjoyed the privilege of a trial before the Court
of Arches. After the absurd proceedings had dragged
their slow length, she was adjudged guilty and was
sentenced to do penance, dressed in a white sheet, on
the following Sunday morning at St. Paul's Cathedral.
Moll was by no means dismayed. On the contrary, she
said that she welcomed the ceremony because it would
attract so great a crowd that her "servants" would secure
a good harvest. The affair came off, but the "penance"
was softened by the fact that Moll was drunk throughout, having fortified herself with three quarts of sack
before leaving her house.

This extraordinary woman had certain artistic tendencies. She loved to fill her house with bizarre *objets
d'art*. Sometimes, when a silver cup or curiously decorated jewel was brought to her in the ordinary way of
"business," she would give the thief his price and retain
the article for her own personal enjoyment. Perhaps one
of her most astonishing traits, when one remembers her
ugliness, was a liking for mirrors. The Fleet Street house
was filled with them, and Moll saw her manly figure and
repulsive features reflected at all angles.

So the years went by. During their passage Moll prospered and took to soft living. She became enormously fat
and bloated. Her ugliness now reached a point that
caused people in the street to cross the road to avoid
this evil-looking, evil-smelling female thing that seemed
neither man nor woman, but an embodiment of the most
repulsive characteristics of both sexes. And just as in the

days of her childhood, when her powers of grimacing had caused people to say that she was inhabited by a devil, so it was now said of Moll that she had sold herself to Satan, for only the fiend himself could have wrought so ugly a shape, so monstrous a face.

In her later years Moll was seized with dropsy and suffered a great deal, but she bore her sufferings with stoic patience, saying that she had had a very enjoyable life and that one must not grumble when bad times came. Almost to the end of her long life, she plied her trade of receiver of stolen property and amassed a great fortune, but at her death only five hundred pounds remained. It is possible that she was robbed, or perhaps she may have speculated rashly. She died of dropsy at the age of seventy-three and was buried near her home in a City churchyard.

Her last wish was characteristic of her eccentric life. She said that she wished to be buried face downwards so that she, who throughout her existence had defied the conventions of life, might also defy the conventions of the grave.

An epitaph attributed to John Milton was placed on her tombstone. That the famous poet should have written an epitaph for a thief will seem incongruous to the modern reader, but no such incongruity would have occurred to Milton. The attitude of even the most cultured persons towards crime in past centuries was an attitude not so much of horror as of resentment. It was the inconvenience of the business rather than its immorality that irritated the honest citizen. The person causing the inconvenience having been decently hanged or burned, there was no reason why the gentlest poet should not celebrate his deeds.

Moll was certainly an unusual person. She stirred, by the force of her personality and her uniqueness, the imagination of the literary minds of her time. Her most distinguished appearance in literature was made when the poet Dekker collaborated with Middleton on the play called *The Roaring Girl.*

Moll Cutpurse was one of Nature's bad bargains. A cynicism, devilish in its intensity, seized her when she was but a child and forced her to crime. She revenged herself on society for the ugliness that shut her off from love and in the very act of vengeance, sustained throughout life, found a grim solace and reward.

Here is a portion of the epitaph attributed to John Milton.

> Here lies under this same marble
> Dust for Time's last sieve to garble;
> Dust to perplex a Sadduccee,
> Whether it rise a He or She,
> Or two in one, a single pair,
> Nature's sport and now her care.
> For her she'll clothe it at Last Day
> Unless she sighs it all away.
> Or where she'll place it, none can tell,
> Some middle place twixt Heaven and Hell.
> Reader, here she lies till then,
> When truly ye shall see her again!

V

MARIE DE BRINVILLIERS

POISON, that instrument of silence and precision, has in all ages been cherished by men and women who have sought to destroy. At certain periods poisoners have been the favorites of kings, princes, prelates and statesmen. Rome under the Caesars was a meeting place for professional poisoners from all parts of the world. In the Middle Ages, poisoners haunted every court in Europe.

On July 22, 1630, there was born in Paris a child who developed into the most notorious woman poisoner of an epoch—an epoch of poisoning. Marie Madeleine Marguerie d'Aubray began life with all things in her favor. The home life and training of this child who, in later years, became a symbol of evil, were wholly admirable.

Her high position in the exalted circles which surrounded the Court of Louis XIV gives added zest to the recital of her crimes. The France of that period was notable for its general corruption and decadence of morals. "A horrible place. Stifling hot, and such a stench." In these words the Princess Palatine summed up seventeenth century Paris. This conveys an accurate impression of the city in which Marie de Brinvilliers lived.

Marie's career must be a very sad blow to those sociologists who are never weary of claiming that environment and education form the principal, if not the exclusive elements of the formation of character.

When she was seventeen, Marie married Antoine Gobelin de Brinvilliers, Marquis de Brinvilliers. They both had estates in Picardy, but also had high connections among the wealthy and fashionable, and shortly after marriage the young couple settled in Paris and soon rose to prominence in the bureaucratic world.

Marie was a woman of great personal attraction. Her skin was extraordinarily white; her hair was very thick and nut-brown, which contrasted well with her blue eyes. She was not tall but was unusually well-built. Her intelligence was above the average, but she had no interest in the spiritual. Her confessor, the Abbé Pirot, found her strangely ignorant of scripture and religious knowledge. She had a strong personality and great courage, and though she had a general air of complete indifference, she was in reality keenly observant. She had a logical mind, spoke sparingly and to the point, and was very clever in finding a way out of a difficulty. Despite all these practical characteristics, she was frivolous and had no power of application. Yet she was always in complete command over herself and seldom lost her self-composure. She tempted fate and was willing to abide by the results.

During the early years of her marriage there was no reason to believe that it was not a serene and peaceful one. However, the marquis, weak and unstable, lacked morals and character. His marriage was probably a *mariage de convenance*.

A few years after their marriage, the marquis, probably wearying of his wife, began to pay attention to other women. With a cynicism characteristic of the times, he hinted to his wife that she was at liberty to take a lover if she chose, and to do as she pleased so long as he was left in peace to follow his own inclinations.

Marie took the hint without too much prompting. Some months previously, there had come to live at the house of the de Brinvilliers a young man by the name of Gaudin de Saint-Croix. He had been a fellow officer of the marquis and they had become friendly in the way of two men who had similar interests. They drank together, gambled together, scoured the town together despite their difference in station. De Saint-Croix' birth was obscure. Even his name was doubtful, and he was by repute the illegitimate child of a noble parent whose name he did not dare assume. He was not a fit companion for a peer, but Marie always accorded him the honorable prefix "de" in all her correspondence, which he was in no way entitled to use.

Bastards are often men of brilliant capacity and Saint-Croix was no exception to the general rule. He was industrious and could suit his manners to the society in which he mixed. He studied theology as well as chemistry, and at times assumed the title and black habit of an abbé. Maitre Vautier, the barrister, states: "He is keenly alive to insults, susceptible of love and, in love, jealous. His expenses are frightful and they were supported by no regular employment. Indeed, his soul prostituted itself to every kind of crime. He wrote books on religion. He spoke divinely of God in whom he did not believe and, assisted by this mask of piety, he seems to have participated in good deeds while in reality he was immersed in wickedness."

Marie, who had for some time been flirting outrageously with a former tutor called Braincourt, now turned her ephemeral fancy towards Saint-Croix. They soon became lovers. So indifferent was the marquis about the goings-on that neither of the lovers made the least attempt to conceal their intrigue. Marie devoted herself entirely to her handsome lover who now began to dominate her household in the Rue Neuve Saint Paul. She made no mystery of her amour. In society she gloried in it, despite the ensuing gossip.

The *ménage à trois* continued for some time to the satisfaction of all. But the marquis' extravagances—to which must be added Marie's—were making rapid inroads upon their joint fortune. Money was becoming scarce. Saint-Croix proposed a radical cure. He advised Marie to take legal steps to separate her fortune from that of her husband. The advice was strongly to his own interest.

Nevertheless, all might have gone pleasantly enough but for the well-meaning action of Marie's father, Dreux d'Aubray. It may be said that his rash and harsh intervention on behalf of morality helped propel his daughter later in the direction of the crimes which blackened her name. Monsieur d'Aubray, having pleaded for some time with Marie to abandon her lover, eventually took an entirely unjustifiable course. He contrived to secure a *lettre de cachet*—an order of arrest—and by means of this document the young Saint-Croix was sent to the Bastille.

In the seventeenth century steel and poison were not the sole methods of ridding oneself of an inconvenient person. Given a certain influence at Court, one could obtain a *lettre de cachet* with hardly any difficulty.

On March 19, 1663, Saint-Croix was arrested while driving through the city and unceremoniously hurried off to prison. He had guessed immediately who had ordered his arrest and the guess was confirmed by his captors. As it turned out, in asking for the arrest of Saint-Croix, Dreux d'Aubray, Marie's father, had signed his own death warrant.

Saint-Croix was placed in a dark cell, where he remained for some time, mouthing prayers for revenge. The Bastille was a mixture of severity and laxity. For instance, despite its harsh aspects, the kitchen was conducted upon a basis of the most extravagant hospitality. Saint-Croix' detention could not have been too unpleasant, for Marie de Brinvilliers probably supplied him with money for his needs.

In the Bastille, Saint-Croix made the acquaintance of a man who offered consolation, telling him that he could help him gain the vengeance for which he prayed. This man, his fellow prisoner, was Exili, the notorious Italian poisoner. Exili was an artist in toxicology and he loved and cherished his sinister profession. He was feared in every court in Europe, and he always had powerful but unknown protectors. When he turned up in France, he was under the guardianship of Sweden. The Italian was imprisoned while the French authorities tried to discover the reason for his visit to France. Every French minister was afraid of death by poisoning.

To cancel in some way the monotony of prison life, Exili taught Saint-Croix many of his secrets—for a price. Not only did he reveal the composition of subtle drugs, but he also explained how they might be administered and how their presence might be hidden. There is no doubt that young Saint-Croix, with his knowledge of chemistry, proved a very admirable pupil. Having learned his lesson, and having gained his freedom after three months by some freak act of an official of the Bastille, Saint-Croix resolved to take immediate vengeance on the father of his mistress.

But Saint-Croix had another motive apart from his desire for vengeance. Monsieur d'Aubray possessed a very considerable estate, a portion of which would pass upon his death to his daughter, Marie de Brinvilliers. Saint-Croix realized that his influence over Marie was such that she would share her fortune with him.

Immediately upon his release from prison, he returned to the arms of Marie. Their affair seemed to be based on a mixture of love and gold. Said Bussy-Rabutin: "The source of all these crimes was love, and then what we other Latins call *Auri sacra fames,* the execrable hunger after gold."

Outwardly, Saint-Croix had come out of the Bastille a changed man. He gave up all loose living. He turned his back upon gambling and card-playing with such debauched and reckless men as the Marquis de Brinvilliers. He became pious, went regularly to church, and his conversation was devout. He gave the cold shoulder to all his former disreputable friends, and he frequented only the most select circles. He began to have business with men of high position.

He turned his private room into a laboratory which led to the investigation of the philosopher's stone. If Saint-Croix had engaged in chemical experiments before his imprisonment, it may well have been in pursuit of the golden dreams of alchemists. But since his association with Exili, his thoughts turned another way. He was exactly the man to avail himself of the "Exili preparations."

Marie de Brinvilliers had been short of money for some time. Her profligate husband was being pursued by his creditors. She herself spent lavishly. So, together with Saint-Croix, she studied two perilous sciences. The first was that of alchemy; the second, that of poison, or the "removing of those who had it in their coffers." Of the two, she soon saw that the second was likely to be more lucrative. But these studies were kept secret.

There now enters upon the scene Christopher Glaser, chief chemist of his time in Paris. In his establishment he taught Saint-Croix and Marie de Brinvilliers the whole theory and practice of poisons. He supplied them with poisons from his drugs, particularly the preparation of arsenic known as "Glaser's receipt."

In pursuit of her deeply laid plans, Marie then began to experiment with the deadly phials and powders Glaser and Saint-Croix had placed within her power. Her first attempts were made in the Hotel Dieu, the great public hospital. The hospital was overcrowded, understaffed, and the surveillance badly organized. Many of the great ladies of Paris faithfully visited the sick and Marie de Brinvilliers was allowed to wander at will. Upon the unfortunate patients, she experimented secretly but freely. She brought and administered sweets, wine and biscuits, all carefully prepared with "Glaser's receipt." Patients who received gifts from her hands invariably died.

The doctors were faced with a mysterious and appalling sickness. Autopsies—as well as they could be performed in that period—were made with the most scrupulous care, but no sign of any poisonous substance was discovered. There was no further investigation. Nobody seemed to have detected Marie or associated her with the deaths. She achieved her end. She had ascertained the dose required to kill. Moreover, she was now confident that she had nothing to fear, for the drugs eluded analysis in the post-mortem examinations.

Still, Marie wanted to proceed cautiously. She decided to experiment upon her servants with the poisons. She made the first test on her maid, Francine Roussel. Saint-Croix had sent her a certain poison which he assured her would defy analysis. She placed a portion of it in some mutton, in some fruit pie, and in the remains of her own meal which the maid usually ate. The girl was immediately seized with horrible pains. An emetic was given her by a doctor and she recovered after a number of hours. The doctor diagnosed it as indigestion and no more was thought of it. The experiment had served its purpose, however, for it had shown Marie that the dose given was not adequate. She resolved to make further experiments. It is clear that from the outset Marie de Brinvilliers went about her tests, at the expense of human lives, in the most cold-blooded manner.

One has to wonder about what went on inside her. How did it happen that this young woman who throughout girlhood and even later had shown no sign of evil, whose disposition was apparently gentle, clinging and kindly, was nevertheless ready at the first appearance of temptation to commit the most appalling of crimes? One can hardly explain her acts by suggesting that Marie was so passionately in love with Saint-Croix that she would stop at nothing to please him. It is far more probable that she was led to consent to the crime in order that she might be rid of her father's constant reproaches. The prospect of the considerable sum which she would inherit no doubt also weighed heavily with her.

Her accomplice, Saint-Croix, had pointed out to Marie that while he would supply the necessary drugs to destroy Monsieur d'Aubray, the actual administration of the poison must be undertaken by her. He emphasized the fact that he had no access to the proposed victim, whereas she was his favorite child and was the last person on earth whom he would suspect of an attempt on his life.

In 1666, when Marie was thirty-six, her opportunity arrived. It happened that Monsieur d'Aubray, feeling unwell, decided to leave Paris for his country house at Compiègne. Marie insisted on accompanying her father, saying that she alone was capable of giving him the care he required. Her father was delighted, for he saw in this action a sign that Marie was now ready to abandon her lover. He kissed her affectionately and said he was certain he would find ease and peace in her society. "You can cure all ills, my cherished darling," said d'Aubray, little dreaming of the irony that lay in his words.

The house at Compiègne was an ideal place to commit a crime. It was isolated; few visitors came there. Marie recognized that here, indeed, was her chance, and having made preparations for the journey, she met her lover who handed her the poison.

Everything went smoothly. The servants were sent away on a pleasure trip to Paris. Marie herself served the dinner. She had already applied the poison to several of the dishes. Monsieur d'Aubray swallowed a few spoonsful of the soup and immediately was seized with violent internal pains. He begged Marie to fetch a doctor. She went out, returning after some time with the story that the only doctor in the village was unable to come till morning. Then she helped the wretched man to bed and sat with him throughout the night, pretending to comfort him.

At eight o'clock next morning, the doctor, an uninformed country practitioner, arrived. He diagnosed the trouble as indigestion and prescribed a simple purgative. However, d'Aubray was growing anxious and refused to stay at Compiègne, insisting on returning at once to Paris where he might have his own physician. Marie was more than agreeable to the suggestion, for it perfectly fitted in with her plan. This way the two doctors would have no opportunity to compare notes; the exactness of the symptoms and their progress would be a matter of hazy conjecture.

Everything happened just as Marie had hoped and expected. After four days of agony, the miserable man died, passing away in the arms of his favorite daughter, blessing her as he went. She cried, sobbed, became almost hysterical, playing her part to perfection.

Monsieur d'Aubray having been a person of importance—a Councillor and at one time a Minister of State—the authorities thought fit to hold an autopsy on his body. No trace of poisonous substance was found in any of the organs. The physicians stated rather vaguely that death was owing to "natural causes." Not for a moment did any suspicion fall upon Marie. Nor was there any apparent reason why suspicion should have fallen. To all appearances, she was the heartbroken daughter.

The eldest son succeeded to his father's position and title, and the estate was parceled out according to his will. Having acquired her portion of the dead man's estate, Marie was not slow in spending the larger part of it with her lover's help.

The death of her father cut off the last thread of restraint, which held back Marie d'Brinvilliers. Her conduct now became thoroughly unbridled. One lover, in the person of Saint-Croix, the father of her two children as later acknowledged was no longer enough for her. She also became the mistress of a certain F. de Pouget, Marquis de Nadaillac, a captain of the light horse and cousin of her husband. In addition, there was a cousin of her own she became friendly with. And Briancourt, the tutor of her children, received more than tutor's fees from her. Her temper became feline in its uncertainty. She quarrelled with Saint-Croix for his unfaithfulness and she savagely stabbed her husband's mistress, a woman called Dufay.

Amidst wild dissipations and excesses, the money left her by her father soon melted away. Creditors dunned her on every side. In 1670, a property at Nourar jointly belonging to her and her husband was sold by order of the court. Rather than let it go towards liquidation of her debts, she tried to set the house on fire.

Again it became absolutely necessary for her to find money. She was next heir after her brothers. The elder brother was a "Civil Lieutenant" and the younger, Counsellor to the Parliament of Paris. It was decided to remove them both, and Marie again plotted with Saint-Croix to secure the entire fortune by the wholesale destruction of the remainder of her family—the two brothers and her young sister.

In order to achieve this goal, the two conspirators took into their confidence a certain La Chaussée, one of Saint-Croix' personal servants. This man, an unmitigated scoundrel, was promised a huge bribe for his co-operation, and he agreed to carry out the crime when the opportunity arose.

The first step was easily arranged. The younger d'-Aubray wanted a valet. His sister Marie heard of it and knew exactly the man to suit him—a faithful and expert servant she could thoroughly recommend. It happened to be La Chaussée. Only one person recognized that the new valet had formerly been in the service of Saint-Croix, a name of evil omen in the d'Aubray household. This person was Cluet, a sergeant at the police depot of the Châtelet, an intelligent officer who was courting a maid in the d'Aubray household.

Accordingly, La Chaussée entered the service of the younger d'Aubray. But before he took up his duties, Marie signed and gave to Saint-Croix two promissory notes, one for twenty-five thousand, the other for thirty thousand livres. La Chaussée was not slow in carrying out his instructions.

During the Easter of 1670, the two brothers went to their estate at Villequoy in Beauce, and La Chaussée, who completely won their confidence, went with them

as their personal servant. He ingratiated himself with
everyone. He even assisted in the kitchen, which was
clearly no part of his duty. The same day a giblet pie
was sent up to the table. Those who ate it were violently
ill; others who had not touched it remained in good
health.

On April 12, six days after Easter, the elder brother
was ill and was rapidly growing worse. He returned to
Paris. He lost all desire for food and wasted away. His
most assiduous nurse was La Chaussée. On June 17,
1670, d'Aubray died of exhaustion, after much agony.
His younger sister was present at his deathbed, but
Marie remained on her estate in Picardy. An autopsy
was held. Death was attributed to a "malignant tumor."
Thus a second murder in this family remained undiscovered.

The success of this attempt urged Marie, Saint-Croix
and La Chaussée to throw all prudence to the winds, for
they considered that they were absolutely secure from
detection. They now decided to make away with the
younger brother without loss of time.

Counsellor d'Aubray was soon ill with identically the
same symptoms as his father and brother. Again La
Chaussée was an excellent nurse, seldom leaving the sick
man. He was so good a servant that when d'Aubray *in
extremis* made his will, La Chaussée was given a leg-
acy of one hundred *écus* for his attention, although he
had been in his service but a short period. The unhappy
patient expired three months after his brother, September, 1670. Marie de Brinvilliers, her young sister, a
Carmelite nun, and the widow of the late lieutenant now
had the entire estate between them.

This time, however, the doctors seem to have been
more searching in their inquires. Three doctors and
an apothecary conducted an autopsy. They evidently
believed the case one of poisoning, but they lacked the
courage or the complete conviction to announce that

fact. They, therefore, drew up and signed a report which today would leave little doubt as the cause of death. It was very strange that they did not push their investigations further. And so another secret crime went unpunished.

Marie and her accomplice, Saint-Croix, had now rid themselves of the senior d'Aubray and his two sons. Only the daughter, the Carmelite nun, remained, and the obliging La Chaussée was charged with her removal. In this case, however, the attempt failed. The chroniclers leave us in doubt as to the cause of the failure. It is possible there was some bungling.

Marie de Brinvilliers could now foresee the time she would be able to restablish the former magnificence of her house. In her own mind, she had arranged that her eldest son should succeed to the family post of "Civil Lieutenant." Her other children she did not care for deeply. Her daughter was not loved. She was ugly and dull-witted. The poor child received several doses of Glaser's receipt." Then Marie repented of her evil intentions and gave her a quantity of milk as an antidote.

The position of the wretched marquis, Marie's husband, was extraordinary. He was undoubtedly well aware of all the evil business. Harassed by creditors, he prepared to avail himself of any sudden inheritance. He lived in constant fear of being poisoned, and several attempts were made to remove him with the aid of Glaser's receipt.

"Madame de Brinvilliers wanted to marry Saint-Croix," wrote Madame de Sévigné. "With that intention she often gave her husband poison. Saint-Croix, not desiring so wicked a woman for his wife, gave antidotes to the poor husband with the result that, shuttlecocked about in this manner five or six times, now poisoned, now unpoisoned, he still remained alive."

His health, however, was not unaffected. He had a weakness in his legs from which he did not recover. He

also always carried theriac, the treacle compound of
some sixty various drugs, which was supposed to be
very effective against poison.

Probably for the same reasons the tutor, Briancourt,
escaped with his life. Marie had every need to destroy
him for, in moments of weakness, this lover had been
made the confidant of all her crimes. He passed through
some exceedingly perilous adventures in her house, as
related at length in his evidence at the trial.

By this time La Chaussée was going freely in and out
of Marie's house. She received him privately in her room
and gave him money. "He is a good fellow and has done
me great service," she used to remark. She was seen "In
great familiarity with him" and on one occasion when
an unexpected visitor was announced, she had to hide
him behind her bed. The rogue had Marie entirely at his
mercy and within his power. It is a wonder that Saint-
Croix did not try to finish him off, but the valet was too
clever, and could not be caught napping.

Marie, having tasted the power of the poisoner, began
to relish the work for its own sake. No man, no woman
was safe. Secure in her passionate egoism and the in-
fallibility of her poisons, she became a wholesale murderess. The smallest trifle served as a pretext for destruction. A woman seated beside her at a reception chanced
to make a jesting remark that annoyed her. A few days
later that woman died in agonies. Another woman who
enraged Marie by accidentally spilling some coffee over
her gown was laughingly reproved and invited to dinner
on the following day. Into her coffee the poison was
introduced and she paid the penalty of her carelessness.
People who merely bored her with weak jokes or long-
winded conversation were likewise dispatched by her
to a region where neither their jests nor their platitudes
could offend.

Meantime, Marie went on her way, joyous, witty, her
eyes sparkling, her lips framing compliments while her

brain stalked new victims. Never had she seemed so
winning, so gentle, so affectionate. Saint-Croix still remained her favored lover. The other men she entertained in a subordinate capacity. When she wearied of
these lesser lovers, when they become importunate, she
fell back upon her invariable remedy. One by one they
vanished, while she herself continued upon her course,
unsuspected, a laugh upon her lips.

At length, the unexpected happened. It came about
with tragic abruptness. Saint-Croix, experimenting in his
laboratory with certain poisons, fell a victim to the
fumes. It had been his habit to wear a glass mask when
thus engaged. The glass, it seems, dropped and smashed
and he was immediately overpowered. He died a few
hours after the accident.

When the authorities arrived at the house, they started
a search for his will and other personal documents. A
casket, crammed full with sealed packages, was soon
discovered. There was also a letter requesting that in
the event of his death, the entire contents of the casket
should be immediately sent, unopened, to the Marquise
Marie de Brinvilliers.

However, the authorities had become suspicious of the
manner in which Saint-Croix died. They decided to open
the sealed packages. They found in each package a drug,
afterwards recognized as a subtle poison. The report of
the analysis, to the effect that the "poison that would
evade detection in the organs," sent the authorities into
a huddle. "This artful and subtle poison," wrote the
chemist, "has been subjected to a long experiment. Contrary to the habit of other poisonous substances, it swims
in water and it eludes the test of fire, leaving only an
innocent residue. After experimenting with animals, *no
trace could be found in any of the organs*. All parts remained sound, but the beasts perished . . ."

After this analysis of the contents of the casket, events
began to move more rapidly. La Chaussée, having been

named by Saint-Croix in certain of the letters as a go-between, was immediately arrested—September, 1672 —and questioned under severe torture. He eventually confessed that he had frequently conveyed poisons from Saint-Croix to the Marquise de Brinvilliers. Moreover, he admitted his part in the murder of the two d'Aubray brothers, but swore he was merely an agent for the woman. His trial followed. He was found guilty, sentenced, and a few days later he was broken on the wheel, one of the most painful methods of execution invented by an age that loved justice a little but vengeance a great deal more.

Like all cruelties of this nature, this atrocious punishment never prevented a single crime. Indeed, the brigands and thieves for whom it was intended were in the habit of hardening their flesh against its agonies, and as a form of practice used to carry out mock but painful tortures of the wheel, which enabled them to suffer on the scaffold with fortitude and resignation.

Four actors thus passed from the stage of this drama— Saint-Croix was dead, a victim of his own instruments; La Chaussée was executed; and both Exili and Glaser had vanished from France. There remained only the Marquise Marie de Brinvilliers.

When the police arrived to execute their order for her arrest, they found the bird had flown. A few nights before, her lawyer, La Marre, had arrived very late at her country house. His news was grave and he counselled such speed that he himself assisted his client to remove many of her goods through the window. All that the police could learn was that Marie and a single maidservant had gone to London. They might have expected such action, and judging from the extreme slowness of their movements they perhaps knew it before they arrived. It is probable that her powerful relatives and friends were behind this in order to avoid the terrible scandal her arrest would create.

The record of the Marquise Marie de Brinvilliers' adventures as a fugitive can never be told, for no record exists. La Reynie, the chief of police, and his agents traced her movements in London until she was swallowed up in the huge city. She then became the subject of diplomatic representations between the statesmen of the two countries in an effort to have England hand her over to France.

Marie, finding her residence in London likely to come to a sudden end, left London for safety in Holland. The French ambassador failed to discover her exact location, but she was evidently informed of the secret negotiations between Paris and London. Probably she had friends in both places. There were many families closely allied to her who had no wish to see their high position sullied by the scandal which would arise out of her public trial. It is more than possible that they sent a warning across the Channel.

For over three years, Marie remained in hiding, her only companion being Genevieve Bourgeois, widow of an old family servant. At various times she was in Cambrai, Valenciennes, and Antwerp, finally settling as a boarder in a convent at Liége, neutral territory under the dominion of a prince-bishop, although the French army was occupying it. She was now extremely poor, and would have been utterly penniless if her sister had not made her an annual allowance of about five hundred livres.

Here she might have remained in devout but irksome solitude until the scandal of her misdeeds had been quite forgotten. But her implacable enemy in Paris, the widow of her dead brother, never lost sight of her vengeance. On the exact day arranged for the evacuation of the French troops from Liége, Marie was arrested.

The story of the arrest belongs to romance. Many historians deny its details, but there is no inherent impossibility in what some claim happened. It seems that Desgrez, the celebrated police agent, arrived at Liége in the habit of a French abbé, "young, amiable and gallant," ostensibly a wanderer. Interested in the history of the Marquise de Brinvilliers, he obtained an introduction to her in the convent and rapidly paid his court to her. Wearied by her peaceful existence, she smiled upon the handsome abbé. Since the arrest could not be made in that place, Desgrez, playing the part of a suitor, performed his role so well that he eventually persuaded Marie to accompany him on a walk along the banks of the river Ourthe.

When they were some distance from the town, they met a coach. At a sign from Desgrez, some hidden police officers sprang out and arrested Marie. Shutting her up in the coach, they quickly brought her to the prison at Liége.

On March 29th, 1676, the first stage of her journey to Paris began. After her unexpected arrest Marie became despondent and gave herself up for lost; and when she saw the box containing her confession in the hands of the hated Desgrez, she relinquished all hope.

Desgrez, it seems, had managed to search Marie's apartment at the convent and had found a box under her bed with a confession she had written. Judged by this confession, Marie stood revealed by her own words as a murderess of the most lurid type.

She had no intention of fighting the case against her. Deprived of a knife at one of her meals, she had seized an opportunity to break her glass and swollow the fragments. Her guard quickly seized her by the throat and prevented her self-destruction. Three times during the journey Marie tried to commit suicide. She was closely guarded against escape by an escort of one hundred cavalry.

Arrived in Paris, Marie was at once driven to the prison—the Montgomery Tower—where she remained for a long time while the formalities connected with her trial

and the marshaling of evidence were arranged. It was
months before the case came to court. When at length
the trial began, Marie created a sensation by withdraw-
ing in its entirety the confession found at the convent
at Liége. Her counsel made an ingenious, if somewhat
futile, attempt to explain away this document. In effect,
this is what he said:

"We have here a woman who flies from Paris and takes
refuge in a convent, knowing that she is suspected of
certain terrible crimes. She is innocent, but the suspicion
of guilt has preyed so strongly upon a susceptible and
half-distraught brain that in an hour of madness she
sets down an imaginary confession . . ."

It is said that this plea caused amusement in the
court and that even the judges smiled. For in view of
the nature of the evidence, it was a farcical attempt.

Witness after witness told convincing stories. First of
all, there was Police Sergeant Cluet. His evidence made
a strong impression. He described the watch he had
kept for some time on the house of Saint-Croix. He stated
that very often he had seen La Chaussée leave that house
carrying small packages to the residence of the prisoner.
Invariably, mysterious deaths soon followed in her
circle of friends.

Marie's maid was then called. Crying bitterly, she related how Madame had once given her the queerly tasting mutton and fruit pie and how, after eating those
foods, she had immediately been seized by sharp pains.

Many other witnesses followed, entirely damning to
Marie. Great interest was aroused by the mistress of
Christopher Glaser, the chemist, who had formerly been
a Court apothecary, and queer stories were told concerning his services to royal patrons. The woman stated that
on a number of occasions she saw Madame de Brinvilliers at the house of Saint-Croix, where the latter
handed her certain packages. Indeed, Madame's footman had frequently suggested jokingly that she had

come there to buy poisonous drugs. The witness, moreover, said that she had overheard conversations with Saint-Croix that clearly pointed to the sinister nature of the visits.

The trial wore to its end. Throughout, Marie remained calm and poised. She smiled affectionately at all her friends in the courtroom; she sent little billets-doux of encouragement to her lawyer who was doing his utmost to save a hopeless cause.

The jury went out but returned after a very brief interval. They found the prisoner guilty of the murder of her father, her two brothers and of attempting the life of her sister. The sentence, however, was deferred. Marie was removed from court and taken to a cell where she was to remain until the judges had arrived at a decision concerning her fate.

She was in the gayest mood. Death still seemed a distant thing. There was the possibility that a term of imprisonment might be substituted for the death penalty. The convicted criminal is almost always an optimist. The behavior of Marie during the time that elapsed between the trial and her execution amazed the entire populace. They said of her in the prison that she behaved like an "angel." The warders loved her; they brought her delicacies forbidden by the prison regulations.

Marie's confessor, the priest Pirot, a man of exceptionally noble character, also fell under the sway of this amazing woman. He admitted he found it hard to believe in her guilt. There was that in her voice, manner and conversation, he said, that suggested a guileless and even saintlike character. But there were her written confessions that could not be denied. She may not have committed all the sins she noted in those confessions, which were written with complete frankness in a country where a spade is always a spade, but she left no doubt regarding the crimes of which she was now accused. It was an extraordinary document which included references to "bizarre and monstrous crimes."

On July 16, 1676, at an early hour, Marie de Brinvilliers was roused and ordered to dress. She was told that the sentence of the court would be communicated to her in a few hours. She became pale for a moment, but quickly smiled and began to dress, making a careful toilette. Friends visited her.

From her cell to the torture chamber where the sentence was to be pronounced was a walk of a few minutes. Officials filed into the room. The clerk immediately read out the pronouncement:

"The Court condemns Marie Madeleine Marguerie d'Aubray de Brinvilliers to make public apology for her crimes before the door of the principal church in Paris, holding in her hand a lighted torch of the weight of two pounds. There on her knees, she shall declare that in order to possess their goods she poisoned her father, her two brothers, and attempted the life of her sister, of all of which she repents and asks pardon of God, the King, and the Law. This done, she shall be immediately conveyed to the Place de la Grève of this city and there her head shall be cut off, her body burned, and the ashes thrown to the winds. She is first to be put to the questions, ordinary and extraordinary, to obtain a disclosure of her accomplices."

The questions under torture were usually administered before and after trial. It was held that many accused persons who would not confess while a chance of acquittal remained, would perhaps admit their crimes when execution was a certain thing.

The torture followed immediately. Marie was placed on the rack. The water torment was applied. Even in that moment of agony, Marie retained her self-possession. On seeing the cans of water, she said to the executioner: "That is a very large quantity for a small person like myself. I cannot drink it all, and perhaps it is intended to drown me."

After a few minutes the agony forced her to speak. "My God! You are killing me!" she moaned. Then she begged them to stop, saying she would reveal all she knew. "Accomplices! I have had none, excepting those who have been named," she told them. "Saint-Croix and La Chaussée. Both are dead. I cannot remember the composition of the poisons. I remember only toad's venom. I know nothing of antidotes. I did not use them. But milk might have served well for that purpose."

That was sufficient. Perceiving that nothing further was to be learned from the pale lips, they unbound her, preparing her for the last journey.

The law decreed that the prisoner should wear a shift and nothing else. But in this case the headsman had all ready a long white gown and he simply threw it over Marie. It enveloped her from head to foot. A white bonnet was given her and tied under her chin. Her hands were shackled and a cord was hung round her neck. She had also to appear barefooted. She felt shame at these preparations and looked to her confessor for sympathy. He was full of compassion. Over fifty important persons had collected to watch Marie undergo the toilette of the condemned. She knew them all, some intimately. Under their cold, relentless gaze, she trembled. Then she left the Conciergerie.

When Marie stood before the vehicle which was to convey her to her doom, her surprise was dreadful to witness. And her horror was shared by her confessor. It was a rough, two-wheeled cart, used for the meanest needs of the stable and was so small that there was barely space for two persons. Some straw had been thrown in the bottom of the cart and Marie and the priest seated themselves with difficulty. The executioner balanced himself on the tailboard, and his legs stuck into the priest's back. The sight was grotesque. The exe-

cutioner thrust into Marie's hand a flaming torch, which
she had to carry at Notre Dame when making her confession.

An enormous crowd surged round the prison. Shame
surrounded Marie like a mist; agony piled upon agony.
It was at this minute that the painter, Le Brun, made his
terrible drawing of her. He said that she looked like a
tigress. The crowd screamed and shouted. Obscene ex-
pressions were shouted at her. She heard them and
winced.

"You must recognize that you deserve to be cursed by
the whole world," said the priest. "Guilty as you are, you
must regard these imprecations more as a punishment
due to your crime than as an insult to your unhappiness."

Tears streamed down Marie's eyes and she fervently
kissed the crucifix. "I take them in that spirit," she replied. "I wish to suffer even more than I do."

When the cortege arrived at the church of Notre
Dame, Marie was dragged into the nave, and having
knelt down, the wretched woman repeated after the reg-
istrar these words:

"I confess that wickedly and for revenge and to secure
possession of their fortunes, I poisoned my father and
two brothers and tried to destroy my sister. I now ask
pardon of God, the King, and the Law of my country."

Then with the priest beside her again, she was driven
to the Place de la Grève, attended by four hundred ser-
geants and archers. All Paris saw her pass by. The crowd
was so large that Madame de Sévigné later wrote that
many narrowly escaped being crushed to death.

The priest accompanied Marie to the scaffold and at
her request held her hand in his own until the moment of
death. He immediately gave her absolution. She then
knelt down and prayed. When she rose, she embraced
the priest.

The crowd hissed and whistled. Every window and
every roof was black with spectators. Marie's eyes and

ears were shut to all her surroundings. She did not appear to notice the pile of faggots, sprinkled with pitch and tar, upon which her body was to be consumed. Nor did she see the executioner's sword resting on one corner of the scaffold, its gleaming edge half-hidden by the coat he had thrown carelessly over it.

The ceremonial of the condemned proceeded leisurely. The executioner cut Marie's hair at the back and sides. He was rather rough, but she did not complain. After this he neatly, but still slowly, cut her chemise, so as to leave her neck and shoulders bare. As the headsman folded the handkerchief to place across her eyes, the priest noticed that she was gazing intently at the twin towers of Notre Dame. He prayed and she prayed with him. She again admitted her sins and asked for divine mercy. Then she kissed the cross. At last she was ready.

"Say the 'Salve,' Monsieur," the executioner said to the priest.

He did so in a loud voice, and one by one the people in the crowd took up the words until the entire throng was repeating the prayer. It was the old custom at French executions for the onlookers to repeat this prayer in the ears of the criminal.

The executioner did his work speedily. The head was severed at the first stroke. Then he turned to the priest and said with satisfaction: "That was a good stroke, sir, was it not? On these occasions I always offer up a prayer for success and the good God has aided me." So justice was done.

The next day, writes Madame de Sévigné, after the body had been burned, hundreds of simple folk gathered, searching for charred bones to preserve as relics. There is supposed to be an occult value in the blood or the bones of a malefactor.

It is not easy to formulate a theory as to the motives of the Marquise Marie de Brinvillers. Though it is clear that greed prompted the murders of her relatives, there seems no obvious motive for the many casual crimes she committed.

That she was sane enough in the common sense is fairly certain. Her control, her equanimity, do not smack of the madhouse. It is equally clear that she must have suffered unconscious guilt feelings, otherwise she would not have written a confession and left it where it could easily be found. But the wellsprings of her crimes were buried with her.

Saint-Croix has been blamed by some historians as the tempter but for whom the marquise might never have become a criminal. But it is just as likely that he was the instrument rather than the instigator.

The piety of the marquise during the last days of life is not unusual in the records of crime. The most depraved criminals often turn to God as the toll of doom comes near.

Marie de Brinvilliers' execution was the final act in a startling tragedy. In her day she was considered the blackest of murderers.

VI

JONATHAN WILD

JONATHAN WILD towers above the ordinary run of scoundrel as a very giant in wickedness. An irrepressible rogue, a monster of deceit, hypocrisy and cruelty, he went his way without a sigh until the end. This cunning rogue, friend and betrayer of rogues, was known as London's master "fence."

Jonathan was a native of Wolverhampton, the son of a wig-maker, and was born about 1682. He received his education at the school at Wolverhampton and learned to read and write. At fifteen, his father apprenticed him to a Birmingham buckle-maker for seven years. While there, he married, but not long afterward he deserted his wife and child, and departed for London, since he felt that a small town was not likely to afford him scope for his talents. There is no doubt that he had decided to live by his wits—to exploit everybody.

His first adventure came en route to London. It seems, the story runs, that on the road he met a "lady doctor." According to this legend, Jonathan possessed the power of dislocating his hip at will and he performed this feat in order to arouse the sympathy of the lady who was passing him in a carriage. She took pity on the "lame" fellow and, inviting him into her conveyance, allowed him to accompany her as far as Warwick.

During the drive Jonathan learned the profession of the lady and he admitted he had tricked her. Slyly suggesting that the trick might be turned to their mutual advantage, he saw she was amused rather than angry at his proposal. They talked it over. In Warwick, together, they produced an ointment which seemed to effect a miraculous and speedy cure. This was Jonathan's first swindle.

They then announced an "exhibition" they had decided to put on. They collected a large crowd, and Jonathan, have carefully dislocated another limb, applied the ointment, and instantly the leg was set right. The innocent yokels were greatly impressed and, during the next few weeks, Jonathan and his partner took in a considerable amount of money. By this time she had confessed to him that she was not a doctor at all—just a fraud, like him—and she became his mistress. For a while they continued to put over their swindle; then Jonathan, restless, left for London and nothing more was heard of this partner of his first swindle.

For a short time Jonathan served as a gentleman's servant. Then, for a brief period, he returned to the bucklemaking trade. But the remuneration earned by this work was not enough to meet the expenses of town life, and before long Jonathan was arrested for debt and placed in the Wood Street Compter, where he remained for four years.

The Compter was nothing less than an academy for incipient scoundrels, and Jonathan was thrown into the society of many persons of both sexes whose life had been somewhat less respectable than his own. While there, he stated: "It was impossible but he must, in some measure, be let into the secrets of the criminals under confinement there." He thus became acquainted with the practices of thieves. For a period of his term, Wild was assistant jailer. Never, at any time, did he lose his natural pleasant manner or his tact. He was genial and could be quite charming, and these qualities stood him in good stead.

In this breeding ground of criminals, Wild met Mary Milliner, an attractive and vivacious woman, notorious as a prostitute and a clever pickpocket. Though young in years, she was old in the ways of crime, and through her Jonathan learned some of the possibilities of roguery. Mary fell in love with him and lived with him as his mistress in prison, which was the custom of the period.

Wild needed only this introduction to the world of crime to make himself a full-fledged member. Once shown the methods, this rogue not only became a master of the trade, but he quickly improved upon them to the admiration of all the cross-coves in London. Jonathan and Mary Milliner were released from jail at the same time.

Immediately they set up an establishment in Lewkenor's Lane, where they both settled down. Mary was to provide the feminine "entertainment"; Jonathan would go out into the byways and bring home suitable clients. Soon the house prospered and, together, Wild and Mary amassed enough money to abandon their bordel and go into another business, which in those days was considered hardly more respectable. They invested in a tavern in Cock Alley, near Cripplegate. Soon they moved into the tavern and settled down there to entertain half of the thieves, footpads, bullies and underworld characters of the town.

While in prison, Wild had made the acquaintance of a subtle rogue, a certain Charles Hitchen, an ex-city marshal who had lost his position through shady dealings and had become an associate of thieves and an expert blackmailer. He used the badge of his office to intimidate those he needed for his purposes. He was demoted to a mere constable. Intrigued by the ill-fame of Wild's tavern, Hitchen decided to visit it in his capacity as constable.

A brief talk with Wild convinced Hitchen that here was a man of talent—a man with whom he might work in harmony to mutual profit. He recognized in Jonathan a brother spirit and, sure he could place complete confidence in Wild, he offered him a job as his assistant. Wild accepted and a partnership was formed that lasted for years. To enable Wild to carry on their "work" with authority, he was invested with a certain insignia of office.

Hitchen was Wild's most efficient instructor in the curious art of acting as intermediary between thieves and those who had been robbed of their goods, or had had their pockets picked of watches and other valuable jewelry. Wild was to thieve and he was also to catch thieves; he was to incite to rob and then to blackmail the robbers. He was to be criminal and detective simultaneously.

After Hitchen explained his duties to Wild, he proceeded to introduce him as his new assistant.

First, they made the rounds of several brandy shops and ale-houses. The proprietors offered their services to their protector—Hitchen—who told them that all he wanted from them was information as to the whereabouts of stolen property that might come into possession of their clients. Then the two associates visited various bagnios, and those off duty were lectured by Hitchen on the impropriety of handing over to anybody but himself—and now also to Wild—pocketbooks and other "trifles" which the girls might extract from gentlemen who sought their society. And, unless all property was delivered up to one or the other of them, every "lady" present might count on being sent to prison. Soon after this visit, the pair came suddenly upon three well-known pickpockets who were ordered to explain their plan of campaign for the night. After promising to give up their booty to either of the two officers, the thieves were allowed to go, promising complete obedience.

From such a congenial introduction to the business, Wild was able to form some idea of his new partner's importance. He liked the occupation, and armed with a staff as a token of his newly acquired authority, Jonathan went on nightly rambles through the city. He bullied unfortunate women and forced them to give him their stolen goods; he swindled honest men who appealed to him for assistance, and he terrified thieves by threats of the Compter—if greater returns were not produced. He disdained no avenue of extorting money.

On one occasion Wild saw a clergyman standing against a wall with his back towards him, and, a woman,. happening to pass by at the moment, Wild seized both and charged the priest with assault. In vain the unfortunate clergyman protested his innocence. Wild insisted that he must either go to prison for the night or give security for his appearance in the morning. It was only the fortunate appearance on the scene of some friends of the clergyman who had sense enough to give the expected fee that prevented the ruin of a good man.

At another time, Wild might see the wife of some honest citizen walking home unattended, and he would seize her as a lewd woman. If she behaved well, she was allowed to empty her purse and depart.

Such incidents as these are only the mildest examples of the shocking methods Hitchen and Wild employed to fill their pockets. They spared none—the poor, the innocent, the respectable.

Meanwhile, Wild was not one to neglect his own business. His new connections with the brotherhood of thieves grew larger daily, and new acquaintances could not do less than patronize his tavern. There, the talk would be of daring exploits done and booty won. After mutual congratulations were over, there generally remained the question of how to get hard cash from the spoils.

All this presented Wild with a hard problem. He could have overheard these tales as an assistant to Constable Hitchen—or he could have eavesdropped as a private citizen. His business sense won over his sense of ethics, and he chose the latter—which meant he took over the property without having to cut Hitchen in on the deal. Thus, from these small beginnings as a receiver of stolen goods, he was on the road to becoming the city's biggest fence.

In his lighter moments, Wild went out with Hitchen at night and took up with different streetwalkers, whom they blackmailed mercilessly after finishing their eve-.ning's amusement. In their business hours, very often the two scoundrels would hide in a doorway near a fashionable tavern. Presently a tipsy gallant would roll along, and a couple of footpads would fall upon him. Instantly Wild and Hitchen would appear, overpower the thieves, and rob them of their booty. The thieves, in a panic, would not only yield up the property to these officers of the law, but would on occasion offer valuable information concerning their friends—information which Wild and Hitchen promptly used for purposes of blackmail.

Much as Wild enjoyed the easy art of blackmail, he realized that the big money was to be made as a disposer and seller of stolen goods, and soon the squalid tavern became a sort of thieves' clearinghouse. Wild would take a footpad or highwayman into his parlor at the back of the tavern, and offer a very low price for what the thief had pilfered—which jewel or plate he would later sell at ten times the amount. If the thief haggled, Wild would point to a pair of handcuffs which, with grotesque humor, he frequently carried on his person. That argument rarely failed to prove convincing. With such enterprise, Wild soon amassed a considerable fortune.

When the organized blackmailing ceased and Wild turned his concentrated attention to the merchandising of stolen goods, he found he could carry on his business without the assistance of his partner in crime, Hitchen. Wild did not believe in dividing spoils.

Wild was a genius in his own way, with a talent for organization never equalled in his "profession" except, perhaps, by Moll Cutpurse. But Moll was loyal to her friends and accomplices, while Wild had no qualms about doublecrossing his intimates, for a price, and sending them to the gallows.

Meanwhile, his connections with the thieving fraternity increased daily. It was not long before Wild, with his highly developed business instincts, beat Hitchen at his own game, and the two friends finally became mortal enemies. Hitchen now began to nurse a very bitter hatred and resentment toward his former partner. It goaded him to see Wild, whom he had met as a very humble "trader" in crime, rising to heights of influence and wealth which he himself had never known. Also, it made him furious when Wild, maintaining his status as an officer, kept himself before the notice of the magistrates by haling before them, from time to time as it suited his purpose, some unimportant footpad or enemy.

The magistrate would then compliment "Honest Mr. Wild" on his capture, and Wild, assuming the expression of a man conscious of virtue, would leave the court with some compensation in his pocket. It was said of this engaging rogue that he was such a consummate actor that he almost believed it himself while he was assuming these honest tendencies. When, on occasion, his clients complained that he had treated them shabbily, Wild would silence their tongues by taking from his pocket a piece of rope which he would dangle before them. "Here is some hemp that has cured several men of your complaint," he would say with a laugh. "I have a doctor at hand, if you compel me to send for him."

Wild's business grew to such a Napoleonic a scale that Hitchen—unable to contain himself any longer at the thought of Wild's beating him at his own larcenous game —brought out an unusual pamphlet, designed to expose the trade. This pamphlet was called "The Regulator, or a Discovery of Thieves, Thief-takers, and Locks," "locks" being known as receivers of stolen property. However, this did not have the desired effect of ruining his rival's business, and Wild continued to thrive amazingly well. As a broker and go-between—a "fence"—in nearly all the crimes committed in and around London, Wild, with masterful irony, carried off his dual roles as both "Receiver-General of stolen goods" and self-styled "Thief-Catcher-General of Great Britain and Ireland." It might seem impossible to pose successfuly at one and the same time as friend and enemy, but this arch-villain achieved the apparently impossible.

It is evident that Wild was a man with great, if perverse, imagination, for he became the brain-center of all the robberies committed at that time in and around London—himself the secret, supreme director of them all, and at the same time the apparently honest broker who, for a consideration, would undertake to restore missing property. Realizing that the original owner of a pilfered item might offer more for it than anybody else, Wild would obtain the owner's name from the thief and politely let him know that something which belonged to him had found its way to his house, and would be restored for a consideration.

Open dealing of this kind started a tremendous growth of criminal activity, with numerous imitators of Wild setting up on a smaller scale, and London was rocked by scandal. The Legislature became obliged to take action. The result was an Act of Parliament, putting the fence, the receiver of stolen goods, on more or less the same level as the thief. (Formerly the receiving of stolen goods was not unlawful.) The new Act made the receiver of stolen goods liable to arrest, and on conviction, to imprisonment for fourteen years. As a result, the "profession," not only of receiving, but of thieving also, staggered. The receivers were now marked men. There remained only the pawnbrokers, and the wretched prices offered by them were not good enough to compensate for the risk run in robbery. The thieves of London lost courage, and starvation or honesty seemed to stare them in the face.

But Jonathan Wild, with his fertile mind, came to the rescue. When the Act went into force, he had been sent for, it was said, by the Recorder—to whom he was known both as a police witness and a receiver—and he was advised to give up his business with thieves and to confine his energies to detecting rogues and thus earning the rewards offered for their discovery. But Wild was not born to settle down to a respectable, and hazardous, existence.

He was determined to use the new law as a stepping-stone to higher things. It occurred to this incredible scoundrel that he might still act as intermediary between the thieves and their victims without actually handling the stolen goods, and he immediately set about organizing his new system. He would abandon the "receiving" branch of his business and concentrate on the "restoration" of stolen goods. He made arrangements with hundreds of thieves to deposit all stolen property in certain specified places. He was to be informed of every robbery and given full details about the victim. By this ingenious manoeuvre, Wild was able to evade the technical label of "receiver of stolen goods."

He, personally, received nothing—he had merely ascertained the whereabouts of certain goods and was ready to reveal the whereabouts at a price. He would be in a position to open up communication with the owner and bargain with him for the return of his property, saying he had chanced to hear of his misfortune and had also happened to hear of a similar article finding its way to an honest broker of his acquaintance. Restitution could be made if the person he was addressing would make a small present to the broker for his trouble—and, of course, would promise not to set the law in motion against the good man who had been unfortunate enough to have come into possession of stolen goods. People had no choice between paying the money or hearing no more of their property.

When an explanation was demanded of this coincidence—how Wild should know of the robbery as well as the whereabouts of the goods—Wild put these inquisitive people to shame by a virtuous indignation: He had come out of pure good nature, thinking to do a service, and if he was suspected of being an accomplice of thieves, he had no more to say except that his name was Jonathan Wild and that he resided in Cock Alley, Cripplegate.

Now Wild's reputation grew in another direction, and people who had been relieved of their property began to come to him for news of it without waiting to be approached by him; all they wanted was to get back their goods, without being too particular about the methods of recovery. On entering his "office," they would find this genius gravely seated behind his registers. They would be requested to pay the nominal fee of five shillings. Then their names and addresses were entered into a book, together with a description of the goods lost and the manner of the robbery—and the amount of reward that would be given. They were then told to return in a few days.

On the return visit, it was announced first, that the goods had been traced and their return demanded, and second, that the thieves pretended the pawnbrokers would give more for them than the owner; therefore, the only way to make sure of recovering the property was to increase the reward. Wild was shrewd enough to know how far this squeezing process could be safely carried, and when the limit was reached, he would ask for payment and the goods would be delivered. To his credit let it be said that in no instance did Wild ever receive payment without restoring the property.

In some cases, Wild would advise his clients to advertise their loss and to offer a reward to any person who should deliver the lost property to Mr. Jonathan Wild, at his office—and no questions asked. Perhaps the most marvelous thing in these negotiations was the assumed disinterestedness of Mr. Jonathan Wild himself who, although the most notorious evildoer in London, posed as the instrument of good, restoring the lost valuables of complete strangers entirely without fee or reward, simply because of the Christian love he bore the human race. Henry Fielding, judge and author of *Tom Jones*, styled him "The Great Man."

So, with his untiring energy and fertile imagination, Wild's business flourished. But he craved expansion of his empire and he started a school for the training of young thieves—homeless, wandering boys. Every art of picking pockets and robbing was taught and rehearsed by Jonathan Wild himself. He was never happier than when engaged in instructing in the felonious arts the young men and women who fell into his hands. He made a great point of encouraging his regiment of thieves to steal only from those who could afford to buy back their stolen property at adequate rates. Moreover, he impressed upon them the frequent value of apparently valueless articles. For instance, a desk might hold documents that would yield a good blackmailing harvest.

"Remember," he would say to some promising young thief, "that a man's secrets are frequently more precious to him than wife, gold, or existence itself. Steal the secrets and you may live upon them in plenty for years!"

Wild had numerous squads assigned to their own specialized work. One attended churches, another visited the theaters. He had a crew trained in the subtle art of shoplifting, and still another to take jobs as servants and, in that capacity, to make away with their employers' plate and jewelry. The stolen property was held for ransom and Wild divided—more or less unfairly, of course—the amounts received. His thieves could not, without running great risks, sell it themselves.

All concerned benefited: the plundered citizens repurchased their valuables; Wild took an excellent commission; and the thieves, pickpockets and highwaymen made a good living without much risk.

The reverse of this charming picture of distributed benefits was the alarming increase of robberies, and the decrease of arrests and convictions. And another serious result of Wild's organization was that he absolutely tyrannized the lives of those who worked for him. No one dared offend this villain who was merciless in his revenge, swearing away the lives of those who dared cross him, and thus sending many men and women to the gallows—some as a result of merely daring to differ in opinion with him on a business deal; others merely for the reason that they had outlasted their usefulness. Everything was possible to the cunning and daring of Jonathan Wild who could not merely bring a man to trial, but could also snatch him from the very jaws of death by making the prosecutor so drunk that he was not present to give evidence at the trial and so the accused was discharged.

Wild reveled in power. He strutted in the streets, put on airs of superiority. As became a man of his influence and position, he wore laced clothes and carried a sword. He is said to have tested the sword's edge by slicing off the ear of his mistress, Mary Milliner, who remained far beneath his new status. No doubt he wanted to get rid of her. They quarrelled and their quarrels suited his purpose. Still, he treated her generously, for he set her up as mistress of a little house in Moorsfields and never failed to come to her assistance when her business was slack.

For himself, Wild had loftier ideas. He left Cock Alley and established a new and grander office at Number 68, Old Bailey, where his clients, coming to him in ever larger numbers, were properly impressed.

Wild was quite a hand with the ladies. He rarely was content with only one woman for any length of time, and although he "remarried" no less than four times, he had many casual affairs in addition. He treated his various women with coarse good nature and was much loved by them all. After he got rid of Mary Milliner, his affections turned to one Mary Reed, with whom he lived in fine style.

But women were a diversion to Wild. All his energies were devoted to the development of his business. This business grew so rapidly, it became too big for his personal supervision. He had to open two branches offices, and in the difficult task of finding the right managers, he showed remarkable judgment and insight into the character of men. He had a genius for delegation, and though his assistants were themselves thieves, or very little better, they faithfully rendered the services expected of them. A careful watch was kept by Wild and his lieutenants on those entrusted with his affairs.

Wild liked to go about with a silver staff as a mark of authority. He let it be known that he was on the watch for thieves and disorderly characters. In fact, he still continued to pose everywhere as an officer of justice. If a suitable reward was offered for a capture, and he had no personal interest in preventing it, Wild would really exert himself. Thus he gained great distinction in the case of the murder of one Mrs. Knapp, who was shot by some thieves who were robbing her son in Gray's Inn Lane, March 31, 1716. He wasn't interested in the case till a reward of fifty guineas was mentioned when, immediately aroused, he exclaimed, "I never pardon murder," and set himself to the task of discovering Mrs. Knapp's assailants. Three of the men involved were hanged through Wild's efforts; another, who had secreted himself in a cellar, was unearthed by Wild, too, and met the same fate as the others.

A man who could make himself so useful was not one on whom the authorities could afford to be too severe. To lay Wild by the heels was to kill the goose with the golden eggs. So, although frequently suspected, and on one occasion even ordered to Newgate, Wild escaped actual punishment and was able to pursue his course practically unmolested. His zeal in tracking down lawbreakers was often praised by newspapers and by justices of the peace.

But Wild's efforts to bring about the arrest and conviction of criminals were as nothing compared with those required for securing their acquittal. If one of his good men was unfortunate enough to come within the clutch of justice, Wild would go to unusual lengths to bring about acquittal: bribing witnesses, and by threats suborn their evidence; and even bribing certain judges, though there is no record that any judge succumbed.

His favorite means of procuring acquittal of his friends was to furnish them with State's evidence. Prisoners who could give information that would convict their accomplices could generally obtain their own release. Wild, therefore, would furnish his man with the detailed history of some less important miscreant whose head would be put in the noose to afford the escape of the other. This, in fact, was the simplest method of revenge on the rebellious members of the profession who had refused to bow to the great Jonathan Wild's authority. Proceedings of this kind were frequent enough to exalt Wild to a very high position in the eyes of the thieves.

Many of Wild's supporters were completely in his power, for they were transported convicts who had returned home before the period of their expatriation had expired, and it was from these ranks that Wild preferred to win recruits. In training his men, the only condition that this Samaritan, who would rescue a man from the gutter, was to receive would be a handsome percentage of the profits. Nothing would probably be said of any penalty for neglecting to observe this condition, but the fool who disregarded it was not long in discovering that in dealing with Wild it paid to be honest.

A certain dissipated cheesemonger had been thus befriended by Wild. He was provided with a horse and started his "business" on the highway, meeting with extraordinary success. He began to doubt the wisdom of sharing his proceeds with Wild, and failed to report his doings. Wild learned through one of his lieutenants of the highwayman's exploits on the Oxford road, and receiving no account from the man himself, determined to make an example of him.

He accordingly set out on the same road, and some miles from Oxford met with a party who had just been robbed. Wild rode on and presently came up with his man. Without waiting to parley or reproach the ex-cheesemonger for his ingratitude, Wild shot him dead. He then cantered on to Oxford to report the service he had rendered the State.

Wild's impudence increased with his success, and he was now found petitioning the city fathers for the Freedom of the City Award to be conferred upon him, in recognition of his great services in bringing criminals to justice. It does not appear that the city responded to this request and Wild was sadly disappointed. He spoke bitterly of the "ingratitude of humanity."

If this arch-villain can be charged with committing an error in judgment, it was in the too ostentatious use of his very considerable wealth. He moved from his house in the Old Bailey to a larger one on the other side of the road, next to the Cooper's Arms, and he maintained the elaborate establishment of a man of great means. The present "Mrs. Wild" went outdoors attended by a footman in livery. They dined in state: "His table was very splendid, he seldom dining under five dishes (courses) . . ." The remains of the meals were sent to the prisoners of Newgate prison.

The authorities knew Wild's real character quite well and they were beginning to think that, despite his services, he was becoming a too prominent character. Again the Legislature made him the special object of attack by passing an act which made it a capital offense to take a reward for restoring stolen effects, unless the thief was apprehended or caused to be apprehended by the person accepting the reward. Face to face with the difficulty, Wild reflected, as became a citizen of the world, that London was not the only place where honest trading might be done, and that in other countries no inconvenient questions would be asked as to the origin of merchandise or the person who wished to dispose of it.

Accordingly, Wild invested part of his savings in the

purchase of a sloop and found a suitable shipmaster in that peerless blackguard, Roger Johnson. The new enterprise worked well. The ship set out with a miscellaneous cargo for Ostend, or sometimes Rotterdam, and after landing the goods, returned to the port of London, or as near to it as she might get without attracting the customhouse officers, laden with a new cargo of contraband. After two or three years' successful trading, the State seized the ship, and its captain was fined seven hundred pounds for smuggling, which expense Wild paid.

Meanwhile, Wild reverted to his old methods of business. But great caution was necessary now and he ran great personal risks. He had some narrow escapes from charges brought against him by former supporters, and he feared he would not always be able to escape. Also, there was a growing insubordination among his thieves who, now that Wild's opportunities were restricted, regarded him with less respect, and thus bred in him a feeling of insecurity. In fact, a letter is extant in which he implores the Earl of Dartmouth to shield him from what he styled the "persecution" of the magistrates who, he declared, had procured thieves and other bad characters to swear false evidence against him. But it was to no purpose, for the authorities were closing in on him.

There is no doubt that if Wild had kept his head; if he had restrained his grandeurs; if he had refrained from offending former allies—all might have been well with him and he might have died in his own bed at a peaceful old age. But obsessed by his own importance, and resenting the smallest affront, he now began to quarrel with his oldest friends.

One of Wild's friends, the notorious "Blueskin"—Joseph Blake—as great a scoundrel as Wild, incurred Wild's disfavor by refusing to deliver up to him a large share of stolen goods. Immediately Wild turned his back on his firmest ally and denounced him to the justices. An indictment was brought against "Blueskin" and he was put in Newgate prison. When Wild went to visit him there, "Blueskin" attacked him and cut his throat from ear to ear. But with his usual invulnerable luck and constitution, Wild soon recovered and was able to give evidence against his old friend. "Blueskin" was found guilty and sentenced to death.

"Blueskin" was not the only sacrifice of a former good friend made by Wild. But he could not afford to quarrel with all his best friends. Moreover, he disliked quarreling, and it was through an effort on his part to act as peacemaker that he started the last chapter of his busy life.

The actual episodes that led to Wild's arrest, and the forces that set the wheels in motion, are obscure. It is more than possible that his old partner in crime, the vindictive Hitchen, had a hand in the business. Also, there were many others who, following Wild's example, turned treacherously upon him and denounced him for having received stolen goods from them. And so his long career of monstrous villainy and deceit was checked on February 15, 1725, when he was arrested and taken to prison under a strong escort.

Wild could not believe that there was any serious intention of interfering with his "career." He felt that he was too valuable and distinguished a person to be imprisoned or hanged. Here are the main charges against Wild:

1. That he had been for many years a confederate of robbers, highwaymen, pickpockets, housebreakers and shoplifters.
2. That he aided and abetted counterfeiters.
3. That he had suborned witnesses.
4. That he had been a receiver of stolen goods, knowing them to be stolen.

5. That he had frequently robbed along with the aforementioned felons.

6. That he had under his care and direction several warehouses for receiving and concealing stolen goods.

7. That he kept in his pay several artists to make alterations, and transform watches, seals, snuff boxes, rings and other valuables.

8. That he had had stolen a large quantity of valuable lace from the house of a Mrs. Stetham on January 22, 1725; and had illegally received from her the sum of ten guineas for its restoration.

The date of Wild's trial was fixed as May 15th. He swaggered arrogantly about the prison as the day approached. When he was brought to the Bar, he seemed confident; he had no fear of the result. His faith in the powers of bribery was as strong as ever. It was decided that only the last two indictments, relating to Mrs. Stetham's property, should be dealt with. They were sufficient to hang Wild.

As the trial proceeded, it began to look very black for Wild. His head sank lower and lower on his chest as the trial progressed. The jury was out only a few minutes considering their verdict. Wild was acquitted on the first charge—the actual stealing of the lace—but he was convicted on the second charge. He was found guilty and was sentenced to be executed at Tyburn, May 24, 1725. The self-appointed enemy of society had at last been vanquished.

However, Wild was not entirely discouraged. There was always the flimsy hope that his friends would—by bribery or influence in the right quarters—obtain commutation of the sentence to transportation or pardon. He himself petitioned the king—"The Humble Petition of Jonathan Wild, Humbly Presented to his Majesty, on Wednesday, May the 19th, at his Royal Palace at St.

James' "—earnestly pleading for a pardon. His optimism, however, was short-lived. After a few days of suspense and hope, his request remained unanswered, and he resigned himself to his fate.

While under the death sentence, Wild frequently declared that his services to the public in returning stolen goods and in apprehending felons was so great as to entitle him to mercy; that he thought it not unreasonable to expect a pardon through the interest of some of the dukes, lords, earls and other persons of distinction who had recovered their stolen property through his means. His disappointment was overwhelming when nobody came forward in his behalf.

Hardly any food had passed his lips since his conviction. He grew increasingly listless and absolutely refused the consolation of religion. His conversation would wander from one topic to another, as if he were talking to empty air. Then suddenly he became aware of the presence of his listener and he would apologize for his obtuseness. His brain, he would say, pointing to bumps in his skull, was disordered by wounds he had received in catching felons, and he had many other scars on his body and legs, received in serving justice.

Each day, he seemed to drift farther from reality, and he took barely enough food to keep him alive. On the day before he was scheduled to die, there was still no reply to his petition. He had never actually given up hope, but now he felt a sense of impending doom. He called for the chaplain and asked to receive the Sacrament. What, he asked the good divine, was the meaning of the words: "Cursed is everyone that hangeth on a tree."

For answer, he was advised to repent of the crimes he had committed. He talked for a long time with the chaplain, praising the behavior of certain Roman heroes who had died on their own swords. He spoke of classic times and revealed a remarkable and deep knowledge.

The chaplain finally said good night to Wild, believing that his suicidal theories were purely academic.

Wild sat brooding for hours. Presently, he took a phial of laudanum from the lining of his coat and took a huge dose of it. The size of the dose prevented it from killing him; it merely made him very sick, and the gallows still awaited him a few hours later. He had failed to cheat the executioner.

He now became a figure of utter despair and terror and had to be carried to the cart that was to take him to his execution at Tyburn. The day of his execution was one of great rejoicing in London. Huge crowds lined the road, pelting Wild with stones, dirt and rotten apples.

Having failed to kill himself, Wild was in no haste to die, for at his arrival at Tyburn, he asked time for meditation and continued to sit with folded arms in the cart, stolidly staring at the multitude that stood around, cursing him—the famous thief-taker. So long did he sit that the mob, thirsting for justice, yelled to the hangman to do his duty. They became so threatening that he was compelled to arouse Wild so he could go about his task. Then, to universal applause, Jonathan Wild swung out of this world.

On the evening of the same day, Wild's body was cut down and buried in St. Pancras churchyard. His bones had no peace, for shortly afterwards, they were secretly disinterred and consigned, it was supposed, to the dissecting room for anatomical research. A skull said to be Wild's was exhibited in London in 1860.

Whatever the judgment on Wild's character—and there is not too much room for difference of opinion—it cannot be denied that he was a man of exceptional ability. His pre-eminence with the law, his knowledge of how to use his men as tools, his organizing skill and resourcefulness were outstanding.

A complex character, he caught the imagination of

noted writers. Daniel Defoe, author of *Robinson Crusoe*, is said to have visited him in prison and to have received from him an authentic confession which he embodied in a little volume published a few months after Wild's execution.

And Henry Fielding, who dubbed him "Jonathan Wild, the Great," in his whimsical biography of Wild, said: ". . . it is the strange adventures of a man's life and art and conduct in the management of things which gives us the curiosity of looking into his history . . . seeing deeper stratagems and plots formed by a fellow without learning and education then are to be met in the conduct of the greatest statesmen."

Elsewhere, Fielding wrote: "He (Wild) laid down several maxims as the certain methods of attaining greatness, to which he constantly adhered. Such as:

1. Never to do more mischief to another than was necessary for his purpose, for mischief was too precious a thing to be thrown away.
2. To sacrifice all men with equal readiness to his interest.
3. Never to communicate more of his business than was necessary to the person who was to execute it.
4. To shun poverty and distress and to ally himself only to power and riches.
5. To foment eternal jealousies among his gang.
6. That a good name, like money, must be parted with or risked to bring the owner any advantage.
7. That virtues, like precious stones, were easily counterfeited and that very few could distinguish the counterfeit from the real.
8. That the heart was the proper seat of hatred, and the countenance of affection and friendship.

This is the creed, of course, of a true cynic.

Wild had many more maxims of a similar nature which were found in his study after his death.

Among the numerous satirical old prints relating to Jonathan Wild there is a gruesome picture of devils lighting him with flaring torches on the red road to hell, together with a group of twenty-five men and women, all duly named and shown hanging by the neck, whom he had brought to the gallows.

The Newgate Calendar, in a brief, official statement, set down the universal, and final, judgment: "Of all the thieves that ever infested London, this man was the most notorious. May the name and memory of Jonathan Wild be ever held in abhorrence as 'The Prince of Robbers.'"

VII

ELIZABETH BROWNRIGG

THOUGH many women have not shrunk from using poison or dagger, the distaff side has generally avoided participation in acts of merciless brutality. There are, of course, exceptions. In our time we have witnessed the unspeakable cruelties of "The Beast of Belsen," whose infamous brutality became known after the Nazi defeat of World War II. Another exception was Elizabeth Brownrigg, a coarse but efficient midwife, ready with quip and jest, always cheering her patients with some obscene stoicism. She became, during the middle period of her life, a tormentor of children and finally achieved the dubious distinction of being tried for the murder of one of these victims.

The life, the surroundings, the profession of this woman were entirely commonplace. She won a place in the hall of infamy because her record exhibits a case where the practice of systematic cruelty became a source of exquisite and unholy delight.

Elizabeth Brownrigg was born in 1720. The name of her family is uncertain, being variously given as Harkly and Hartley. As a child she appears to have been normal. She grew up amid ordinary surroundings of working-class people, and she became a servant in the household of a merchant living in Goodman's Fields, London. Here she formed the acquaintance of James Brownrigg, an apprentice to a housepainter of the neighborhood who, when his term of apprenticeship was over, set up for himself and married Elizabeth.

The pair first lived in Greenwich, but five years later returned to London, where they ultimately settled in Fleur de Lys Court, Fetter Lane. Her husband prospered and she became the mother of sixteen children. Less success attended her efforts in bringing them up—thirteen of her offspring died in their early years.

Her fertility exhausted or in abeyance, Mrs. Brownrigg directed her energies to acquiring some extra money and she chose the career of a midwife. She is said to have become quite proficient in her work, and was rewarded by being officially appointed to usher into life those destined to be born in the workhouse of the Parish of St. Dunstan's-in-the-West. She extended the sphere of her good work by receiving private patients at her home.

Mrs. Brownrigg's patients were well cared for, and although it was afterwards claimed that none of the little creatures who first breathed the air of Fleur de Lys Court ever emerged any further into the world, none of the mothers made accusations of the kind against the accommodating midwife.

One may perhaps hazard a guess that nature was not

altogether unassisted in these infantile collapses. A woman capable of flogging her apprentices for two hours on end would probably not hesitate to take the life of a child if the bribe were sufficiently tempting.

By the year 1765, business was so thriving with Mrs. Brownrigg that she found it necessary to have assistance in the house and determined to keep a servant. Her connections with the workhouse had taught her that young girls were bound as apprentices from that establishment and that it was the practice to give five pounds to the mistress of each girl. She decided that an apprentice of this sort would be the most economical sort of servant she could obtain.

Mary Mitchell, a child of fourteen years, was therefore introduced into the Brownriggs' house "upon liking," as it was called, the meaning being that if, after a month's experience, both maid and mistress were satisfactory, the indentures were signed and the apprenticeship began.

Now let it be noted that until this moment Mrs. Brownrigg had never experienced the pleasure of wielding authority. The coming of an apprentice over whom the law gave her a parental and almost absolute control probably stirred in her some latent impulse which until that time had not had means to develop.

In the case of Mary Mitchell, the month passed pleasantly and the girl was so pleased with the treatment she received and the good food that was served her at the same table as the family that she was perfectly content to be bound. That ceremony over, Mary's position in the household at once changed. She became a drudge.

Hardly had a day elapsed after the signing of the contract when Mrs. Brownrigg, reveling in the sense of newly gained power, entered the kitchen and in a harsh voice ordered the wretched girl to strip off her clothes and dress herself in some hideous rags she gave her.

Instead of eating with the Brownriggs and their three

sons, Mary now learned to be thankful if scraps were thrown at her, or if she could find an opportunity to steal a crust of bread. On the pretense of laziness or of work inefficiently done, Mary was flogged almost daily by her mistress, quite unmercifully. She was allowed no rest except when she was ordered to her mat for sleep at night.

On some occasions, this monstrous woman would pull the girl's hair, call her a dirty slut, slap her face and bestow kicks upon her. She would joke coarsely as she performed these outrages, while her husband, weary of house decorating, who in the beginning took no active part in the persecution, would sit grinning at his wife's antics, and his son, who still remained at home, would share the enjoyment. The trio had found a new and exhilarating diversion.

Mrs. Brownrigg was so delighted at being able to act the tyrant that shortly after the engagement of Mary Mitchell, she obtained another girl, Mary Jones, also fourteen, on similar terms. Mary Jones, she took from the Foundling Hospital.

Mary Jones soon became the favorite victim of Mrs. Brownrigg's cruelty, and being unable to satisfy her mistress's demands, she was forced to submit to continual punishment. Ordinary whipping no longer appeased Mrs. Brownrigg's lust for inflicting pain; it enraged her if the object of her passion could for a moment elude her grasp. Exercising a fiendish ingenuity, she devised an arrangement of two chairs on which Mary Jones, after having by command taken off her clothing, was stretched out and tied down. Then, at her leisure, Mrs. Brownrigg flogged the child till exhaustion overtook her.

It now came to the knowledge of this child-torturer that Mary Jones had an obsessive fear of drowning, and Mrs. Brownrigg lost no time in acting on the information. She would steal behind the child while she was engaged in scrubbing a floor, seize her by the heels and, lifting her up, plunge her forcibly, head downwards, into the pail of water. The girl's shrieks and terror at the constant repetition of this drowning game caused this fiendish woman great amusement, and even Mr. Brownrigg and his son sometimes joined in the sport.

Soon Mrs. Brownrigg devised some improvements on the game.

On the pretense of some fault, real or imaginary, committed by Mary Jones, Mary Mitchell would be ordered to bring a large tub and fill it with cold water, and in this the naked victim was totally immersed until the diminution of her struggles for air and life warned Mrs. Brownrigg to stop. A short breathing space would be given the wretched girl and then the bathing began all over again.

It was fortunate for the unhappy little slave that she was able to preserve not only the will to live, but the determination to carry out the dictates of that will. But her desire to escape had been anticipated by her tormentor, so sleeping accommodations had been allotted to her under a dresser in Mrs. Brownrigg's bedroom on the ground floor, and this led to a front room which opened directly onto the street.

One morning, awaking early, Mary Jones noticed that the key of the street door was in the lock instead of under the pillow of her slumbering mistress. She crept from her kennel, opened, the door, sprang into the kindlier air of Fetter Lane, and found her way to the Foundling Hospital. It was only two months since she had left it and she now returned nearly blind in one eye, covered with wounds and bruises, her shoulders deeply scarred by the rim of the pail into which she had so often dived against her will.

The surgeon of the Hospital described the girl's injuries as alarming and dangerous, whereupon the governors instructed their solicitor to write to Mrs. Brownrigg, demanding that some reparation be made. As a result, the Brownriggs consented to cancel the indenture of Mary Jones, thus freeing her of enforced apprenticeship.

Mere cruelty was so commonplace an incident in those times that if the inflicter of it stopped short of actual murder, he frequently escaped punishment.

Mrs. Brownrigg, not discouraged by this experiment, looked about for a third apprentice and shortly found one in the workhouse at Whitefriars. This time the potential victim was a child of somewhat feeble intellect, named Mary Clifford. Once again the farce of the probation period was gone through with due solemnity and the new apprentice was bound to her mistress for the customary period. It was destined, however, that this time the contract was to be cancelled by an authority more far-reaching than the governers of the Foundling Hospital.

From the moment this third Mary entered her house, Mrs. Brownrigg conceived a deep dislike for her, which she had not entertained for the other apprentices, and the punishment inflicted on the poor girl became violently sadistic. Toward Mary Clifford there had developed a violent personal hatred. The child was stupid and made blunders that involved the household in expense. All Mrs. Brownrigg's vitriol became directed against her. She was thrashed several times daily. Her sleeping place was the coal-hole; her bed was a mat that swarmed with vermin. A few filthy clothes were given her. She wore these day and night, removing them only when she was to receive her daily floggings.

Usually, from the afternoon of Saturday to Monday, the family spent the week end in Islington. Throughout the entire period, both girls would be locked in the cellar without light or food, with the exception of a few crusts of bread, and deprived of a drop of water.

It seems that father and son rarely took an active part

in the flagellations, but they derived great amusement from the spectacle, and on occasion would relieve Mrs. Brownrigg when fatigue overcame that usually tireless person.

This monstrous creature derived great pleasure from the agony of her victims. She also possessed a certain grim sense of humor, for she sometimes impressed upon the apprentices that the whippings were performed for their benefit, so that when they encountered the hardships of the world outside Fetter Lane, they might be more ready to endure those hardships. Perhaps she starved them on the same principle.

In addition to flogging poor Mary Clifford, Mrs. Brownrigg devised a method of inflicting upon her some of the preliminary sensations of strangulation. On one occasion, when the girl had broken open a cupboard door to procure some food, the door itself was used as a means of punishment. One end of a chain was fastened nooselike round the girl's neck, the other end was attached to the door. The door was then opened and shut with abrupt movements, and each time the noose tightened, Mary received the harrowing sensation of abrupt strangulation. For a whole day Mrs. Browning continued this torture.

Mrs. Brownrigg devised remarkably ingenious methods to give variety to her sadistic pleasures. One of her favorites was the suspension trick. Across the ceiling of the kitchen ran a water pipe and to this she—having first tied together the hands of the girl whose turn it was for punishment—hauled her up with the surplus cord till her feet were off the ground. Mrs. Brownrigg was thus left free to beat the girl till her arm wearied. With frequent use, the pipe finally gave way and then the resourceful woman instructed her husband to screw into a beam a large iron hook to which the cord was attached, the girls strung up till their feet were suspended in the air and again flogged until they became unconscious.

The demon that possessed Mrs. Brownrigg gave her no rest but continually inspired her to fresh acts of senseless barbarities. One of her common practices with Mary Clifford was to seize her by the head and, forcing down with her thumbs the upper part of her cheeks, wait deliberately till the blood rushed from the eyes. She seems, in fact, to have reached such a pass that she was unable to bring herself to believe in the pain she caused unless her eyes, too, were gratified by the sight of fresh-drawn blood.

Possibly the most hideous example of utter lack of restraint took place when tale-bearing was involved. Mary Clifford one day found an opportunity to bemoan her sad lot to a French lady who was living temporarily at a house that Mrs. Brownrigg was servicing as midwife. The lady remonstrated with Mrs. Brownrigg and ventured to point out that her conduct towards her apprentices was scarcely kind. But no sooner did Mrs. Brownrigg escape from the lecture than she rushed to find Mary Clifford and cut her tongue in two places with a pair of scissors. She actually threatened to remove the tongue entirely if this did not cure the girl of tattling.

The outer world knew nothing of what went on in the house in Fleur de Lys Court and no possible chance of communicating with it was given the young prisoners. Most of Mrs. Brownrigg's patients did not stir from their rooms. And when cries of distress reached them, they were told some plausible story. The neighbors were requested by Mrs. Brownrigg to inform any inquisitive persons who might inquire of them about the girls that Mrs. Brownrigg kept no apprentices and that she had never done so.

This was the information given to Mary Clifford's stepmother who had asked for her and had been told that no such person was known. When she pressed her inquiries, she was threatened by Mr. Brownrigg who heatedly informed her he would complain to the police. She started to leave, discomfited, when a neighbor, Mrs. Deacon, came out and learning of Mrs. Clifford's errand, assured her that apprentices were kept by the Brownriggs and, from the frequent groans and moans overheard, she suspected that they were not too well treated. She promised to investigate and to communicate with Mrs. Clifford, who went away baffled, little knowing what her intrusion would cost her stepdaughter.

Mrs. Brownrigg was not one to miss an opportunity for reprisal. On the following morning, July 13, she summoned Mary Clifford to the kitchen, forced her to strip—a painful procedure since the girl's clothing stuck to her former wounds—and then she strung her up by her tied hands to the hook in the beam. She now flogged her till the blood flowed and then, untying her, ordered her to wash in a tub of water brought by Mary Mitchell. Even while the washing went on, she continued to rain down blows with the butt end of her whip. Several times on the same day this brutal punishment was repeated, in every detail, before Mrs. Brownrigg was satisfied that the poor child had paid the price of the uneasiness caused by her stepmother's visit. Fortunately, release, though it came too late to be of much good, was not now far off.

It seems that Mr. Brownrigg had bought a hog at an auction sale and, having no place to keep it, put it in the back yard of his house. This yard was covered with a roof which effectually screened it from the observation of neighbors, but the presence of the hog made it advisable to remove part of a skylight from the roof. Thus the long-awaited opportunity was given to the Deacon family next door to see something of what was going on next door. They set a servant girl on watch and after awhile she saw, in the Brownrigg's yard, a shapeless mass which turned out to be the bare, raw, half-mortified body of Mary Clifford. No response other than inarticulate sounds and moans came from that poor creature.

The Deacons immediately sent word to Mrs. Clifford, who came at once with the Parish overseers to the Brownrigg house. On the first appearance of the officers, Mrs. Brownrigg quickly slipped out of the house, but not, however, before first instructing her husband to hide the body of the girl.

Mr. Brownrigg prepared to lie the matter out. He produced Mary Mitchell, who was in pitiable condition, and she was instantly removed to the workhouse. On being told that this Mary was not Mary Clifford, the girl they were seeking, Brownrigg swore by God there was no other in the house. He tried all sorts of lies and ruses to forestall the officers, and finally he threatened them. But the officers, unfaltering, searched the place high and low but still could find no trace of Mary Clifford.

Brownrigg, feeling triumphant, again threatened to prosecute the whole invading party, but he was informed that since the girl could not be found, he would be arrested on a charge of having made away with her, and a coach was called to carry him off to jail. Brownrigg then recognized the real situation and promised to produce the girl if the coach was sent away. Then, from a small cupboard underneath the sideboard in the dining room, he reluctantly drew out the anguished, ulcerated body of Mary Clifford.

Mary Clifford, too, was taken to the workhouse, where her condition aroused anger and indignation in the surgeons who examined her. Besides the indescribable injuries of her body and limbs, her head was found to be covered with frightful gashes, and the head and throat were so swollen as to form one continuous line; her mouth was extended in such a manner that she neither could close her lips nor speak.

Mr. Brownrigg was brought up to Guildhall. Both girls

were brought into court, delirious, and Mary Clifford, though regaining her senses, was unable to do more than signify "yes" or "no." Brownrigg was committed for trial at the Old Bailey, and a warrant for the arrest of his wife and son was issued. Their victims were sent to St. Bartholomew's Hospital where, four days later, on August 9, 1767, Mary Clifford died, less than eighteen months after her first introduction to Mrs. Brownrigg.

Mrs. Brownrigg had gone into hiding, where she was followed by her son with money and clothing. For some days they lodged in a side street in East Smithfield, living on bread and water and hardly venturing out. Then, after purchasing disguises, they made their way to Wandsworth, where they took a bedroom in the house of one Dunbar, a chandler.

Meanwhile, the hue and cry was being loudly raised and was redoubled when, after the inquest on Mary Clifford's body, the charge against the Brownriggs was wilful murder. Advertisements for them appeared in all the newspapers of the day, and considerable rewards were offered for their capture. Mrs. Brownrigg was described as "a middle-aged, middle-sized woman of a swarthy complexion, remarkably smooth of speech." Her dress, when she disappeared, was "a black silk crepe or bombazine, a black silk whalebone bonnet, and a purple petticoat flounced."

For five days the culprits remained in their one room till the chandler, who was a reader of newspapers, connected his lodgers with the persons wanted for the murder of Mary Clifford. He lost no time in communicating with the authorities in London. The wretched pair were arrested at once.

The following day Mrs. Brownrigg was scheduled to appear at the Mansion House for magisterial examination, but the news of her capture had spread and such a crowd of excited, indignant citizens filled the street which separated the prison and the court that it was considered impossible to bring her safely through it. She was therefore committed to Newgate to take her trial on the coroner's warrant. It was some time before this change of the prisoner's quarters would be carried out, since not only did the unfriendly mob threaten throughout the day, but Mrs. Brownrigg herself was thought to be in no fit condition to be moved since—due to her refusal to take food and to a habit she had suddenly developed of falling, or affecting to fall, into fits—she became quite ill.

An opportunity to transfer her peacefully occurred one night, and thereafter for nearly a month Mrs. Brownrigg awaited her trial at Newgate. She refused to be visited by the chaplain and continued to simulate ill-health. The authorities did not allow her to see her husband or son, but they both were in custody, and on September 14, 1767, appeared with her in the dock of the Old Bailey. All three were indicted "for that being moved by the instigation of the Devil they did on different dates from the 1st of May, 1766, to the 4th of August, 1767, so assault Mary Clifford that she did pine and languish till she died."

The trial lasted eleven hours and consisted chiefly of the evidence of Mary Mitchell, now somewhat recovered and able to describe in detail the many scenes of sickening cruelty which she had witnessed. There was practically no defence.

Mrs. Brownrigg was found guilty of murder and sentenced to be hanged the following day. Her husband and son, however, for some reason best known to the jury, were acquitted.

During the one whole day of life that remained to her, Mrs. Brownrigg became penitent, listened with patience to the chaplain and acknowledge the righteousness of the judgment passed on her.

The next morning, she was placed in a cart and conducted to Tyburn through a crowd which was never equalled for size at any execution.

The crowd was very unruly. The hoots, the imprecations, the jeers were appalling. Even the soldiers, accustomed to barrack-room language, were said to have been horrified by the curses of the enraged Londoners.

The chaplain, the Reverend Joseph Moore, recorded some of his impressions in the following words: "On my way to Tyburn, my ears were dinned with the horrid imprecations of the people. One said to me he hoped I should pray for her damnation and not for her salvation. Others exclaimed that they hoped she would go to Hell and were sure the Devil would fetch her." Mrs. Brownrigg seemed to have been more affected by the curses and insults of the mob than by the prayers of the chaplain, and in order to appease them and leave the world in peace, she told him to announce that she freely admitted her guilt.

The executioner duly performed his duty and Mrs. Brownrigg's body was carried to Surgeon's Hall for dissection. Her skeleton was preserved entire, and placed in a niche facing the front door of the anatomy auditorium.

The bare facts of Elizabeth Brownrigg's incredible brutalities may be sickening, but she is hardly alone in her urge to inflict savage cruelties on others. The inflicting of physical pain affords—in varying degrees—an exquisite if horrible, pleasure to certain warped persons. There are many, of both sexes, of the order of Elizabeth Brownrigg. But her name stands as the symbol of those who revel in orgies of savagery because of the staggering enormity of her unnatural urges.

VIII

ANNA MARIA ZWANZIGER

Poison, a silent and certain destroyer, has from the beginning of recorded history been a weapon very dear to the killer of his fellow-creatures. In remote ages poisoners were held in high esteem by kings, prelates and other powerful figures who desired a convenient method of removing inconvenient people.

Of all methods of dealing out death, poison is perhaps the means that has been used most treacherously, because the administration of it, in the majority of cases, is made possible by a certain closeness and friendship.

One of the great virtues of poison, from the murderer's point of view, is that its effects were often attributed to purely natural causes. In former days, when autopsies were rare and inadequate, when many doctors were careless, it is conceivable that hundreds of persons passed beyond reach of earthly cares, sped in that direction by certificates that bore a record of "Natural Causes," whereas they had been the victims of poisons.

In the case of Anna Maria Zwanziger, perhaps the most notorious woman poisoner of the nineteenth century, there is little doubt that she would have escaped justice and have died in quiet and proper respectability had the bodies of her victims been cremated. Her story reveals an extraordinary tendency of a certain criminal temperament—a temperament that impelled her to embark on a life of evil with a view to gaining certain practical ends and to continue it for the mere joy of dealing out death.

110

Anna Maria was of middle age, ugly, stunted, a misshapen woman whom some people likened to a toad—who deliberately killed certain women so that she might win their husbands. Obsessed by vanity and deluded in the magnification of her charms, she believed that she had the power to win men and, dominated by that belief, she broke down every obstacle in her road.

Anna Maria Zwanziger was born about 1760, in the city of Nuremberg, and lived during her youth at her father's inn. The Zwanzigers appear to have been decent people of the lower middle class—the sort of people who go to church twice on Sundays and consume the other sections of the day with heavy eating and heavy sleeping. Anna had an uneventful childhood. Glad to escape from the monotony of home, she married the first man who came her way, a young lawyer. He turned out to be a drunkard and a bully. For years she endured a life of misery, and when at length he died, she would have been quite pleased, if only he had left her with some resources. She was without money and without friends.

Having scraped together some meager funds, Anna opened a small confectionery shop. This was a failure, and after a while she became housekeeper to a well-known politician. Wearying of this work, she joined a traveling circus as cook. Throughout this period of her life, Anna Maria was intensely gloomy and more than once tried to kill herself. She had a great love for gloomy fiction of the romantic type, crying over the pages.

This sentimentality of the murderer is not a rare thing. Anna Maria was always a prey to this sentimentality, and at a later stage would often weep with apparent sincerity over the bed of the person she had killed.

It was at Weimar, where she stayed for some time after traveling through various cities, that Anna Maria committed her first crime—a comparatively trivial affair. She stole a valuable jewel from the house where she was employed. She took refuge in the home of a relative, but was driven out when the relative discovered why she was hiding. It is possible that this action, added to the misery she suffered at the hands of a brutal husband, may have induced in her a certain hatred of humanity, a hatred that afterwards crystallized into wholesale destruction.

Once again Anna Maria took to the road and tried her hand at many things. She taught needlework in a girls' school; she cooked for restaurants; she was a nursemaid in tradesmen's houses. Eventually, she settled down in Pegnitz, a small town near Bayreuth, and it was in this town that Anna first turned her thoughts towards murder.

She had suddenly developed an almost insane desire for being admired by men, and for marriage. She was now nearing fifty, and at a time when the average woman is shedding her vanities, Anna Maria was assuming them. She longed for men, but she knew that her unshapely figure and her dull, unattractive features could not arouse their interest. It seemed to her that her only chance of finding a husband would be by means of strategy. She must find a place as housekeeper to some wealthy bachelor or widower, and by special kindnesses and catering to his comfort, prevail upon him to marry her.

To this end, Anna Maria soon established herself in the house of an important person, a certain Judge Glaser. She believed him to be a widower, and was horrified to discover that his wife was living. The judge and Frau Glaser had quarreled and had agreed to live apart, but Anna Maria soon ascertained that the quarrel had not effected a final break and that there was a possibility of a reconciliation. She pondered this possibility. In that moment there was born in her brain the first dim thought of murder.

How does that nebulous thought develop, one wonders. It is conceivable that the potential murderer deals with it according to his temperament. One man will thrust it aside with horror and come back to it later, with the horror melting into interest and eventually into desire. Another will trifle with it as a cat trifles with a mouse. It is possible that Anna Maria, a woman of enormous resolution, did neither of these things, but that having conceived the nebulous scheme, she proceeded to build it up in all its details.

Her first move was to cajole Glaser into taking back his wife. She urged upon him the falsity of the position of the husband who lives apart from his mate. She pointed out, moreover, that scandal might attach to him if he retained her as a housekeeper while his wife remained under another roof. She played upon his feelings, even going to the length of showing him mementoes of his wife, which she had found in her room, hoping that these reminders would awaken something of his old affection for his wife.

The subtle scheme succeeded. Glaser at length yielded and Anna, delighted, wrote to Frau Glaser explaining the situation with much sentimentality and ornate phrasing. The wife came back to her home and Anna arranged for a sort of triumphant welcome. The house was made to look like a flower garden; festoons were hung upon the walls. One would have said that here was a woman of sublime altruism, rejoicing in the reunion of a man and woman whom she had brought together.

Why had she done this? Because she realized that if Frau Glaser was to be destroyed by her, she must have constant access to the woman. Within a few days of the return of the wife, Anna set to work administering doses of arsenic. She placed the poison in tea, coffee and wine.

Arsenic has always been a favorite poison for two excellent reasons. It is easy to obtain, being sold for many legitimate purposes, and it may easily be mistaken for illness when it begins to assert itself in the body of the potential victim. However, it is quickly and easily detected in the body, which most murderers forget—to their ruination—and even decomposition will not affect its presence. There are cases where arsenic has been found in persons who have been buried for more than fourteen years.

Arsenic can be administered in very small doses and the poisoning process can be extended over many weeks. On the other hand, it can be given in fairly large doses and bring about death within a few days. In the case of Frau Glaser, this last course was followed by Anna Maria, and the wretched Frau Glaser died in great agonies at the end of the third day after the first dose had been swallowed.

Anna was now ready to console the husband and to cajole him into marriage. She had imagined that this would be an easy thing—that he would turn to her as a natural solace, seeing that he had come to rely upon her friendship before the reunion with his wife. But a terrible disappointment was at hand. Glaser showed no signs of friendliness, but became morose and unresponsive. It is possible that he reproached himself for having caused his wife so much sorrow and was in no mood to marry again. Anna Maria finally realized there was nothing she could look forward to in this house. She calmly decided to seek her fortune elsewhere.

No suspicion had been aroused by the death of Frau Glaser. It had been attributed by the doctor to some internal trouble. Feeling that she was secure from associa-. tion with the crime, Anna Maria found another job as housekeeper. Her second master, like the first, was a legal official, a Judge Grohmann. He was a bachelor, thirty-eight years old, who suffered from gout. By being especially considerate of, and attentive to his infirmity, Anna Maria soon won his confidence and learned that he was engaged to be married. Horrified by this discovery, she set herself to intercepting the letters from his fiancée. She played other tricks to bring about a breakdown of the engagement, but these failed. Enraged by the judge's indifference to her, she coolly planned his destruction.

Before carrying out this second crime, however, Anna Maria experimented on two of the servants, giving them small doses of arsenic in their tea. They were seized with violent pains but recovered. Perceiving that no suspicion followed these temporary illnesses, she told herself that she was immune.

Judge Grohmann was not so fortunate. It was not long before he sickened and died. Once again the innocent doctors diagnosed the death as resulting from natural causes, and the second victim was carried to the grave. But Anna Maria came through with flying colors. So assiduously had she nursed her master during his last illness that she became a sort of heroine in the small town. People spoke of her as a self-sacrificing little angel. As a result of the supposed devotion, a colleague of the dead man, a magistrate called Gebhard, looking for a nurse for his wife who was about to have a child, called on Anna Maria and asked her to come work for him.

Anna Maria was delighted. This was the very opportunity she had been waiting for. Gebhard was comparatively young, rich and good-looking. She had fancied that he had looked at her with more than a mere employer's interest when he had engaged her as nurse. Encouraged by this delusion, she entered the house and proceeded to nurse Frau Gebhard. The nursing was so efficient that the young woman soon became a corpse.

During the process of the poisoning by arsenic, the victim had more than once developed a suspicion that something sinister was being done to her by the nurse, but the remarks which she made to her husband were waved aside as the delusions of an hysterical, sick woman.

Three deaths had now been brought about by this

woman, but she went her way undisturbed. People pitied her for having been associated with houses where so much mourning had entered. After the murder of her young mistress, Anna Maria remained in the house of Herr Gebhard as housekeeper to the unhappy man whom she consoled with her usual comforting indulgence.

In addition to superintending the household, Anna Maria undertook to prepare meals. It was no culinary interest that urged this action. She had now been seized with an extraordinary obsession—an obsession to poison unoffending persons. She availed herself of the role as cook to introduce arsenic into many of the dishes. It has been thought by some that, embittered by her failures to gain a husband, she wanted to take wholesale revenge on all with whom she came in contact. No doubt there had also begun to grow in her a lust for power.

The poisoner revels in power. In time, if he continues sufficiently long at his trade, he comes to look upon himself as a sort of deity dealing out death—sparing some, destroying others. To that point Anna Maria Zwanziger had now come. She was beginning to abandon her ambition to get a husband and was concentrating on destruction. The servants in the Gebhard household were seized with agonizing pains, and the guests who came to dinner were also attacked. Even the tradesmen bringing articles to the house did not escape her interest.

Eventually Herr Gebhard asked her to go. Not for a moment did the ingenuous man suspect his housekeeper, but he pointed out to her that he could hardly retain a cook who made so many blunders. Whenever any symptoms of poisoning appeared in guests or servants, Anna Maria was ready with a glib story. She had used the wrong ingredient in the cooking and it had produced violent indigestion. The lies were invariably accepted without arousing suspicion.

But the end was now approaching. That she was able to continue her operations for so long is a reflection on the man and his times. People living quiet, uneventful lives are rarely ready to suspect drama. They read in the papers of tragedy, but it does not occur to them that tragedy may enter their own houses.

Enraged by the dismissal, Anna Maria decided to take a final revenge. On the eve of her departure, she went to the salt box and interspersed the contents with arsenic. The coffee tins and the sugar canisters were also sprinkled with the poison. Not content with this distribution of death, she gave to the Gebhard infant a poisoned sweet as she kissed the child in farewell. Then, carrying with her testimonials from her employer that stated that she was "a model housekeeper and trusted friend," Anna Maria set out for Bayreuth.

Soon afterwards, the entire Gebhard household was seized with illness. Since the outbreak occurred within a few hours of Anna Maria's departure and attacked everybody in the house, suspicion at last began to assert itself. Even the trusting Herr Gebhard was roused to action. The police were sent for. On their arrival with a surgeon, they searched the house and examined the receptacles in the kitchen. The arsenic in the salt box was soon detected; the sugar canister revealed the poison. Meanwhile, emetics had been given to the sufferers and they soon recovered.

Bavarian police methods in the early part of the nineteenth century were absurdly slow. The deliberation and almost metaphysical meanderings that are an essential part of the true Teutonic temperament seemed to have entered the stolid officers of the law. For some weeks no attempt was made to arrest Anna Maria, not even to exercise a watch over her movements. That she did not escape was due to the fact that in her supreme vanity and self-confidence, it did not occur to her for an instant that she would be suspected of murder and attempted murder.

At last the police decided that it might be advisable

to exhume the bodies of the three people who had died while Anna Maria was in their houses. After many formalities had been gone through, this was done. The remains of Frau Glaser, Judge Grohmann and Frau Gebhard, were dug up.

Meanwhile, Anna Maria, quietly living at Bayreuth, wrote several letters to her late employer, bitterly reproaching him for "ingratitude." She had been a faithful servant, she wrote; she had nursed his wife with selfless devotion, and yet her reward was a dismissal from his service. She begged to be received back into his household.

It is possible that the absence of any reply from Herr Gebhard may have induced in Anna Maria the first emotion of fear. She left Bayreuth and went suddenly to Nuremburg. Restless and perhaps anxious, she soon left that city and went to Mainfernheim, but a few days later returned to Nuremburg. By this time the authorities had come to the conclusion that a strong *prima facie* case had been made out against the woman. A detachment of police went to Nuremburg on October 18, 1809, and arrested Anna Maria on the charge of willful murder.

Poisoners are frequently rash people. So attached do they become to their poisons that they love to carry them on their persons, sometimes indeed taking out the drugs to gloat over the powders or liquids. Thus, when Anna Maria was searched at the police station, a quantity of arsenic and a quantity of tartar emetic were found in her pockets. Had she had the foresight to hide or get rid of her poisons, it is possible that she would not have been convicted for, after all, the defence might have convinced the court that the three deaths were mere coincidences. But the presence of the poisons in her pockets spoke for itself.

After several preliminary examinations, Anna Maria was sent back to prison to await her trial. She was very calm and confident, feeling certain that she would be acquitted.

Bavarian criminal trials in former days were on lines different in one essential respect from trials by jury in this country. For the judge acted not only as the presiding official of the court, but also as the prosecutor, putting before the jury all the facts and allegations on behalf of the Crown. It was also his duty to present any facts that might be in favor of the accused. The counsel for the defense would then avail himself of those facts and call his witnesses.

Anna Maria's first action was to implicate Glaser in the murder of his wife. The man was arrested, but after questioning, was able to satisfy the magistrates of his innocence. Anna Maria was then placed on trial. Throughout its course she denied everything. She showed remarkable skill and cunning not only in her replies to questions, but by her cleverness in evading certain queries.

The trial ended but no conviction was registered. So impartial, so admirable was Bavarian administration of justice that it was held that a person could not be convicted of murder unless some sort of confession was extracted. Nevertheless, the affair could not be abandoned, and so trial follow trial and two years went by. It seemed to the authorities that Anna Maria would escape them and that they would be compelled in the final event to send her back to the world a free woman, when the unexpected happened.

Anna Maria, without giving the slightest indication of what was going to happen, collapsed suddenly and made a full confession as she stood writhing in the dock. With a loud scream, she proclaimed her guilt. The accumulated courage and endurance of years died. She was no longer the callous, clever witness; she was a shrieking, baffled, huddled-up bundle of faded clothes. The face seemed to have died, the hunched shoulders shook with misery.

"Yes, I killed them all, and would have killed more if I had had the chance," she shrieked. Then, suddenly, she collapsed and rolled over and over on the floor of the court.

The trial had stretched over a period of two years, but now that the confession had been made, there was no further delay and the law hastened to visit justice on this diabolical woman.

On a blazing hot day in July, 1811, Anna Maria Zwanziger was roused from sleep and told that she was to prepare for the end. During the three days that had elapsed since the announcement of the sentence, she had behaved very admirably, showing the apparent penitence and religious fervor that are so often evident on these occasions. Anna Maria could find no words sufficiently strong to describe her crimes and her remorse.

Nevertheless, this woman went to the block with a lie on her lips, for again she protested that Glaser had killed his wife. Having said this, she helped the executioner to remove her neck covering. Her hair was then cut short at the back, and the short, squat figure knelt down to die. She muttered a prayer. The axe fell and human justice had said its last word to Anna Maria Zwanziger.

Of her prison life, certain anecdotes are told—stories that reveal the dreadful depths to which she had sunk. A day or two before the execution, she smiled and said that it was perhaps a very fortunate thing for many people that she was to die, for had she lived she would have continued to poison men and women indiscriminately.

When the arsenic was found on her person after the arrest, Anna Maria had seized the packet and gloated over the powder, looking at it, the chronicler assures us, as a woman looks at a lover. When the attendants asked her how she could have brought herself calmly to kill people with whom she was living—whose meals and amusements she shared—she replied that their faces were so stupidly healthy and happy that she desired to see them change into faces of pain and despair.

Some students of criminal types believe that when a woman is of a cruel nature, she is frequently more so than a man. Lombroso, the criminologist, tells us that some of their methods of torture are so horrible that they cannot be described without outraging the laws of decency. He mentions also a woman who, having trapped a rival, compelled her to die slowly of starvation while chained to a table on which was displayed a variety of tempting foods. Another woman forced a man who had wronged her to swallow portions of his own roasted flesh.

Anna Zwanziger did not employ tortures of this kind, because her poisons sufficed her cravings. It is possible that even in the hour of death she found a certain satisfaction in the reflection that she was dying as a martyr to the cause of the poisoning force that she had served so well.

IX

GAETANO MAMMONE

Most brigands, living hard, dangerous lives and menaced by authorities on one side and hotheaded subordinates on the other, rarely live to a ripe old age. But one man—an Italian robber, perhaps the most monstrous and vicious of his tribe—passed from illicit brigandage to the more respectable brigandage of war, became an officer in the Royal Army and lived to a very advanced age.

Gaetano Mammone, born about 1769, began to prey upon travelers in the valleys and mountains of his native land when he was little more than a boy. He married young, but finding that wife and child were useless encumbrances, he decided to free himself of family restraint by murdering both of them. The child had annoyed him by its wailings during an illness. The killing of his wife followed because she had vexed Gaetano's peace with lamentations concerning the infant.

Gaetano was an enormous man, with a strength of limb and muscle that caused legends to cling to his name. It was said of him that he could lift a horse with ease, could bend a thick iron bar across his knee. It was also claimed that he appeared to absorb vitality from all men and women with whom he came in contact, leaving them exhausted. This mental and emotional vampirism was eclipsed by a more literal and horrible vampirism to which we must refer at a later stage.

Gaetano's methods were extraordinarily simple. Having waylaid a traveler, he would order him to deliver up his property. If the property was not sufficiently valuable, or if Gaetano had reason to believe that something was being withhheld, he would order his gang to inflict horrible tortures upon the wretched man to get him to disclose the treasure Gaetano thought he was concealing.

Thus, on one occasion, Gaetano encountered an old man and his daughter whom he forced to dismount from their mules while the gang searched their persons. Nothing of value was found. Gaetano then produced his torture implements, whereupon the half-fainting traveler pointed to his boots. The boots were wrenched off and found to hold a quantity of gold. For this act of "deceit," as the brigand termed it, the wretched old man was immediately put to death. The daughter was outraged and, a few days later, followed her father.

Gaetano was no respecter of persons. Having learned that the French ambassador was on his way to the court of King Ferdinand, his gang lay in wait for the diplomat, who at length came into view while the brigands were in close ambush. For some reason which the records do not state, the ambassador was riding alone, unaccompanied by secretary or retinue. Not only did Gaetano rob the ambassador of his purse and his jewelry, but he actually stripped the man naked so that his richly embroidered clothing might be added to the booty. To cover his nudity, the man was given a filthy cloak, old and dirty, and in this guise was allowed to depart for Naples.

The ambassador was furious and complained bitterly to the king. Ferdinand sent for his minister and charged him to take "immediate steps for the capture of the brigand." But at this point, diplomacy intervened to save the head of Gaetano Mammone. The minister explained that Gaetano was far too valuable an asset to the safety of the throne to be sacrificed to an ambassador's wish for vengeance.

Rebellion was making itself felt, and at any time an attempt might be made to destroy the monarchy. Gaetano, the minister pointed out, was a very useful person in that his journeyings and his adventures frequently enabled him to gain valuable information regarding the doings of the revolutionaries. "Destroy this brigand," said the minister in effect, "and we lose a spy whom we cannot afford to lose."

Eventually, the king resigned himself to the sending of a message to the brigand—by means of one of his gang who had been captured and was then set free—to the effect that his robberies would be ignored in high quarters, provided he took care in the future not to molest "high officials en route to the court, or personal friends of his Majesty." To this message, Gaetano replied with exaggerated courtesy. He humbly begged the pardon of the king for the insult placed on the ambassador, offering to return his clothing—but not his gold—and vowed he would exercise scrupulous care in his future dealings with travelers. He ended by protesting that the king had no more loyal subject than himself.

Brigandage in Italy had political origins; peasants, harshly exploited and suppressed by lord and landowner, had early banded together in sporadic little revolts. Hence, even centuries later, the life of a brigand in Italy was a more pleasant affair than the life of the highwayman in England. The highwayman was a solitary creature, little more than a street thief who had taken to the road; the brigand had the solace of friends and a certain prestige. The brigand frequently was a member of some semi-political association whose aims were not entirely connected with personal gain. Sometimes revenge formed the leading motive of a gang. They lived generally in good style: they had their campfires and their songs, their romances and their women. Not often were they monstrous villains of the Gaetano type.

Gaetano claimed no virtues. He knew himself for what he was—a desperate brute who laughed at patriotism except when it served his purpose, who reveled in cruelty for its own sake, who frequently killed a man in order that he might watch the agonies of his dying.

In 1799, Gaetano had rendered certain services to the reigning house that actually gained him the rank of captain in the army. It is an ironical reflection on the ethics of war that we find the brigand rejoicing in his new occupation because it would afford him greater chances of stealing and killing. Gaetano was now free to carry on these trades without fear of interruption, and in the years that followed he gratified his thirst for blood to the extreme.

Blood in its literal sense had become a sort of obsession with this monster. For some time he had made a practice of drinking it on certain occasions when he believed that his tremendous strength was failing him. He said that the taste of it was more delightful than the taste of the most exquisite wines of France or Italy, and that the man who had once formed an affection for the "scarlet vintage" would not exchange it for the juice of the grape.

He had two horrible methods of enjoying this blood-drinking. Sometimes he would sever the artery of a victim and then, bending down beside the wretched man, would suck the blood while the wretch was still living, uttering cries of joy between the draughts. When in a more leisurely mood, he would cut off the head of a victim—excising the brains—and having made a sort of drinking cup of the interior of the skull, would fill it with blood and proceed to quench his disgusting thirst.

His health was wonderful. Plagues passed him by, leaving him untouched. He went his way unworried, unconcerned. He said sometimes that he ought to have been miserable because of his crimes, but that, fortunately, he had not been burdened with a conscience. He came to look upon himself as a privileged person, one to whom there were no such problems as right and wrong.

Undoubtedly, he was successful as a soldier and a strategist. He performed many remarkable feats and proved himself a man of great courage. He would go into battle armed with a short dagger, and seeking the most perilous position, would stab with a ferocity that so terrified the enemy that many of them fled without coming to grips with him. King Ferdinand was enchanted with his new officer, and the brigand's crimes were quickly forgotten.

Gaetano now had an opportunity to win distinction for himself by the use of his strategic gifts; but with the natural preference of a cruel man, he relied upon savagery even when less brutal methods would have served his purpose. He loved to know that people became sick with terror at his approach. Some twist in his make-up made him enjoy the inflicting of pain, and if he had the choice of putting a man to death quickly and mercifully, or protracting his agonies with brutality, he always chose the latter.

Sometimes this monster organized spectacular horrors that would have delighted a Nero. Thus, on one occasion when he had taken a number of prisoners after a skirmish, he drove them all into a large barn. Their hands were then nailed to tables and walls. An hour later, the barn was filled with straw and oil, the doors were locked, and the prisoners were burned to death.

He loved blasphemies and frequently committed hideous sacrilege. After the capture of Altamara, Gaetano entered the principal church of the town and organized a burlesque Mass. In that church there were two people —an old man and an old woman—who feebly protested against the procedure. The reply of Gaetano was characteristic. With his own hands, he slaughtered both of them. The dead man was then flayed. A scrap of his skin was used as a wafer, a portion of his blood for the Communion Cup, and Gaetano, roaring with laughter, improvised a Mass for his soul.

The passing of years brought no avenger after Gaetano. He went from success to success, rising high in the Royal esteem and piling up a very considerable fortune. He was fortunate in having been born in that era—he lived at a time when evil government and lawlessness brought many ruthless adventurers to a harbor of safety and riches.

Of his last years, there is no exact record, but one can conclude that he died as he had lived, remorseless, content, conscienceless. His abnormal vitality saw him through his long career untouched by illness—the man

who had never known a day's suffering was able to
laugh at the sufferings of other men. Yet in some deep
recess of his mind, it is possible that his boast that he
knew no qualms was bluff. Otherwise, why would he
have to insist upon it?

Brigands like Gaetano are now few, and brigandage,
once almost universal, has of recent years been confined in Europe to Italy, Spain, Corsica and Greece, although there have been isolated cases in other countries.
Those countries by reason of their geographical characteristics have afforded shelters and refuges to bands of
robbers and murderers.

In the case of Italy, there was in former times an additional security for breakers of the law, because the
presence of a number of small states afforded a refuge.
The brigand had merely to cross a frontier and was at
once immune. Again, the political situation was often in
his favor, for by offering his assistance to one party or
the other, he gained a sort of official recognition and
aid.

While hills and fastnesses and insecure governments
remain, the brigand will perhaps always have a certain
existence, in spite of radio, trains, automobiles and other
civilized contrivances that appear to render brigandage
an anachronism.

The monstrous savagery of a Gaetano Mammono may
find its repetition in the future. But the brigand as an
institution is dead, and even the most romantic-minded
lover of the past would not wish for his resurrection.
His picturesqueness was perhaps his only possession;
remove that and there is nothing left but a skulking
thief and a cold-blooded murderer.

X

BURKE AND HARE

In the social history of Scotland there is perhaps no more curious chapter than that of the rise, development and ultimate downfall of the Resurrectionist Movement. This practice of violating sepulchers came about for a number of reasons. The principal of these was undoubtedly the discovery by the medical profession that what little was known of the human body was founded upon uncertain tradition rather than upon empirical science; that they were practically ignorant of anatomy, and that if they hoped to make any advances in healing human diseases they must devote more attention to the study of the dead subject—to dissection of the dead body itself.

However, a great difficulty was encountered here. The people of Scotland even in the most lawless ages had a great reverence for the dead, and the bodies were carefully entombed to await the last call. The prejudices of the people would not permit offering or selling the bodies of their deceased. It was considered high sacrilege to disturb the dead. As a result, doctors and students could not obtain the subjects upon which to experiment and were compelled to rely on men who rifled graveyards.

Two names stand out starkly in this grave-robbing era —Burke and Hare—the most notorious offenders in this traffic of cemetery pillage and cadaver vending.

William Burke was the son of Neil Burke, a laborer, and was born in the early part of the year 1792, in the parish of Orrey, County Tyrone, Ireland. After receiving a fair education, he became a servant to a Presbyterian minister, although he himself was a Catholic of Catholic parentage. Finding this work not to his liking, he tried his hand as a baker and then as a weaver. None of these trades agreed with him and ultimately he enlisted in the Donegal Militia as a fifer, having acquired a local reputation as an excellent player on the flute. He married a young woman from Ballina. Then an event occurred which may be regarded as the turning point of what had hitherto been a life of respectability.

Burke was anxious to obtain the subtenancy of a piece of land from his father-in-law, but they quarrelled over the matter so violently that Burke left his wife and family and emigrated to Scotland, under conditions that made it impossible for him to return again.

Burke arrived in Scotland in 1818 and obtained employment as a laborer on the Union Canal, which was then in the course of construction. He found a place to live in the village of Maddiston. It was here that he met Helen McDougal, who became the partner of his wretched "body-snatching."

The record of Helen McDougal's career up to her meeting with Burke is somewhat spotty. In early life she made the acquaintance of a sawyer named McDougal, by whom she had a child during his wife's lifetime. When McDougal became a widower, Helen went to live with him, and though they had never gone through a regular marriage ceremony, cohabitation was sufficient to constitute them man and wife and she bore McDougal's name. He died of typhus fever and Helen was left with two children, a boy and a girl.

Helen was of middle size, but thin and large-boned. Her features were long, and the upper half of her face was out of proportion to the lower. She was of a dour and sullen disposition, jealous, and gloomily wicked.

Burke was rather below middle-size, stout, and with

a hard, determined expression. His face was round with high cheekbones; he had sunken grey eyes, a short snubbish nose and a round chin. His hair and whiskers were of a light sandy color. He dressed in shabby blue surtout, buttoned close to the throat. The expression in his eyes was far from inviting.

Helen McDougal seems to have been living rather dissolutely when she met William Burke. They soon threw in their lot together and lived as husband and wife. Their irregular life came to the knowledge of the priest of the district, who advised Burke to return to his lawful wife in Ireland. Burke refused to do this and was consequently excommunicated.

It is worth remembering, however, that Burke was a man of a naturally religious turn of mind, though not bound up in any particular form of faith, and that in all his later actions, brutal and godless though they were, the inward voice never left him at peace, except when his senses were steeped in drink. Both he and Helen McDougal drank heavily, and throughout his life liquor held a compelling spot.

They decided to move to Edinburgh, where they lodged at the Beggar's Hotel in the Portsburgh section. Here Burke worked as a shoemaker to earn a livelihood. He now formed a relationship with a young woman, a friend of Helen McDougal, who became very jealous of her. The three lived in one room. There were frequent fierce quarrels, and once Burke turned on Helen and beat her brutally.

Burke's moral character, never very upright, was now on the decline, and gradually he began to associate with men and women whose experience in wickedness was greater than anything to which he had as yet sunk.

In 1827, when he was thirty-five, Burke and McDougal went to live in Tanner's Close, the lodginghouse in Edinburgh kept by William and Mrs. Hare—the companions and participators in the crimes that afterwards embroiled them all. Here Burke again set up business as a shoemaker in the cellar attached to the house.

William Hare, a hawker, was about the same age as Burke and was also a native of Ireland. Brought up without any education or proper moral training, he had rapidly slipped into a life of aimless vagabondage. His temper was brutal and ferocious, and when he was drinking he was unbearable. In Ireland, he had done farm work. Then he came to Scotland where he became a laborer, then a "lumper" and finally a hawker. In 1826, he married a widow who had one child—and a lodging-house. The lodginghouse, possession of which Hare had assumed on his marriage, contained seven beds, and the earnings from it gave him the means of drinking without the necessity of working. He took full advantage of his position, became even more dissolute and went about bullying and fighting with all around him. Mrs. Hare was equally dissolute and brutal, and though she had a streak of vivacity, she was equally vicious.

Hare had dull blackish eyes, one higher than the other; a thick, coarse-lipped mouth, high broad cheekbones, and sunken cheeks. He was sluggish and inert, and unconcerned and callous about the consequences of his diabolical acts.

Of the two men, William Burke seems to have been the more dangerous, because mentally he was the abler man. Of the two women, Mrs. Hare was definitely the abler. All four were given to drink and greed. They formed a close-knit companionship.

In Hare's house one day an old pensioner died, owing him about four pounds. Casting about for some means of recovering the debt, it occurred to the resentful Hare that by selling the body to the doctors at the medical school in Surgeon's Square, he would more than realize his loss. He was well acquainted with the readiness of the doctors to deal in such "wares."

Hare communicated his plan to Burke, since a confederate was required to help carry through his plan, and promised him to share in the proceeds. Burke agreed to the scheme, and then and there the sinister partnership between the two men was formed.

The coffin which had been screwed down was opened and tanners' bark substituted for the body of the pensioner, which was concealed in a bed. Hare then nailed down the lid again, and the obsequies were in due course completed.

In the evening, the two men visited the medical school at Surgeon's Square, Hare remaining near at hand while Burke advanced towards the room of Dr. Robert Knox, the celebrated scientist and lecturer on anatomy. There was a consultation with some of his students, after which Burke and Hare returned home.

They now put the body into a sack and carried it to Surgeon's Square. In accordance with their instructions, they carried the corpse into the dissecting room. Dr. Knox then examined the body and proposed to the paymaster that the men should get seven pounds, ten shillings for the body. This was promptly paid, the paymaster saying that he would be glad to see them again when they had any other body to dispose of.

This was the first transaction these two men had with the doctors, and it is curious to notice how an incident of so little moment in itself should be to them the first step in a long and terrible course of crime—long in the sense that they kept out of the reach of the law, and were considered nothing worse than pitiful "Resurrectionists" who were willing to robe graves for a few paltry pounds.

For the two scoundrels, a new road to riches had opened. They saw in this new business an easier method of making a comfortable livelihood than any they had yet tried. They prowled around graveyards and became regular providers of subjects for Dr. Knox and his students. They were not, however, too successful, for the sextons resented this interference with their trade and bloody fights resulted.

It was Hare who now suggested to Burke that they should abandon the slow business of graveyard body-snatching for more direct methods, even though it involved murder. They seemed completely indifferent to the consequences of such a course of action.

It would be well to give a description of the den of iniquity in which these mass murders were to be enacted. Hare's lodginghouse was a dirty, low, wretched place called Tanner's Close. It was a one-story house, and though the interior might be observed by any passerby, it was not connected to any other dwelling. It was fitted up as a lodging for beggars and wanderers, and a *Beds to Let* sign invited vagrants to enter, frequently to their destruction. So, far from any concealment being practiced, the door generally stood open. But there was one small inner room or den, the window of which looked out on a pigsty and a dead wall, into which it is asserted they were accustomed to conduct their prey to be murdered. No surprise could have been excited by cries of murder issuing from such a riotous and disorderly house. And it was unlikely that any could reach the ear from the interior den. The very character of the house, the continued scenes of violence and fights that took place there, saved it from observation which a more respectable dwelling might demand.

So the two confederates made their compact. They took for their motto the significant question Burke put to a student when he was negotiating for the sale of the pensioner's body: "Wouldn't you give a pound more for a fresh wun?" It is doubtful if the two women knew anything about the original pact. Hare began by prowling about the streets to see if he could fall in with any person who would make a likely subject upon whom they could practice. For a time he was unsuccessful, but at length an opportunity arrived. This was, according to Burke's confession, early in the spring of 1828.

One afternoon Hare met an old woman, the worse for drink, in the grassmarket. She was Abigail Simpson of Gilmerton, a village on the outskirts of Edinburgh, who had come into the city to obtain a small pension due her. He considered her a fitting subject—old and weakly and with little strength of mind and body left after her drinking bout. Hare spoke to her, claiming that he had seen her before, and she readily entered into conversation with him. Speedily they became friends and he easily persuaded her to accompany him to his house, where they would have a "dram" together in honor of their happy meeting.

Once in the house, Mrs. Simpson was treated with overflowing kindness. She was introduced to Burke as an old friend, and the whiskey was placed before her. The fun became fast and furious as the drinking went on. When morning dawned, the woman was sick and helpless. The time had now arrived. The house was quiet, and the courage of the two men, urged on by whiskey, was sufficient for the deed they contemplated. Hare placed his hand over Mrs. Simpson's mouth and nose to stop her breathing, and Burke laid himself across her body to prevent her making any disturbance. There was no resistance. The wretched woman was beyond resisting, and any noise she might have been able to make was stifled by the method they adopted to effect her death. In a few minutes, she was dead. The men lifted the body out of bed, undressed it and bundled it up in a chest.

Later, one of the men informed Dr. Knox's students that they had another subject to give them, and it was agreed that a porter from Surgeons' Square should meet them at the back of the "Castle" in the evening. Burke and Hare carried the chest with its ghastly contents to the meeting place and then the porter assisted them with it to the rooms of Dr. Knox. "Dr. Knox came in.

The body was cold and stiff. The Doctor approved of its being so fresh, but did not ask any questions." So admitted Burke. The price paid the murderers for the corpse of Abigail Simpson—their first experiment in killing—was ten pounds.

The work of wholesale murder was now begun, and the monstrous confederates had gained confidence by the success of the first effort. There were no qualms of conscience. If there were, they were speedily drowned in drink, strong enough to stop them. The fear of discovery, too, had passed away when they saw how easily and quietly they could work, and the desire for more victims became a mania.

The next unfortunate victim who fell into their hands was a miller known to Burke simply as "Joseph," who resided in Hare's house. Joseph contracted an infectious fever. Hare and his wife were alarmed lest the rumor should damage the reputation of their house and keep lodgers away. So it was agreed that Joseph should be put out of the way as quickly as possible—and by the same remedy they had applied so successfully in the case of Abigail Simpson.

Burke placed a small pillow over the sick man's mouth and Hare lay across the body to keep down his arms and legs. Death followed as a matter of course, and the body was sold in Surgeons' Square for ten pounds.

Within a very short time another victim, a native of Cheshire, England, also a lodger in Hare's house, became ill with jaundice. He was a very tall man, about forty years old, and made a livelihood by selling "spunks," or matches, on the streets of Edinburgh. His death was caused by the same efficient plan now adopted by Burke and Hare, who obtained the customary ten pounds from Dr. Knox for the body, and no questions asked.

It is remarkable that at so early a period in their career of crime, Burke and Hare should have shown so much boldness as they exhibited in the murder of Mary

Paterson, a young woman unfortunately too well known on the streets of Edinburgh. And it is equally remarkable how, considering the circumstances, they were able to carry out the crime and dispose of the body without detection.

There is little reason to doubt that Burke was a man of finer nature than Hare, though their guilt in the end was at least equal. Hare could play his part in the slaughter of a fellow mortal without any qualms of conscience, and he slept as quietly the night after he had provided a "subject" for the doctors, as if his soul were spotless.

Burke, however, was a man of different temperament, and reckless though he was, he could not altogether banish the moral teachings of his church from his mind. "Thou shalt not kill" rang in his ears, but under the numbing influences of drink the Command was forgotten and broken, and then followed the fearful looking for judgment. He could not sleep without a bottle of whiskey by his bedside, and he kept a candle burning on the table all night. When he wakened sometimes in fright, he would take a deep draught at the bottle, which finally induced sleep, or rather, stupor.

Early one morning, April 9, 1828, Burke went to a public house in the neighborhood of the Canongate. While he sat drinking, two young women, of apparently doubtful character, entered the house and ordered a gill of whiskey. They were Mary Paterson and Janet Brown. The two women and Burke were strangers, but he—his conscience quieted by liquor—thought that he saw in them two fine subjects for the doctors. In his most winning manner, Burke went over and spoke to them, asked them to have a drink with him, and ordered a round of rum and bitters. They were not at all averse to the treat, so they sat down and consumed three gills, at the expense of their smooth-spoken stranger. At last Burke had ingratiated himself so much with the girls that when he proposed that they accompany him to his lodgings for breakfast, they agreed.

Purchasing two bottles of whiskey, he gave one to each of the girls and then the trio set off for Constantine Burke's house in Gibb's Close, off the Canongate. Constantine was Burke's brother, married and with a family. It was never known whether he and his wife had any complicity in the murders, but it was suspected that they were at least aware of them, especially of the one that was committed in their house.

Burke told the girls he was a pensioner, and to Janet Brown, who had some objection to going with him, he said he could keep her comfortably for life.

When Burke and his two companions arrived at the house, he found his brother and sister-in-law just out of bed, and the place looked rather gloomy for receiving guests. Burke upbraided his sister-in-law—or landlady, as he wished her to appear—for her carelessness. Mrs. Constantine Burke then set about preparing breakfast. The company sat down, and what with the drink they had imbibed and the warmth of their reception, the girls began to feel quite happy. Constantine soon left for his work—that of a scavenger in the Edinburgh Police Department—and the breakfast dishes were cleared away.

Then the two whiskey bottles were produced and the debauch, begun so early in the morning, was renewed. Burke and Mary Paterson drank recklessly, the former to keep up his courage for the murder he contemplated. Janet Brown drank more temperately than either. Mary at length felt the effects of the whiskey and fell asleep in her chair. Regarding her now as certain prey, Burke turned his attention to his other prospective victim, Janet.

At Burke's suggestion, he and Janet went out for a walk and soon the couple were seated in a public house, with pies and porter before them. The mixture of the drinks made Janet stupid and after a while she went back to the house in Gibb's Close with Burke, in a very drunken condition. More whiskey was produced. While they sat drinking, Helen McDougal, who had entered the house while they were out, broke in upon them. Mrs. Constantine Burke whispered to Janet that this was Burke's wife. McDougal reviled the girls, accusing them of attempting to corrupt her husband. While this was going on, Mrs. Constantine Burke rushed out of the house and went, it has been assumed, for Hare.

Mary, now completely besotted, lay prone across the truckle bed. Janet, however, apologized to McDougal, explaining that they had not known that Burke was married. Helen McDougal then turned her full fury upon her husband, breaking dishes on the table. Burke threw a glass which, striking her on the forehead, caused an ugly gash. He then threw her out, locking the door after her.

Alone with Janet, Burke tried to persuade her to lie down on the bed, but her terror of Helen McDougal, who was hammering on the door, made her want to leave the house. On her promise to come back when the coast was clear, Burke allowed her to go, escorting her at her request past his indignant lady. It has been suspected that this connubial interlude with McDougal was prearranged.

Hare arrived soon afterwards and the two men put their fatal skill to work on the intoxicated, unconscious girl. Within a few minutes the job was done. Mary Paterson was dead. McDougal and Mrs. Hare were conveniently outside and when they came in, the corpse was lying on the bed, covered up. They asked no questions— no doubt knowing what had taken place—and the men left the house.

In the meantime, Janet Brown made her way to the house of a Mrs. Laurie, with whom she had once lodged and whom she had visited with Mary Paterson immediately before meeting Burke, and related to her the day's adventures. Mrs. Laurie sent a servant along with Janet to bring Mary away. Befuddled with drink, Janet had difficulty finding the house and applied to one Swanston at the tavern for information. Finding the place at last, she was met at the door by McDougal and the two Hares. She asked for Mary Paterson and was told she was out with Burke.

On the invitation of Hare and his wife and McDougal, Janet again agreed to join them in a few more drinks. Mrs. Laurie's servant, seeing the state of matters, left Janet and returned to her mistress.

Hare, meanwhile, was figuring on a second victim and he plied Janet with more liquor. The poor girl was within a foot or two of the bed on which lay, covered with a sheet, the still warm body of her dead companion. Fortunately for Janet, the servant had informed Mrs. Laurie of how matters stood and she, rather alarmed, sent the girl back to bring Janet away. In this the girl succeeded and Hare, frustrated, left the house shortly afterwards.

Later in the afternoon Janet, partially sobered, returned again, and once more inquired for Mary. The answer she received this time was that Burke and her friend had never returned. When later she once more returned for an explanation, she was told that Mary had gone away with a packman to Glasgow. This explanation was unsatisfactory to Janet, and though she saw no more of the Burkes and Hares, she continued from time to time to make inquiries for the missing Mary Paterson, but without result.

About four hours after Mary Paterson's death, her murderers had her body in Dr. Knox's dissecting room and had received eight pounds for their forenoon's work. This expedition was rather foolhardy, for while the corpse was cold, it was not very rigid and it presented the appearance of recent death.

Burke and Hare had been considered at Surgeon's Square as mere resurrectionists of the old type, men who robbed graves of their contents. But now Ferguson and another student had second thoughts. To them the girl seemed familiar. One of them said she looked like a girl he had seen in the Canongate only a few hours before. Also, the girl's hair was in curl papers, and the general appearance indicated that the body was fresh and had not been buried. They asked Burke where he had obtained the body and his reply was that he had purchased it from an old woman residing at the back of the Canongate, and that the girl had killed herself with drink. This explanation was feasible since Mary's body still reeked of whiskey. Evidently satisfied, one of the students gave Burke a pair of scissors and he cut off the girl's hair. This he would probably sell to a hairdresser to be made up for the use of some proud dame.

But this was not all. In life, Mary Paterson had been an exceedingly beautiful girl. Her handsome figure and well-shaped limbs so attracted the attention of Dr. Knox that he preserved the body for three months in spirits and invited a painter to see it. Knox wanted the best example of the female form and muscular development for his lectures. Dr. Lonsdale, one of Dr. Knox's students, makes the following interesting reference: "The body of the girl could not fail to attract attention by its voluptuous form and beauty; students crowded around the table on which she lay, and artists came to study a model worthy of Phidias and the best Greek art."

Murder multiplies quickly and soon there was another death—an old woman whom Mrs. Hare in the course of her peregrinations persuaded to go home with her and whom she plied with liquor. When Hare came home for dinner, his wife had her unknown acquaintance in bed, helplessly intoxicated. Hare carefully place part of a bed-tick over her mouth and nose and in the evening the woman was dead. Burke had no part in this murder, but he assisted Hare in conveying it that night to Dr. Knox's rooms, where they received and divided the usual fee. The name of this woman was not known.

For his part, Burke by himself then also did away with another old woman. She came into the house as a lodger, and of her own accord drank until she became insensible. Hare was not in the house at the time and Burke, by the usual method of suffocation, brought about her death. No time was lost in conveying the body to Surgeons' Square.

On their next victim, they went back to their original collaboration. This woman, known as Effy, would search for small pieces of leather which she was in the habit of selling to Burke, who used them for mending shoes. One day he took her into Hare's stable, which he used as a workshop, and gave her some drink. It may have been in part payment of scraps of leather he had received from her, for a murder never seems to have been committed except when funds were at a low ebb, and at the rate at which the confederates were carousing and indulging in finery, that was very frequent. Hare joined his companion in the work of making the woman insensible, and soon she lay down to sleep on a heap of straw. Their time for action had again arrived, and they carefully placed a cloth over her head to stop her breathing. "She was then," proceeds the confession, "carried to Dr. Knox's rooms and sold for ten pounds."

In spite of his drunken habits and loose way of living, Burke had a "good character" with the police, and on one occasion he made it the means of obtaining another victim. A "good character with the police" in the area in which he lived was of some consideration. The locale was inhabited by the lowest classes of the community, and the criminal element was prominent. The police looked upon Burke as a poor workman, a little foolish perhaps, but still, as the place went, comparatively respectable. This attitude, together with his winning tongue, enabled Burke to pull off one of his cleverest jobs.

It actually came about by accident.

Early one morning, when probably on the lookout for some poor unfortunate whom he might drug with whiskey and put to death, Burke came across Andrew Williamson, a policeman, dragging a drunken woman to the watch-house in West Post. Burke saw in her a victim, so he said, "Let the woman go to her lodgings," and he volunteered his services to take her home. The policeman gladly handed over his loathsome burden, and Burke took his valuable prize to Hare's house. That night she was murdered by Burke and Hare in "the same way as they did the others," and for her body they received ten pounds from Dr. Knox.

Sometime in the midsummer of 1828 Burke and his wife moved to the house of one John Broggan, evidently after a quarrel between the two partners over some underhanded doings by Hare concerning their "business." However, they did not keep up the ill feeling long, for they soon were together at work again, and the wholesale slaughter of weak human beings went on.

The murderers, be it noted, never sought a strong, able man upon whom to try their fatal skill. They always chose the old and the silly in body or in mind—those who could be rendered insensible with drink.

And so the list of victims continued to mount: old Mary Haldane and her daughter Margaret; and after them two strangers, an aged grandmother who had walked all the way from Glasgow with her deaf-mute twelve-year-old grandson, whose back Burke broke the day after they did away with his "nanny." Even kinship did not deter them, for their next victim was the pretty young cousin of Helen McDougal's former husband, who had come on a visit to Edinburgh. Truly Poe's lines seem most aptly applied to Burke and Hare:

> "They are neither man nor woman—
> They are neither brute nor human—
> They are Ghouls."

While all this was going on, the four fiends, bound together, as they were, by the joint commission of terrible crimes, had their little disagreements amongst themselves. The women were jealous of each other, and there is reason to believe that each man was suspicious that his partner, in case of discovery, would turn informer, as was afterwards proved. To those around them, however, they all appeared contented and most prosperous. The women dressed themselves in a style that was considered highly superior in the locality in which they lived; the men also were better clad than members of the same class usually were. And their mode of living showed that somehow they had plenty of money. These things attracted the attention of the neighbors, but if they had any suspicion that matters were altogether right, they did not give expression to it.

But the criminals were gradually approaching their doom. They had become reckless and bold. They had been so successful thus far that they hoped to be equally so in the future, forgetting that the mills of God grind slow but sure. But before they were actually discovered they managed a killing that aroused much public interest, and it is amazing they were not then apprehended. This was the murder of James Wilson, known as "Daft Jamie," a lad of about eighteen. He was one of those wandering "naturals" known to everybody and, being a lad who, though mentally retarded, was kind at heart, he was a universal favorite. The murder of so well-known a character as Daft Jamie can only be regarded as rash and foolish and, like the killing of Mary Paterson, it courted discovery.

One day early in October, 1828, Daft Jamie was wandering about the Grassmarket, asking all if they had

seen his mother. During his search for her he was met
by Mrs. Hare. She quickly formed a plan. Yes, she had
seen his mother and if Jamie went with her he would
find her in her house in Tanner's Close. Jamie, in all
innocence, followed the woman to her lodging, where
Hare was sitting idle. Of course, the visitor was welcomed in the most kindly fashion, asked to sit down until
his mother should appear. To keep him from being
bored, he was invited to help himself with the contents
of a whiskey bottle. Although fond of an occasional
dram, Jamie was hesitant; he had a great fear of "get-
tin' fou." At last he was induced to take some.

In the meantime, Mrs. Hare went down to Mr. Rymer's
shop for some provisions. She found Burke there. She
pressed his foot; he understood the signal. He knew
what was wanted of him and went back with her to the
house. More whiskey was brought in and Jamie was
induced to take more than he could handle. Then they
managed to get him into the little room where so many
tragedies had been enacted, and he lay down on the
bed in a half-dazed state. Burke and Hare kept watch
on his every movement to see when it would be safe
for them to carry out their diabolical design. Mrs. Hare
knew it was not for her to stay in the house when "business" was being transacted, so she went out, carefully
locking the door behind her.

The two men were eagerly watching their victim, but
they felt that this case would not be too easy. Jamie,
though witless, was young and physically strong, and he
had not taken enough liquor to make him absolutely
helpless, even in the hands of two robust and desperate
men. Finally Burke, tired of waiting, furiously threw
himself on the prostrate body of the dozing lad. Jamie
was no sooner touched than the natural instinct for
self-preservation made him try to defend himself. He
threw Burke off and climbed to his feet. Burke then
closed in on him again, but now Jamie was awake and

fighting for his life, and it seemed he was more than a match for the killer.

Hare, meantime, was standing aside, idly watching the contest, and it was only when Burke threatened to "put a knife in Jamie" that he roused himself and threw his strength in the scale against the boy. Jamie had nearly overcome Burke when Hare jumped in and tripped him up. The poor lad fell heavily on the floor and before he had time to recover himself, the two men were upon him—Hare, as usual, holding his mouth and nose, and Burke lying over his body, keeping down his legs and arms. Still Jamie struggled, but their combined strength was too much for him. His murderers had him too securely beneath them, and gradually his strength waned, until at last the tragedy was completed. They had not, however, come off unhurt; he had got in a few telling blows.

Before the body was taken to Surgeons' Square, it was stripped of its clothing. This was a blunder that could have proved fatal. In all the other murders, the clothes of the victims were destroyed to prevent detection, but in this case Burke gave Jamie's clothes to his brother Constantine's children, and it is said that a baker who had given the murdered lad the pair of trousers he wore at the time of his death recognized them on one of Burke's nephews. But Burke and Hare were too immersed in their deed and in their routine of disposing of the body to worry about detection. In the course of the afternoon the body was conveyed to Dr. Knox's rooms and the sum of ten pounds was obtained for it. No questions seem to have been asked as to how Burke and Hare became possessed of the body of Daft Jamie, though there can be little doubt that some of the students recognized it.

The public, when Jamie's death was known, wondered about this. In a popular work published at the time, there was this very pertinent sentence: "Certainly those scientific individuals who attended the class in which he was dissected must be very hardened men, when they saw Jamie lying on the dissecting table for anatomy; for they could not but know, when they saw him, that he had been murdered; and not only that, the report of his being missing went through the whole town on the following day; there could not be any one of them but must know him by sight."

Shortly after Jamie was missed, the statement was circulated that one of Dr. Knox's students claimed that he'd seen Jamie on the dissecting table. Jamie's mother and her friends searched everywhere for the poor boy, but they could find no trace of him. There seemed to be a tendency to treat the statement of the body having been seen on a table in the rooms in Surgeons' Square as mere idle rumor, arising out of the general uneasiness and fear because of the disappearances that had lately been taking place. A sense of insecurity had been building up gradually among the inhabitants.

The mysterious fate of Daft Jamie caught the public mind and heart, and when the mystery was solved, the murder of the poor lad bulked larger than all the other crimes put together. Pamphlets and chap books, quickly and coarsely printed, were sold in great amounts, and the story of poor Jamie was on everyone's lips. One writer caught the mood of the people in a widely repeated couplet:

> "The ruffian dogs—the hellish pair—
> The villain Burke—the meagre Hare . . ."

But Burke and Hare again got away with murder. They even began to think of expanding their "business" —of opening a "branch" in Glasgow or Ireland, and forwarding the bodies to Dr. Knox from there. For they were quite pleased with their work, which was easier than cobbling boots and shoes, or traveling about the country as a peddler. In his confession Burke described the simplicity of their operations: "When they kept the mouth and the nose shut a very few minutes, they (the victims) could make no resistance, but would convulse and make a rumbling noise in their bellies for some time; after they ceased crying and making resistance, they (the murderers) left them to die by themselves; but their bodies would often move afterwards, and for some time they would have long breathings before life went away."

But, though Burke and Hare found their chosen work particularly suited to their tastes, their plans for expansion were not put into effect. Retribution was creeping up on them.

The last of the tragedies was the murder of Mary Campbell—or Docherty, as she was better known—an old Irishwoman who had come to Edinburgh to look for her son. On the morning of October 31st—the Friday of Sacrament Week—Burke was in Rymer's grocery store talking to the shop boy while he sipped a tumbler of liquor. As he was doing this, the old woman entered and asked for information. Burke, ever on the lookout for a victim, saw that the poor creature was in every way suitable for his purpose—she was an old and frail stranger who would never be missed because she was not known, and her very frailty would make her an easy victim. He soon got into conversation with her and invited her to his house for a little nourishment. The poor woman, delighted to find a friend who would help her, accompanied him to the house.

There, she was made welcome by Helen McDougal, who seemed to understand everything, and Burke went in search of Hare. When they returned, they found that McDougal and the old woman had, after their breakfast, set about cleaning up the room and had everything as neat and tidy as the ill-furnished, tumbledown place could be, and preparations were made for a night's junketing, to be followed by the usual tragedy.

But there was one difficulty they had to overcome. At that time there were lodging with Burke an old soldier named James Gray and his wife. Burke had to get this couple out of the house without creating suspicion, for they could not be trusted. Burke explained to them that the old woman was a relation of his mother and, of course, it would not do for Mrs. Docherty to seek accommodation elsewhere, and it would be a matter of "obligement if Mr. and Mrs. Gray would find quarters in some other place for a night or two." Gray and his wife obliged, and obtained lodging in Hare's house. Now the way was clear and the tragedy could begin at once.

In the evening Mrs. Hare joined the company and the fun began. The whiskey circulated rapidly. Burke sang his favorite songs and the old woman crooned some Irish ballads she had learned in her youth. Dancing, too, was engaged in. Once or twice, visits were paid to the house of a neighbor, where the revelry continued and where Mrs. Docherty hurt her foot trying to emulate the sprightliness of her youthful companions. As the night wore on, they kept more to their own house.

Between ten and eleven o'clock the neighbors heard a great disturbance from Burke's dwelling, and some of them, though used to the sounds of drunken riot from that quarter, had the curiosity to look through the key-hole of the door to see what was going on. One of them, a woman, saw—or thought she saw—Helen Mc-Dougal holding a bottle to the mouth of the old lady, pouring whiskey down her throat.

After a while the disturbance ceased, but not for long. Soon Hare quarreled with Burke and the dispute could only be settled by blows. Whether this was a real quarrel or not, it would be difficult to say, but while the two men were fighting, Mrs. Docherty, tipsy though she was, tried to interfere as she did not wish to see Burke abused. The fight, however, continued, and Hare, whether by design or not, knocked the old woman over a stool. She fell heavily and, owing to the amount of drink she had taken, was unable to rise. The fighting ceased.

Mrs. Hare and Helen McDougal slipped out of the house, and Burke and Hare set to work on the prostrate, helpless woman. It was along the lines of the old method, but a fatal mistake was made. One of them grasped the old woman violently by the throat, leaving marks of the undue pressure. Soon the woman was dead. Burke undressed the body, doubled it up and laid it among a quantity of straw beside the bed. The women then returned to the room and all four resumed their debauch, and for the last time together they spent a riotous night. The murder was committed on Hallowe'en night and they brought in the month of November with heavy drinking.

About midnight they were joined in their cups by a young fellow named Broggan, a son of the man to whom the house had once belonged and who was bought off by Burke and Hare when the murder of Helen McDougal's kin was committed in it. At last, when morning was far advanced, they were all overcome by sleep and they lay down to rest, with the body of the murdered woman beside them.

The next morning Burke went to Hare's house and brought Mr. and Mrs. Gray back. When they returned they found a Mrs. Law and Mrs. Connoway, two neighbors, visiting with Broggan and Helen McDougal. The Grays naturally missed the old woman for whom they had been shifted, and Mrs. Gray asked where the "little old woman" had gone. The reply was that Mrs. Docherty had grown very impudent to Burke and they had found it necessary to put her out. Then breakfast was served.

After breakfast, in the course of her search for an article of clothing, Mrs. Gray, smoking a pipe, went to the corner of the room where the body of Mrs. Docherty was lying covered with straw, but Burke called to her to keep out of there. When she attempted to go beneath the bed to get some potatoes, he asked her what she was doing there with a lighted pipe. He offered to help, but Mrs. Gray dispensed with his help and collected the potatoes without disturbing anything. All this created a suspicion in the woman's mind that something was wrong.

Later in the day this suspicion was strengthened by Burke when, as he was about to go out, he told Broggan to sit on a chair which was near the straw until he returned. Broggan either did not know of the mystery underneath the straw or he did not care, for he shortly went out also. Helen McDougal after a while left the house, too. Mrs. Gray now had an opportunity to clear up her suspicions. The straw in the corner had appeared to be the great object of attention and she went directly there.

Mrs. Gray lifted the straw and the first thing she caught hold of was the arm of a dead woman. Mr. Gray then joined her and together they saw the naked body of the old Irishwoman who had been brought into the house by Burke the day before. The horrified couple hastily threw the straw over the corpse, collected what property they had in the house in order to leave it immediately. Gray went out first, leaving his wife to complete the packing. On the stairs he met Helen McDougal, who was returning, and asked her what it was she had in the house. The woman made a feeble pretence at ignorance, but when Gray said to her, "I suppose you know very well what it is," she begged him not to say anything about it, and offered him five or six shillings to carry him over till Monday. She insisted that the woman's death had been caused by an overdose of drink— alcoholic poisoning—and then tried to make Gray believe that the incident was not uncommon and could happen anywhere.

But Gray was hard to convince, so Helen McDougal told him there would never be a week after that but what he might be worth ten pounds. Evidently she thought Gray might be induced to join their murdering gang. He, however, replied that his conscience would not allow him to remain silent. Mrs. Gray now came out and she was offered the same inducements, but all to no effect. She exclaimed: "God forbid that I should be worth money because of dead people!"

The couple then left the place together and Gray made his way to the police with his information.

In the meantime, Burke and Hare were busy making arrangements for the removal of the body to Dr. Knox's premises. Burke purchased an empty tea-chest in Rymer's shop and engaged John McCulloch, a street porter, who carried it to Surgeons' Square, where Paterson, "the keeper of Knox's museum," had it placed in the cellar.

The end had now at long last come. The murdering career of Burke and Hare was about to close.

When Sergeant-Major Fisher heard Gray's story, he thought it was merely the discontent of a tenant trying to make trouble for a landlord, but nevertheless he and Constable Finlay accompanied Gray to Burke's house. What took place there can best be told in Fisher's own words:

"I asked Burke what had become of his lodgers, and he replied that there was one of them—pointing to Gray —and that he had turned Gray and his wife out for bad conduct. I then asked what had become of the little woman who had been there the day before and he said she left the house about seven o'clock that *morning*. He said Hare saw her go away. I then looked around to see if there were any marks in the bed and I saw marks of blood on a number of things there. I asked Mrs. Burke (Helen McDougal) how they came there and she replied that a woman had lain there about a fortnight before and the bed had not been washed since. A stricter search of the premises resulted in the discovery of clothing, afterwards identified as worn by Mrs. Docherty when last seen alive, and there was a quantity of fresh blood among the straw. I asked McDougal then what time the woman had left the house and she said seven o'clock at *night*. When I found them to vary over the time, I thought the best way was to take both Burke and his wife to the Police Office."

The next morning, November 2nd, Fisher went to the premises of Dr. Knox and found there a box containing the body of a woman. Gray was sent for and he recognized the corpse as that of the old woman he had seen in Burke's house. The authorities now thought it was time they had Hare and his wife in custody, too, and they were immediately arrested and placed in separate cells. When the four malefactors were confronted with the corpse of their last victim, they all denied that they had ever seen the woman before, either alive or dead.

Burke and McDougal offered to make statements before Sheriff Tait, but they turned out to be contradictory and obviously false. Mr. and Mrs. Hare's declarations were equally stupid and false, though more defiant. Young Broggan by this time had also been arrested on a charge of complicity in the murder, and the authorities were busy making inquiries into the case, and lining up witnesses.

The public had begun to think that Burke and Hare were responsible for the disappearance of Daft Jamie and Mary Paterson, especially the latter, as she had been seen in Burke's company. The authorities also pursued their inquiries along these lines.

On November 10th, the two men and their wives were committed by the sheriff to stand trial for the murder of Mrs. Docherty. Young Broggan, however, was freed, his innocence being apparent. The four fiends, though repeatedly examined, positively denied any knowledge of the murder.

The evidence against the killers was actually insufficient to obtain a conviction. From the legal standpoint, the proof was defective both as to the fact of the murder and as to who was the actual perpetrator.

There was, of course, the evidence of the Grays and of other neighbors, but it was all entirely circumstantial and might fail to convict. There were fifty-five witnesses in all named.

Hare, ever wily and cunning, saw how matters stood and he agreed to an offer to turn King's evidence, after being given assurances that he and his wife would be safe from any prosecution. This was a way out of the difficulty which the Lord Advocate, after consideration, was glad to accept as the only one possible. As a result of Hare's treachery, Burke and McDougal, on December 8th, were formally charged with the murder of Docherty, Daft Jamie and Mary Paterson. The trial before the High Court of Justiciary was to be held at Edinburgh, December 24th, at ten o'clock in the forenoon.

As the day for the trial drew near, the public excitement became more and more intense. The feeling against the culprits was very strong, and while the statement that Hare and his wife were to be accepted as informers was received with displeasure, it was thought that the revelations they would make would compensate for their escape from punishment. But the authorities decided to take every precaution to prevent a disturbance at the trial. Police were reinforced by three hundred men, and the infantry and the calavry were held in readiness for an emergency.

Early on the morning of the trial, December 24th, Burke and McDougal were placed in cells beneath the High Court of Justiciary in Parliament Square. The inhabitants of the city were early afoot and crowded to the Square, anxious to gain admittance to the courtroom. The best men of the Scottish Bar engaged in the trial. The defense, of course, had been understaken gratuitously by eminent counsel. The trial proceeded.

When Hare was brought forward to testify, his appearance caused quite a sensation, since it was on his evidence and that of his wife that the case for the Crown principally rested. Mrs. Hare's appearance caused quite as much interest when she was ushered into the witness box, carrying her infant child in her arms. Her evidence contained only one point calling for special notice. When, after relating how she ran out of the house when she saw Burke get upon Docherty and returned later to the house and did not see the woman, she made a very revealing admission. She was asked: "Seeing nothing of her, what did you suppose?" Her answer was: "I had a supposition that she had been murdered. *I have seen such tricks before.*"

The remarkable fact about her testimony was that it corroborated, with exception of one or two points, that of her husband. There can be no doubt that they had conned their story together before they were apprehended.

Finally, the evidence was summed up and the jury retired to consider their verdict at 8:30 in the morning of December 25th—Christmas Day. Burke seemed to consider a conviction certain not only in his case but also in that of Helen McDougal, for he is said to have given her directions on how to conduct herself when sentence was being pronounced. After an absence of fifty minutes, the jury returned and the chancellor, or foreman, gave the following verdict:

"The Jury find the pannel, William Burke, guilty of the third charge in the indictment, and find the indictment not proven against the pannel, Helen McDougal."

The audience applauded the findings and the news was conveyed to the enormous crowd waiting outside in Parliament Square who cheered to the echo.

Burke remained cool and, turning to his companion, he remarked: "Nellie, you're out of the scrape." Mc-Dougal was free from the pains of the law.

The Justice-Clerk then addressed Burke on the magnitude of his guilt. The only doubt, said his Lordship, which the Court entertained was whether his body should not be exhibited in chains. But the sentence was that Burke be hanged in the usual way on January 28th, next, and his body be publicly dissected and anatomized.

The sentence was formally recorded in the books of the Court, the place of execution was specified as the Lawnmarket of Edinburgh, and the body of Burke was ordered to be delivered to Dr. Alenxander Munro, Professor of Anatomy in the University of Edinburgh, to be by him publicly dissected and anatomized.

The trial was concluded. There was no need for further proceedings against Burke on the first and second charges on the indictment, since he had been condemned on the third. But everybody felt he was guilty also of the murders of Daft Jamie and Mary Paterson.

The *Edinburgh Evening Courant* of December 27th thus described the appearance of the prisoners when the Lord Justice-Clerk addressed them: "The scene was altogether awful and impressive. The prisoner stood up with unshaken firmness. Not a muscle of his features was discomposed during the solemn address of the Lord Justice-Clerk consigning him to his doom. The female prisoner was much agitated and was drowned in tears during the whole course of the melancholy procedure."

The result of the trial was received with mixed feelings. The greatest satisfaction was felt at the conviction of Burke, but the dismissal of McDougal and the probable escape of Hare and his wife through having become informers, caused a great deal of resentment. The evidence given by the two principal witnesses showed that they were as guilty as Burke himself, and people began to feel that Hare was, after all, the leading spirit in the conspiracy and he had, as the counsel for Burke had suggested, made Burke his last victim. The public hoped the Crown would be able to put Hare and his wife on trial, too, for their crimes.

The limitation of the indictment confined the informers' evidence, one-sided though it undoubtedly was, to one crime and, further, that limitation did away with the necessity of calling Dr. Knox and other medical men who were supposed to be involved in the transaction.

"Where are the doctors?" came the question when the trial had ended without their appearance. And it was repeated with threatening emphasis and critical comment. In the case that went to trial and on which Burke was condemned, there was no need for them. The body had been recovered and identified. There was no doubt as to the murder. The whole subject of the inquiry was: by whom was it committed? Had the other charges in the indictment gone to judicial inquiry, the evidence of the doctors and their assistants would have been required, for only they could have testified as to the probable identity of the unfortunate subjects supplied them. Then they would have been indispensable.

A strong feeling of resentment began to mount, and on Sunday, December 28th, a band of young men attacked Dr. Knox's house on Minto Street and they were only driven off by a strong force of police after they had broken most of the windows.

Immediately upon Helen McDougal's release, she returned to her house and remained unmolested until the next night, when she went out to purchase some whiskey. She was recognized by a number of boys. "There's McDougal!" Speedily a rough crowd assembled. The police had to rescue her from the infuriated mob. She barely escaped lynching. She was taken for safety to the watch-house in Wester Portsburgh.

But even there she was not safe, for a huge crowd attacked the place, determined to gain admittance and mete out their own brand of justice to her. So threatening did the situation become that the officers decided to get rid of her. Hastily, they dressed her in men's clothing and allowed her to escape by a back window, unobserved, and she was accompanied outside the city on her way to Stirlingshire. She had about twelve pounds in her possession. But wherever she went she was recognized and constantly had to be rescued by the police who always gave her safe conduct from one place to another in order to get rid of the "accursed thing."

There is no record of what became of her later. One authority was of the opinion that she died in Australia in 1868.

When all hope of prosecuting Hare for murder had finally been abandoned, Mrs. Hare was released from prison on January 19, 1829. On her way to the Old Town she was recognized and attacked by a hostile crowd who pelted her unmercifully with snowballs, mud and stones. Only pity for her child, whom she carried in her arms, saved her from the violence of the mob. Finally, she was rescued by the police, and a few days later she betook herself to the West Country, wandering the district incognito. But one morning a woman recognized her, shouted, "Hare's wife!" and threw a large stone at her. A mob soon gathered and again she was rescued by the police. The authorities made arrangements for her passage to Ireland, and on February 12th she sailed for Belfast. What became of her thereafter is unknown.

Meanwhile, Burke was removed quietly to Calton Hill Prison and placed in the condemned cell. The thirst for vengeance against Hare had been constantly mounting in him and he would break out into curses against his former partner. Hare, he declared now, was more guilty than he was. "Hare murdered the first woman. He persuaded me to join him, and now he has murdered me."

On January 3rd, Burke, at his own request, made what is known as his official confession, to which several weeks afterward he added a short supplement. Later, however, someone got a fuller and more detailed account of his crimes than the official version, and this is known as the "Courant Confession."

One day, sitting quietly in his cell, he startled his attendant by saying: "I think I am entitled to, and ought to get that five pounds from Dr. Knox which is still unpaid on the body of Docherty."

"Why, Dr. Knox lost by the transaction, as the body was taken from him," was the reply of the amazed attendant.

"That was not my business. I delivered the subject and he ought to have kept it."

"But you forget that were the money paid, Hare would have the right to half of it," argued the other.

"I have got a tolerable pair of trousers," explained Burke, "and since I am to appear before the public, I should like to be respectable. I have not a coat and waistcoat that I can appear in, and if I got that five pounds, I could buy them."

Between his condemnation and execution Burke was visited by Protestant and Roman Catholic clergymen and he received the ministrations of both calmly.

The hour for the final scene had almost come and to this event the people looked forward with ghastly satisfaction. Indeed, it was thought prudent to remove Burke to the jail in Liberton's Wynd a day before the execution or the probability was that he would have been torn to pieces by an infuriated mob.

The vicinity of the scaffold was occupied by one of the largest crowds ever assembled on the streets of Edinburgh. From twenty to twenty-five thousand people were estimated to be present, many of the best people in the city among them. Every window giving a view of the execution had been bought up. All fashionable Edinburgh had a seat, the well-known Charles Kirkpatrick Sharpe among the number. It is probable that he was accompanied by Sir Walter Scott, who had had every intention of attending Burke's execution, as appears certain from a letter to Sharpe by one Robert Seton, an Edinburgh bookbinder, dated January 14th, 1829, in which the writer says: "Mr. Stevenson, bookseller, wished one window for Sir Walter Scott and yourself, but on account of the number that had applied that will be out of my power. But I shall be happy to accommodate (sic) Sir Walter and yourself with a share of one."

Burke had slept soundly the greater part of the night before the execution and arose about five o'clock Wednesday morning. He lamented his connection with the murders to which he had confessed. Then, holding up his hands, he remarked with real earnestness, "Oh, that the hour was come which shall separate me from this world!"

An incident even more dramatic, but similar in character, occurred shortly afterward. He expressed a desire to be free of his irons. The warders proceeded to knock them off and the fetters fell with a clank on the floor of the cell. "So may all my earthly chains fall!" Burke exclaimed.

Two priests undertook the last religious exercises. The condemned man joined in the devotions with apparent fervor, and he seemed deeply affected by the exhortation to "confide in the mercy of God." He was ready now and accepted a glass of wine which was offered him, and on putting it to his lips, he gave his last toast: "Farewell to all my friends!" Burke then expressed his gratitude to the magistrates for their kindness to him, and also to the prison officials. The solemn procession then formed and marched out of the jail to the scaffold.

The enormous crowd sent up a loud roar. Burke was afraid the mob might break through and tear him to pieces, and he hastily ascended the scaffold. His appearance there was the signal for another outburst of hate and condemnation from the multitude. Shouts of "Burke him! Choke him! No mercy, Hangie," came from all sides. There were frequent shouts of "Hare! Hare! Bring out Hare!" "Hang Knox, he's a *noxious morsel!*" "Wash the blood from the land!" "You'll see Daft Jamie in a minute!"

Burke, with an air of firmness, began the recitation of the creed. When he came to the Holy Name, he gave the signal, the bolt was drawn, and the most vicious murderer of his time—except perhaps for his associate Hare—was swinging on the gallows. The mob set up a fearful yell, and every time the body of the dying man gave a convulsive twitch, the crowd cheered to the echo.

The time was now a quarter past eight and Burke had been "separated from this world." The body was allowed to hang until five minutes to nine, when the executioner cut it down amid the gloating yells of the people, who tried to rush forward as if to lay hold of the corpse of the murderer. Thus the curtain fell on the scene of the West Port murders—the gruesome Burke and Hare tragedies.

Sir Walter Scott briefly recorded in his diary: "Burke the murderer hanged this morning."

There was an ironic sequel to Burke's end. The man who had been so active a participant in the horrible murders, and who had supplied so many "subjects" for dissection, was himself a "subject"—after death by strangulation.

At the College of Edinburgh, the body was laid out on a table and several eminent scientists—and a sculptor, who made a cast for a bust—examined it. Dr. Munro gave a lecture on it, and for this purpose the upper part of the head was sawed off and the brain exposed.

An informant gives the following description of the subsequent treatment of the fiend. ". . . Burke was cut

up and put in pickle for the lecture table. He was cut up
in quarters, or rather portions, and salted, and, with a
strange aptness of poetic justice, put into barrels." Thus
was Burke's body destroyed. The dissection gave rise to
excited discussions between phrenologists and their
opponents. Combe, the apostle of phrenology, and Sir
William Hamilton, the metaphysician, waged violent ar-
guments over the conclusions to be drawn from the
measurements of Burke's head.

Previously, arrangements had been made for a grand
public exhibition. An estimated thirty thousand people
passed through to view the body. Sir Walter Scott wrote:
"The corpse of the murderer Burke is now lying in state
at the College, in the anatomical class, and all the world
flock to see him. . . . The strange means by which the
wretch made money are scarce more disgusting than
the eager curiosity with which the public have licked
up all the carrion details of this business."

After the trial's end, the position of Hare remained
one of great danger, notwithstanding the protection
which his evidence afforded him, and he was recom-
mitted to prison. It was believed the Lord Advocate was
conducting investigations in order to see if he could
find some means to proceed against the informer. The
press and the public clamored for the indictment of the
wily and vicious Hare. The belief persisted that of the
two culprits, Hare was the greater villain.

But finally the Lord Advocate came to the reluctant
conclusion that he had no legal grounds for prosecuting
Hare. The warrant of imprisonment against Hare had
been withdrawn because no crime could be laid at his
door other than those for which his evidence gave him
immunity. However, there were lengthy deliberations,
and long and elaborate opinions were delivered by six
judges. By a majority of four to two, the Court held that
Hare could not be prosecuted, ordered him set at liberty, and quashed the proceedings taken against him.

On February 5th, Hare was set free. The prison officials arranged passage for him, under the appropriate
name of Mr. Black, on the coach for England. He was
accompanied by the head turnkey who was charged to
see him safely out of Edinburgh. This was carried out in
the strictest secrecy, for the people were still clamoring
for retribution and death.

When the coach stopped at the King's Arms in Dumfries for four hours, Hare had already been recognized
on the coach, and the news spread rapidly that Hare was
a passenger. Soon a crowd of some eight thousand surrounded the inn where Hare was drinking ale. The mob
intended stopping the coach after it departed and throw-
ing Hare into the river. But the coach left the inn empty.
The mob surrounded it and their fury was intensified
when they found the murderer was not in it.

They turned back to the inn and found Hare in hiding.
An old woman attempted to strike him with her um-
brella; another seized him by the collar and nearly
strangled him. As Hare crouched in a corner a small boy
menaced him, backed up by the crowd. It was impossible
to tell what might happen on the part of the enraged
people. In desperate attempt to avoid bloody violence,
Hare was spirited away to the local prison. But the populace followed and laid siege to him there. A hundred
additional special police were drafted to assist in pre-
serving the peace. This force cleared the streets, and
the people, tired and exhausted, reluctantly went home,
leaving a great amount of wreckage about the town, with
scarcely a window in the prison intact.

Soon the authorities sent Hare secretly and quickly
on his way. Trembling violently, he set out on foot at
one o'clock in the morning. Two hours later he was seen
by a boy passing Dodbeck. On Saturday, it was reported
that Hare's identity had been discovered at Annan and
that he had been stoned to death. But this report was
unfounded for he was seen on the roadside on Sunday

beyond Carlisle, where the residents were prepared to give him the same reception he had received at Dumfries. It is believed that after this, Hare turned eastward to Newcastle, but as a matter of fact nothing is authoritatively known of his subsequent movements—how he lived or where he went.

The ballad-makers had another version of Hare's departure from Scotland. Here are a few of the verses that indicated the popular mood.

Dark was the midnight when Hare fled away,
Not a star in the sky gave him one cheering ray,
But still now and then blue lightning did glare,
And strange shrieks assailed him like shrieks of despair.

But still as the fugitive ran down the wild glen,
Not a place did he fear like the dwellings of men;
Where a heap lay before him all dismal and bare
The ghost of Daft Jamie appeared to him there.

"I am come, says the shade from the land of the dead,
Though there be for poor Jamie no grass-covered bed;
O'er hills and o'er valleys I'll watch thee for ill,
I will haunt all thy wanderings, and follow thee still."

Dr. Robert Knox, who had bought the bodies from Burke and Hare, was likewise haunted. The violent outbreak of public feeling against him caused him to take some means to clear himself. A committee of investigation, at his own request, was appointed to make a study of his dealings with the criminals, and in their long, full report they unanimously agreed: "The Committee have seen no evidence that Dr. Knox or his assistants knew that murder was committed in procuring any of the subjects brought to his rooms. . . . No evidence whatever has come before the Committee that any suspicion of murder was expressed to Dr. Knox by his assistants or students, or other persons . . ."

However, Dr. Knox, the most brilliant and popular lecturer on anatomy in his day in Edinburgh, lost public confidence and his career began to ebb. In 1839, he left his old quarters in Surgeons' Square to lecture on anatomy at the Argyle Square Medical School. It was not a change for the better. In 1844, he removed to Glasgow, where his class was so small that he returned the fees to the pupils. No university would appoint him a chair, no medical school in Scotland would open its gates to him. He moved to London where he found occasional work as a lecturer; to the end he devoted himself to writing on his favorite subjects. He died of apoplexy December 20, 1862.

The occasion of the doctor's downfall had a far-reaching consequence: The passing of the Anatomy Act, in 1832, which put an end to all secret sources of supply to the anatomical schools of Great Britain and Ireland, and was directly due to the situation brought about by Dr. Knox's "incautious" and "unfortunate" conduct.

The body-snatcher's occupation was gone, the minds of the living were relieved, and the dead slept securely in their resting graves, too. But, even if people do not know its origin, there exists today a reminder of the monstrous deeds of Burke and Hare. Language has kept them alive. A "burker" was unknown before the crimes of William Burke were made public; "burking" was an undiscovered art until then.

The ruthless fiends of Edinburgh made their own ghoulish immortality.

XI

ANDREW BICHEL

IT IS A surprising thing that the case of Andrew Bichel, a Bavarian murderer, has often been overlooked by chroniclers of notorious and infamous criminals. The man was quite unique in some ways. Unique, because he appears to have lived an entirely honest and decent domestic life for many years, suddenly developing a taste for murder without any clear reason for this abrupt degeneration. The mass-murderer, even if he began to destroy life late in his career, has usually paved the way to crime by previous acts of instability or violence.

Bichel was a typical, hard-working peasant of over a hundred years ago, toiling honestly enough in a small inn; he was a good husband and father, a regular worshiper at his parish church. He neither drank, gambled nor quarreled. His solitary vice throughout those years of honesty—a vice that developed to an extreme degree when he became a criminal—was avarice. Avarice of the hardest and most uncompromising sort. The loss of a trifling coin would send Bichel into despair; the chance finding of a similar coin in the street or in a tavern would make him happy for many days afterwards.

Here again, Bichel was unique. The criminal is very rarely a miser. He spends his money as swiftly as he earns it, is frequently very generous, and is usually hard up. Bichel, a true miser, loved money as a thing in itself.

Moreover, Bichel was an abnormally cowardly person. Even when he was leading an honest and harmless life, he walked in terror of the authorities, fearing that they might arrest him on some imaginary charge. It is possible that he never would have got up the courage to commit murder had he not first of all protected himself from retaliation on the part of his projected victims by a diabolically clever and subtle trick.

So, judging by his character and personality, it would seem that there were three features that distinguished Bichel from the majority of his fellow murderers.

First, there was no paving of the way to crime. He seems to have become a thief and murderer without any previous history of instability or violence. Second, he was an inordinate miser. And thirdly, he was a complete coward.

Bichel was not ambitious in the direction of gain. Like many men of the miser type, he was more concerned with hoarding a few coins than in amassing a large fortune. It is not surprising, therefore, that when he began to murder for profit, he was ready to content himself with absurdly small returns.

He was shrewd enough to realize that the more humble his victims, the less would be his chances of detection. A rich—an important person—cannot vanish suddenly without a mass of friends making swift inquiries. On the other hand, a poor and obscure servant girl, many miles from home, may go out one night, fail to return, and arouse by her disappearance little more than a few perfunctory official inquiries. This truth was more apparent a hundred years ago than today, because the world was then a less democratic place than the world as we know it, and the value of human life was largely appraised in terms of pounds, shillings and pence.

Superstition, generally strongly entrenched among the poor and ignorant, seemed to Bichel a means to an end. A very wide reader of books dealing with magic, he hit upon the idea of posing as a fortuneteller and astrologer. By this means he would be able to bring many women to his house. He did not want to deal with men, for their physical strength might make killing them a dangerous business. But a foolish, pliant young domestic servant, seamstress or shop assistant was in another class from the aggressive male. She would come to his house ready to acquiesce in all the demands of the supposed "reader of the future."

Moreover, in order to protect himself still further, Bichel decided that he would choose for his victims, as a rule, women who did not belong to the little town of Regendorf in Bavaria, where he contemplated carrying on his new trade. He reasoned that a native of the town was more likely to be missed than a casual visitor. Again, a girl on a holiday would doubtless carry all her money on her person, afraid to leave it at her lodging. A subtle rogue, this Bichel, who was not ready to begin the business of murder until he had protected himself from the smallest risk.

Everything went according to plan. To the stuffy little room, furnished with cheap Oriental trappings and scented with stupefying perfumes, came many women, young and old, the majority of the lower middle class. They came to Bichel to ask questions concerning possible husbands, babies, money matters, travel, health, and sometimes to put to him questions on matters of a medical nature. Sometimes private secrets would come out during the "readings," and he would then add to his income as a fortuneteller by a little blackmail. But here again, he was cautious. He did not terrify and drive away the victims by asking big sums. The man seemed temperamentally unable to think in terms of vastness. A few silver coins would in most cases satisfy his demands. He was dealing, of course, with persons of small means, but it is likely that had a very rich woman come to his house, mere force of habit would have held him from asking a considerable amount.

And so Andrew Bichel prospered. He showed a canny sense in choosing his victims, knowing that murder

would not always be his best investment. The majority
of his clients came, put their questions, received the
answers, paid the small fees and departed safely enough.
But when Bichel, with a certain diabolical intuition, had
satisfied himself that a client was carrying on her person
a fair amount of money, then he would decide that she
must die.

The actual business of killing depended on the ignorance and gullibility of his victims.

Bichel, having received his client with great politeness
and with an air of mystery that doubtless impressed the
foolish young woman, would presently produce an elab-
orately decorated mirror which he would place upon
the table. The girl would be seated in a high-backed
chair and required to look into the glass so that the
concentration might evoke the images which Bichel assured her would soon develop.

But when the images failed to appear, Bichel, feign-
ing annoyance, would proceed to point out that he had
omitted a very essential detail of the ritual. The mystic
powers would not reveal the future in the mirror unless
the eyes of the seeker after knowledge were bandaged
so that they might not be distracted by outward things.
Moreover, in order to maintain the rigidity of body necessary for the best results, her hands must be tied behind
the chair.

Today such a thing might be possible with only a few
very foolish persons. But a hundred years ago Bavarian
peasants were uninformed, superstitious, and completely ignorant about everything except their daily toil. On
occasions, however, when a more sensible woman refused to undergo the blindfolding and the binding,
Bichel abandoned his murderous intention and, having
told them a few meaningless predictions, took their fees
and let them go.

But with a girl easily swayed, once she had been rendered harmless, Bichel would suddenly take up his posi-

tion behind her and with two swift movements would end her life. He would cut through the spinal cord at the junction of the neck and spine, and finish the horrible business by stabbing the woman in the lung. After the murder, Bichel would remove all the clothing and take the money and trifling jewelry of the victim. His avarice made him save the clothing with a view to selling it at a later time.

To increase the number of salable garments, Bichel would sometimes impress upon a prospective client that she must bring with her to the "sitting" three changes of dress. So picayune was Bichel's idea of gain. It was this passion for small profits resulting from the murders that subsequently led to his detection. Had he been less avaricious, had he been content to murder and steal money only, he might have escaped his ultimate arrest for many years. But his miserliness was of such stuff that the tiniest possession of the victims, if marketable, had to be kept.

The burial place of the poor girl was a woodshed at the rear of the house. The dead woman was buried in a shallow grave which, after the earth was replaced, was covered with shavings and litter. From time to time, when girls vanished, apathetic inquiries were made, but no suspicion attached itself to Bichel. Made confident by his immunity from detection, he continued to murder and rob whenever the potential victim proved sufficiently gullible.

The relatives and friends of the women who vanished were hard-working people of the poorer class who had neither the time nor the money to instigate energetic searches for the missing person. An exception finally occurred in the case of Catherine Seidel, murdered by Bichel in 1808. The girl's sister had been very devoted to Catherine and had vowed that she would not leave off her efforts to discover her whereabouts if she were alive.

She seems to have been a woman of character, this sister, for she went from place to place, seeking information, enduring all sorts of rebuffs and insults during the search. At certain houses where she appeared, she was driven away on the plea that she sought to blackmail. At other houses, it was believed that she came there to rob. But she was not discouraged, and day by day she went on with her search.

She had almost despaired of finding any clue when chance came to her assistance, and it was that chance which brought Bichel to justice. It happened that while the sister was in a tailor's shop in Regendorf, talking to the tailor, she was observant enough to notice that he was making up a waistcoat from a piece of unusual dimity. She uttered a cry of amazement, for in that dimity she had recognized the material which her sister Catherine had worn as a petticoat when she was dressed in her best clothes.

She immediately questioned the tailor, asking him how and where he had obtained that material. The man told her he had bought it from Andrew Bichel, the fortuneteller. Hearing this, the sister recalled the fact that Catherine had told her long ago that she intended consulting Bichel about her future. Here was a strange coincidence, she told herself—a coincidence that was perhaps too remarkable to be overlooked.

She recalled an interview which she herself had had with Bichel soon after the disappearance of Catherine. The man had admitted that Catherine had come to him as a client, but had sworn that the girl had eloped with a certain man whom she had met there. At the time, the sister accepted this statement because she was well aware of Catherine's erratic and amorous nature; but now the material in the tailor's shop had developed in her a sudden suspicion. Bichel had lied to her, she told herself, and he must have had a very sound reason for the falsehood.

She went immediately to the police and told her story. Now the authorities had never looked with favor on Bichel, whose trade they disliked, but in view of the fact that he had always been well-behaved, regular in his attendance at church and never creating any disturbance, they had decided to leave him alone. Nevertheless, they were not sorry to have an opportunity to investigate his practices, and, accompanied by the girl, they went in force to Bichel's house, informed him of their suspicions and began a rigorous search.

In a large trunk in the bedroom they soon discovered a mass of women's clothes—shoes, undergarments and corsets. Bichel, as we have said, had preserved all these things so that they might bring him a profit when enough time had elapsed to make their sale wholly safe. He had been foolish enough to sell the dimity too soon. Witnesses were shortly found who were able to swear that certain of the garments had been worn by Catherine Seidel on the day they had last seen her alive.

Questioned as to how the contents of the trunk had come into his hands, Bichel, trembling with fear but assuming an air of profound innocence, replied that the garments had been sold to him by their owners. There was no obvious reason why this very commonplace explanation should not be accepted, and the police were on the point of leaving the house when they suddenly paused, held back by the barking of the dog they had brought with them—a very sharp-nosed animal, trained in criminal hunting.

The dog was in the woodshed at the back of the house. Instantly, the police made for the shed. Finding that the dog refused to budge and remained rooted over a certain spot, they resolved to dig. Spades were sent for, and in a few minutes, a quantity of human bones was unearthed, together with dismembered arms, legs and feet. A severed head of a young woman was found later. This head was afterwards identified as the head of Barbara Reisinger who had disappeared in 1807.

Bichel, having stolidly refused to make a confession, was confronted a few days later with the remains of the victims; the authorities were convinced that this revelation might bring him to speak. During this horrible encounter, Bichel showed great terror. His face was very white and he showed signs of actual physical distress, but he refused to speak a word that would incriminate him. It is conceivable that some sort of torture would have been applied to force his confession, but that last, brutal recourse was not required. For, after he had been taken back to his cell, a strong reaction set in. He burst into tears, quite uncontrollably, and for a while he was unable to speak. Before the day was over, however, he had made a complete confession.

Bichel revealed everything—the bringing of the victims to the chair, the blindfolding, the binding, the stabbing. He denied, however, that he had murdered all the women who had disappeared. He admitted the killing of Barbara Reisinger, Catherine Seidel, and several others, but swore that he had let many escape because he had been afraid to kill them.

"I would not touch them unless they were securely bound," he naively added.

His trial was, of course, a mere matter of form. He was found guilty and sentenced to be broken on the wheel. This is a horribly cruel punishment wherein the victim, stripped naked, is bound to a section of a wheel. Stretched on a partial circumference, his body tied so tightly that the cords bite into his flesh, his bones are broken, one by one, by a heavy hammer. But in the case of Bichel, the sentence of the wheel was eventually abandoned, and he suffered the minor penalty of decapitation.

A few minutes before the end, Bichel, whose face was contorted with terror, told the priest who was attending him that he feared he might meet in the next world his victims who would inflict horrible vengeance on his defenseless soul. The priest, helpless in the face of this inner torment, could only mumble words concerning pardon and repentance.

"Do not tell me of repentance," whined Bichel, "but tell me if the dead can tear and injure?"

"We are all of us, living and dead, in the hands of God," replied the priest, and with that half-hearted consolation, Bichel was thrust forward to meet his punishment.

A fortuneteller, of course, cannot read his own fortune, as Andrew Bichel discovered.

XII

CHARLES PEACE

CHARLES PEACE is one of the most astonishing figures in the story of crime, as well as being one of England's most notorious criminals. To students of criminal psychology, his has been a fascinating personality.

Peace was an accomplished burglar and general thief, and a pugnacious murderer. He possessed every quality that goes to make the complete criminal: he was liar, braggart and actor, as conceited as he was cunning; a lecher without scruple, he seemed in every way to be without conscience or remorse.

There is little accurate information about Peace's

childhood or early background—about his friends, companions, or relationship with his parents. In a general way, one can only judge what kind of boy Peace was from what he became as a man.

According to a statement accredited to him by an intimate friend, Charles Peace "was born in Angel Court, Sheffield, of respectable parents." The date was May 14, 1832. He was the youngest of a family of four. His father, a shoemaker, had previously been an excellent tamer of wild animals. Peace stated, as reported by one of his mistresses: "I have been, and my father before me, a tamer of wild animals, and I think I shall tame you, my lady." According to this informant, his father was a caretaker of the animals in Wombwell's Menagerie, which the father and son had accompanied up and down the country. His father died when Peace was thirteen years old. Of his mother, nothing has been learned.

Judging by his correspondence, Peace did not have much education. That he could read and write to some extent is all that can be definitely said. The defects in his education were certainly not due to lack of ability and, judging by his later career and achievements, he had artistic and musical leanings, and would have attained considerable success as an actor. He wrote the following obituary notice of his father:

> In peace he lived,
> In peace he died.
> Life was our desire,
> But God denied.

Peace had a pronounced mechanical bent, which helped him devise a number of the tools he used in his practice of burglar. It is said that in his youth he worked as a tinsmith, and he was employed for some time in the Millsands Rolling Mills, near Sheffield. There, in 1846, his leg was injured in an accident which left him permanently lame. Another story tells that he lost a finger. A later version has it that this maiming of his hand was the result of his being shot by another young blackguard. Of the accident at the mill, he later said: "I never cared to work after that." This, at least, seems to be true.

When he was imprisoned at Dartmoor, he suggested some improvements in the machinery then in use, which were adopted there and in other prisons in England.

According to "Mrs. Thompson," one of Peace's many mistresses, after the death of his father, Peace "started on his own account. Even then, he admitted to me that his tastes were depraved and disgusting. But I cannot tell you of that; it is too bad. There is one thing I will say which will give you an idea of his character at that age. There was a fête at Sheffield, and for purposes of plunder, Peace attended it, and concealed himself in the ladies' lavatory. There he had to remain the whole day for, the place being constantly occupied, he was unable to escape without being discovered. He used to gloat over this when telling it to me." On this occasion, Peace relieved an old gentleman of his gold watch, his first recorded crime.

So, at fourteen, Peace had already started on his crime career. Even then, he boasted that he worked alone, to which fact may be attributed his prolonged success. "A man has more to fear from his pals than from the police," he would say. The number of thefts and burglaries he committed will never be fully known.

Usually a criminal leans toward a particular specialty —he will go in for picking pockets, or burglarizing homes, or holding up victims. But Peace refused to be catalogued. At Sheffield Fair, he picked pockets; at other times he functioned as a portico-thief, entering the homes he wished to rob by way of the porticos over the hall doors. He used whatever opportunities came to hand.

To his unlawful pursuits, Peace added those of carver,

gilder, and frame-maker. He also sold small wares when he had to, and he even played a one-string violin and sang and performed as an entertainer! He billed himself "The Modern Paganini" and "The Great Ethiopian Musician," and is said to have composed a song he often sang, "My Own Sweet Will." In later life, when he became wealthy, the violin and the harmonium were his constant companions. He performed mostly at public house "sing-songs," fairs, and similar entertainments. Occasionally he even offered his services as a reciter at private schools.

He had a knack for making himself liked. He was a glib and amusing talker, and he had a way with women.

In 1851, when he was little more than nineteen years old, Peace robbed a home in Sheffield, was convicted of burglary and sentenced to a month's imprisonment. After this, he seems to have gone completely over to the side of crime, enjoying the company of criminals to the extent that police began to mark him as a fellow to watch.

Three years later, when Peace was twenty-two, their watchfulness paid off. Peace was arrested once more, and with him a girl with whom he was keeping company, and his sister Mary Ann, for stealing some rings, brooches and other jewelry. Peace was sentenced this time to four years' penal servitude, and the ladies got six months each.

In 1858, Peace was again free to pursue his multifarious avocations. He resumed his fiddling, spent his afternoons playing in taverns, but it was now no more than a musical accompaniment to burglary. The call of crime was so insistent, he could not shut it out.

The next year Peace married a Mrs. Hannah Ward, a widow who had one son, Willie. This unlucky woman is said to have been unaware of the character of the man who had vowed eternally to cherish her. During Peace's next imprisonment, a son was born to him, but the son died shortly after birth and was never seen by his father. But the boy, John Charles, in these verses was immortalized by his father, who did not find religion at odds with crime:

Farewell, my dear son, by us all beloved,
Thou art gone to dwell in the mansions above.
In the bosom of Jesus who sits on the throne,
Thou art anxiously waiting to welcome us home.

Peace confessed to the following faith: "I believe in God, and I believe in the Devil, but I don't fear either." Truly, a rare insight into the mind of this unusual criminal.

At times, Peace would work under the name of John Ward, and would also extend his activities beyond the limits of his native town.

On one such occasion, plying his trade in Manchester, he was outmaneuvered by the police. One night, he broke into the house of Mrs. Elizabeth Brooks and removed a large number of articles from the house. Unable to carry all the booty off, he concealed part of it in a hole in a field, believing he had carefully hidden the place of burial.

Here the police discovered it, but left it as bait while they kept a careful watch for the robber's return. At night, Peace came to retrieve his booty. After a desperate fight in which Peace nearly killed one of the officers, he was handcuffed and arrested. At the police station Peace facetiously gave his occupation as "a professor of music." His "mother, an aged woman," came all the way from Sheffield to swear that her son had been with her there on the night of the crime. In spite of this loyal act of perjury, Peace was given six years' penal servitude.

It was a harsh sentence but, of course, the severity of the punishment seemed to have little effect as a deterrent to crime. Prisons are not merely places of punish-

ment and of possible reformation, they are too often—
and were then too—schools of criminal development. A
man frequently leaves prison knowing much more about
crime than when he entered.

Peace was discharged from prison in 1864 and returned for some time to his native city of Sheffield,
which seems to have had an everlasting attraction for
him.

During the eight years that followed his release,
Peace seems to have engaged in a number of burglaries.
He was caught and convicted more than once, serving
sentences in various prisons. When caught in the act
of robbing a house once, he admitted that at the time
he was fuddled with whiskey; otherwise, his capture
would have been more difficult and dangerous. Usually
a temperate man, Peace realized on this occasion the
value of sobriety even in burglary and never after allowed intemperance to interfere with his success.

At Chatham, Peace was flogged for taking part in a
mutiny. When confined in Wakefield Prison, he made a
daring attempt to escape, an attempt that almost succeeded. While doing repairs in the prison, he smuggled a
small ladder into his cell. With the help of a saw made
out of some tin, Peace cut a hole through the ceiling of
the cell and was about to get out on to the roof when
a turnkey came in. As the latter attempted to seize the
ladder, Peace knocked him down, ran along the wall of
the prison, fell off on the inside, owing to the looseness
of the bricks, and slipped into the warden's house.

He now appropriated a suit of civilian clothes in
which he coolly dressed himself, having chosen a convenient bedroom for his change of clothing, and here
he waited for an opportunity to escape. However, he
was caught on the threshold of the room and promptly
taken back to his cell, being rewarded for his achieve-
ment by a period of bread-and-water and a remission
of good conduct marks.

In August, 1872, Peace was released from prison on ticket-of-leave.

So far, Peace had been but a commonplace and not too successful practitioner of crime—an apprentice, actually. He now entered a period in which he made his name as a masterly exponent of the fine art of burglary and as a ruthless murderer.

After regaining his freedom, Peace reappeared in Sheffield where he lived with his family, pursuing the somewhat unexciting occupation of picture-framer. It has been said that sometimes he would actually refuse to frame a picture that seemed to him an outrageous daub. He himself frequently painted in watercolors and dabbled in designing.

During this period—a short one—his standards of honesty seem to have aproached his standards of artistic criticism, for he committed no robbery and lived a quiet, decent life, encouraging his family to attend church regularly and even taking part in their religious training. His devotion was so marked that it seems he even assisted as a teacher in Sunday school.

However, the path of honesty was not one that Peace could tread for long. He moved his family to Darnall, a suburb of Sheffield, in 1875, and here he made the fatal acquaintance of a man and a woman, Mr. and Mrs. Dyson, who were destined to play tragic parts in his later career.

Mr. and Mrs. Arthur Dyson, an entirely commonplace couple, lived in a house near the Peaces. Mrs. Dyson was good-looking and was endowed in general with more than her rightful share of physical appeal. Peace immediately found himself strongly attracted to her and began to pay her more than neighborly attentions. She was about twenty-five years old, had met her husband in America and went back to England with him to live.

In later years, Peace swore that Mrs. Dyson had been his mistress, but Mrs. Dyson denied it with a vehemence that convinced everybody she was telling the truth. The chances are that, weary of the monotony of home and her tame husband, and being a woman who liked excitement, she had accepted Peace's invitations to music halls, taverns and other places, and never let the relationship get out of bounds.

Peace evidently had some kind of attraction for women. An undersized little "rat of a man," as he was described by more than one person, he relied on his agile tongue and his glib humor. He was an acute and subtle flatterer who knew the weak side of women and was quick to appeal to it.

Peace was now forty-three years old but he appeared much older. In the following year, he was described by the police as "thin and slightly built, five feet four inches or five high, grey (nearly white) hair, beard and whiskers. He lacked one or more fingers off the left hand, walked with his legs rather wide apart, spoke somewhat peculiarly, as though his tongue was too large for his mouth—and is a great boaster. He is a picture-frame maker. He occasionally cleans and repairs clocks and watches, and sometimes deals in oleographs, engravings and pictures." To which description was later added this line: "Alias George Parker, Alexander Mann, 'Paganini.'" He had the extraordinary power of altering his features so as to make his face unrecognizable even to close friends and relations. Cunning and cruel, absolutely selfish, his thoughts were centered wholly on satisfying his every immediate desire.

It was on account of the very obvious injury to his hand that Peace adopted his famous false lower arm, a sort of sheath of cloth and wood, which he held in his hand and to which a stout iron hook was attached. Not that he attributed any great importance to the appearance of his hands, for he said: "A policeman goes by the face. He never thinks of looking at people's hands." Identification was not then so careful as now.

Slight as was his frame, his strength was enormous. As an example of Peace's pluck and brawn, the following story is revealing as well as amusing. "He met two men one day who said to him, 'Charley, 'as ta got any brass wi' thee? We are about as dry as a lime basket. Gi' us a pint.' Peace was not complaisant so they made a grab for him. Upshot—two lusty men spent some time in a hospital!" Again: "One day he had been going his rounds as a hawker and visited some farms, it being his delight to sell some of his fancy wear to the lassies—besides putting a few fowls into the bottom of his basket. On his homeward way, he met a farmer, a big, burly, strong chap, to whom he offered a watch which had on its face a picture of a man ploughing with two horses. 'It wanted winding up every time you had a look at it.' The farmer's fancy was tickled and he acquired the seeming treasure in exchange for his own watch and the sum of two pounds. When they met again a few weeks later, there was a small pantomime, but Charley Peace won. There were not many who could beat him in a rough and tumble."

And Sir William Clegg provides the following: "While Peace was in custody here (Sheffield), he informed me that on many occasions he went to Scotland Yard for the purpose of reading the notice offering a reward for his own apprehension, but that by manipulating his jaw, he could escape detection. He had no very great belief in the efficiency of the police and, on occasions, he daringly put himself in their way. He was an expert in the use of a revolver."

Many such stories are still current along the Yorkshire and Lancashire countryside, stories that tickled the public imagination.

Meanwhile, his attentions to Mrs. Dyson increased. Arthur Dyson bore the humiliation of Peace's "friendship" for his wife with patience. Eventually, he had a scene with his wife, ordered her to drop Peace, and sent a brief note to the disturber of his domestic harmony asking him to stop seeing his wife.

Peace was not the man to obey a request of this kind. On the contrary, he set himself to pursuing Mrs. Dyson with more attentions than before, and he even threatened on more than one occasion to blow Dyson's brains out.

Dyson, growing afraid, applied for a warrant against Peace. The warrant was issued, but before it could be served, Peace had decided to leave Sheffield. Why he took this step is something of a mystery. A man who had undergone long terms of imprisonment for serious crimes could hardly have dreaded a visit to a local county or police court. The fact remains that he went, and the family, having settled at Hull, Peace opened a small restaurant for workingmen, presided over by Mrs. Peace.

Peace, however, had no intention of settling down as a restaurateur. The old lure got him and he broke into houses whenever a convenient opportunity came his way.

It was while engaged on a burglary job in a suburb of Manchester that Peace committed the first murder of his career. He had always boasted that he shrank from taking life, that he had never fired on any man. But perhaps this immunity from bloodshed was due to luck rather than to any humanitarian principle. This time, however, about to be caught in the act of robbery, he fired and killed.

It happened as he was emerging from the house, and he almost ran into the arms of a constable who had seen a light and was about to whistle for help. This constable, Cock by name, was a plucky fellow. Without waiting for aid, he ran after Peace who, covering the policeman with his revolver, shouted at him to stand back. Cock, undismayed, advanced, and Peace then fired wide of him. But since Cock kept advancing, Peace, desperate and determined not to be caught, again pulled the trigger, this time fatally. Cock fell instantly, and Peace made good his escape without difficulty.

Peace returned to Hull and learned shortly after, to his intense relief, that two brothers, John and William Habron, living near the scene of the murder, had been arrested and charged with the killing of Constable Cock.

The two brothers were tried. John Habron was acquitted, but William Habron was sent to jail for life.

Peace actually attended the two days' trial of the brothers, probably gloating over the miscarriage of justice.

Neither burglary nor murder, however, let him forget Mrs. Dyson, and from time to time Peace paid visits to Sheffield where he continued to molest her. She must have become an obsession with him. He once said to her: "I am never beaten when I have made up my mind. If I make up my mind to a thing, I am bound to have it even if it cost me my life."

It certainly cost him a certain amount of peace at home. On one occasion his daughter made a remark about Mrs. Dyson which Peace resented. He was about to hit her, but his wife intervened, with the result that Peace struck her cruelly, severely disfiguring her face.

Peace always believed in applying beatings as a means of keeping order at home. Pleasant and entertaining as he could be, he was also feared. It was very dangerous to incur his anger. "Be sure," his wife would say, "you do nothing to offend our Charley, or you will suffer for it."

At one time Peace and a friend passed Dyson in the street. Peace took out his revolver. "If he offers to come near me," he said, "I will make him stand back." But Dyson took no notice of him and passed on. Dyson little knew it, but he had only another month to live.

Whatever the other motives of Peace may have been—devouring passion, spite, jealousy or revenge—it must not be forgotten that Dyson, by having taken out a warrant against him, had driven him from his home in Sheffield. This, Peace bitterly resented. According to many witnesses, he was at this time in a state of constant irritation because of Dyson.

He certainly could not get Dyson's wife out of his mind. On the night of November 29th, 1876, Peace was watching their house from a passageway that led to the rear of the houses in the area where the Dysons lived. He saw Mrs. Dyson come out the back door and go to an outhouse some yards distant. He waited. As soon as she opened the door to come out, she found herself confronted by Peace, holding a revolver in his hand. There was talk, then a sharp quarrel, with Peace threatening her. Dyson, hearing the disturbance, came quickly into the yard. Peace made for the passageway. Dyson followed him.

Peace fired once, the shot striking the lintel of the passage doorway. Dyson, undaunted, still pursued. Then Peace, according to his custom, fired a second time to hit. Dyson fell, shot through the temple. Two hours later he was dead.

Once again luck favored Peace and he managed to escape. He arrived at Hull and went straight to the restaurant kept by his wife and demanded some dinner, which he proceeded to eat very calmly in the rear of the restaurant. While eating, he heard two detectives enter and ask his wife if a man called Charles Peace was lodging with her. Mrs. Peace said that that was her husband's name, but that she had not seen him in two months.

The detectives decided to search the house. Peace fled upstairs, got out onto an adjoining roof and hid behind a chimney stack where he remained until the detectives had finished their search. Later that same day, the whole procedure was repeated, but Pace kept out of sight on the roof. For some three weeks he remained in Hull, hiding. He shaved his grey beard, which he had been wearing at the time of Dyson's murder, dyed his hair and stained his face with walnut juice, put on a pair of spectacles, and for the first time made use of his unusual ability to contort his features in such a way as to change the appearance of his face. He had disguised himself beyond much chance of recognition into a thin, wiry, benevolent-looking old buffer.

But the police did not let up in their chase. They put a price of one hundred pounds on his head and sent out a complete description of him. It is worth noting that they estimated his age as between fifty-five and sixty, though in reality he was only forty-four at the time.

Marked man as he was, Peace soon began to keep perpetually on the move. In the company of a sergeant of police, he traveled from Bath to Oxford. The officer had in his custody a young woman charged with stealing forty pounds, and Peace and the sergeant discussed the case during the journey. "He seemed a smart chap," said Peace, describing the incident, "but not smart enough to know me."

He did not let the murder of Dyson interfere with his chosen career as burglar. Between November, 1876, and October, 1878, Peace kept pulling off robbery after robbery with enormous—and to the police, disconcerting —success. And all the while he was being hunted for the murder of Dyson.

At Nottingham, Peace found what seemed to be safe lodging at the house of one Mrs. Adamson, a lady who carried on the convenient side line of receiving stolen goods. It was there that Peace met the woman who became his mistress and subsequently was to betray his identity to the police. Her maiden name was Susan Gray.

Susan Gray was at this time about thirty-five years old, rather fetching in appearance, with both a fair complexion and fair education. She had led a somewhat checkered married life with a man named Bailey. Her first meeting with Peace took place at Mrs. Adamson's.

At first, Peace passed himself off as a hawker of goods, but before long he openly admitted his real character as an accomplished burglar.

With characteristic insistence he declared his passion for Susan by threatening to shoot her if she did not become his mistress. The next day he apologized. She changed her mind, too, and did become his mistress, assuming in the process the more dignified title of "Mrs. Thompson," another name sometimes assumed by Peace.

Life in Nottingham was relieved of monotony, for Peace, by a number of burglaries, carried out with the help of information supplied by Mrs. Adamson. In 1877, Peace was nearly caught while on a job, the act of brandishing his revolver enabled him to get away, and soon after returned for a while to Hull.

Here, still hunted for murder, he took rooms for himself and "Mrs. Thompson," his mistress, at the house of a sergeant of police. To the sergeant he described himself as an agent. But a number of sensational burglaries at the houses of city officials and other well-to-do citizens of Hull revealed the presence in their midst of no ordinary robber. Peace had some narrow escapes, but with the help of his revolver and, on one occasion, the hesitation and fear of a policeman, he succeeded in getting away in safety. The bills offering a reward for his capture were still to be seen in the shop windows of Hull, so after a while he gathered up his "Mrs. Thompson" and returned with her to Nottingham.

He was not long there when a pair of detectives came into the room where he and Susan were in bed. One of the officers asked Peace his name. He gave it as John Ward and described himself as a hawker of spectacles. He refused to get up and dress in the presence of detectives and they were obliging enough to go downstairs and await his convenience. Peace seized the opportunity to slip out of the house and get away to another part of town. From there he sent a note to Susan, insisting on her joining him.

Before the year was out, he somehow had found his way, under the name of Thompson, to a suburb of London. Here he donned the manners of solemn respectability, was a regular churchgoer, and described himself as a dealer in musical instruments, explaining that he had independent means. His home, however, was somewhat less respectable than his manner. For with him were Mrs. Peace, who went by the name of Mrs. Ward, and her son Willie, to whom the basement was allotted. The better rooms were occupied by Peace and his mistress, "Mrs. Thompson."

The house was fitted with Venetian blinds. The drawing room was gorgeously appointed—a costly suite of walnut furniture, rich Turkish carpet, many mirrors, a bijou piano, a Spanish guitar, said to have been looted from a countess, and by the side of an elegant table, the beaded slippers of the good master of the house to complete the elegance of the room.

Everything confirmed Mr. Thompson's description of himself as a gentleman of independent means, with a taste for scientific inventions. In fact, with a person named Brion, Peace did patent an invention for raising sunken vessels, and it is said that in pursuing their project, the two men had obtained an interview with Mr. Plunsoll at the House of Commons. And at the time of his final capture, Peace was engaged on other inventions, among them a smoke helmet for firemen. To the anxious policeman who seeing a light in Mr. Thompson's house in the small hours of the morning, rang the bell to warn the old gentleman of the possible presence of burglars, this business of scientific inventions was sufficient explanation.

Here Peace entertained his friends at musical parties, he himself playing the violin. He was proud of his collection of violins, banjos and other musical instruments.

He was busy with his dogs, cats, rabbits, canaries, parrots and cockatoos. By way of conversational diversion, he was profoundly curious as to why a Christian nation should support the very unchristian Turks against the Christian Russians.

Family life at No. 5 East Terrace, though, was not without its discordant notes. These were due chiefly to the drunken habits of Peace's mistress who had an unfortunate tendency to slip out under the influence of too much liquor and chat away freely with the neighbors. Since she was the repository of many a dangerous secret, her neighborly visits were regarded by Peace with certain misgivings. On these occasions Susan was followed by Peace or his wife, brought back home and soundly beaten. To Mrs. Peace there must have been some satisfaction in spying on her rival for, in her own words, "Peace never refused his mistress anything; he did not care what she cost him in dress; she could swim in gold if she liked."

Through all dangers and difficulties, and notwithstanding his roles as gentleman and churchgoer the master was busy in the practice of his "art," plundering and robbing. Night after night, though it was early to bed, it was not to sleep, for Peace must be out at his trade. If the job was a distant one, he would take his pony and trap. He was devoted to his pony, and great was his grief when, at the end of six month's devotion to duty, the pony died after a few days' sickness, during which his master attended him with unremitting care.

Besides the pony and trap, Peace would take with him on his expeditions a violin case containing his tools; at other times they would be stuffed into odd pockets made for the purpose in his trousers. These tools consisted of ten in all—a skeleton key, two picklocks, a centre-bit, gimlet, gouge, chisel, vice-jimmy and knife; a portable ladder, a revolver and life preserver completed his equipment.

Though he transgressed laws with impunity, right under the very noses of the police, they never entertained a shadow of suspicion that Mr. Thompson of Peckham was Charles Peace of Sheffield. They knew him only as a polite and chatty old gentleman of scientific turn of mind, who drove his own pony and trap and had a fondness for music and his pet animals.

Peace was now at the summit of his career. It was possible, he told himself, that he would live to be eighty, and die in the odor of Peckham sanctity, to be remembered hereafter as an inventor and a benefactor of ship owners, firemen and hydraulic tank merchants. But this admirable, if somewhat commonplace, finale was not destined for Charles Peace.

On the night of October 10, 1878, Peace set out to break into a house in St. John's Park, Blackheath. He entered the building and set to work. Meanwhile, a constable, Charles Robinson, had seen a light in a window —unusual at that hour. Suspicious of the light and by the fact that Blackheath had been the scene of several burglaries recently, he at once called to a colleague. Before, however, the other policeman could arrive, Peace had leaped through the window, had caught sight of the policeman and had made off.

Robinson followed him. Peace turned, leveled his revolver and, having uttered a sharp warning, fired three shots in succession. The plucky constable then closed with his man, receiving a bullet in his arm. However, he managed to hold on to his prisoner and get him on the ground, where he held him securely until assistance arrived.

Peace fought desperately, but was soon overpowered, handcuffed and conveyed to the local station. Next morning, when brought up at Greenwich Police Court, he refused to give his name or any information. He was wearing a walnut juice make-up that gave him a semi-Negroid appearance.

In these days of fingerprint records, the local authorities would have been in possession of Peace's name, aliases, and every conviction registered against him within twenty-four hours. In 1878, the Bertillon method was yet to be discovered. However, the police had their methods, crude but not altogether fruitless. A letter which the unknown "half-caste" contrived to send to his mistress during his first week of detention put them all on the track of his identity. It led them from the house in Peckham to Nottingham, to Hull, and finally to Sheffield, where Mrs. Peace now lived, after leaving London when her husband was arrested. The villa had been shut up and the "happy family" scattered.

In that house, after close and thorough search, they found evidence which proved the identity of the Blackheath burglar—Charles Peace, the man wanted for the murder of Arthur Dyson two years ago.

Later, Mrs. Peace was arrested and charged with being in possession of stolen property. She was taken to London and tried at the Old Bailey, but acquitted on the ground of her having acted under the compulsion of her husband.

Justice works with a certain formality. It was necessary that before Peace could stand trial for the alleged murder of Dyson, he must be indicted on the charge of burglary and attempted killing of the constable at Blackheath. The trial opened November 19, 1878, before Mr. Justice Hawkins, one of the severest judges who ever sat on the bench of the Old Bailey and who was the terror of every professional criminal. The jury found the prisoner guilty of burglary and of attempted murder.

Asked if he had anything to say why sentence should not be passed upon him, Peace began to whine and mumbled some words to the effect that he had disgraced himself; that he was not fit to live or die; and, finally, that he hoped the judge would show him some mercy.

The judge instantly showed his appreciation of the request by sentencing the prisoner to penal servitude for life. Peace was completely crushed.

But the climax was yet to come. With as little delay as possible, Peace was to be called on to answer for the murder of Arthur Dyson. A member of the Criminal Investigation Department had gone to America and traced Mrs. Dyson to Cleveland, where she had returned after her husband's death. She was brought back to England to give evidence against her old admirer and husband's murderer.

On January 17, 1879, Peace was taken from Pentonville Prison, where he was serving his sentence, and conveyed to Sheffield. There he was charged with the murder of Arthur Dyson. When he saw Mrs. Dyson enter the witness box and tell her story of the crime, Peace must have realized the true, desperate picture. Without her evidence, the case against Peace would have been weak. Her cross-examination was adjourned to the next hearing and Peace was taken back to London.

On the twenty-second, the day of the second hearing in Sheffield, an enormous crowd had assembled outside the Town Hall. Inside the court, an anxious and expectant audience, among them Mrs. Dyson, "stylish and cheerful," awaited the appearance of Peace. Great was the disappointment and eager the excitement when the magistrate entered and announced that Peace had attempted to escape that morning on the journey from London to Sheffield, and that as a result of his injuries the case would be adjourned for eight days.

What happened was this: Peace, from the very beginning of the journey, had been wilful and troublesome, behaving in a crude and beastly manner. He kept making excuses for leaving the carriage whenever the train stopped. To put a halt to this behavior, the guards provided a number of paper bags, and whenever Peace required one it was given him and then thrown out of the window. These details are disgusting, but assist the realization of the brutish nature of the convict.

After passing Workshop—the route would be familiar to Peace between Shireoaks and Kiveton stations—Peace demanded another of these bags. His back was toward the guard, and when the window was lowered for him to throw out the bag, Peace at once started to go through the window. The train was then going at about forty-five miles an hour. The guard caught him by the left foot, and there Peace hung, struggling and kicking with his free foot. The chief guard, unable to give his partner any assistance, pulled the alarm cord to stop the train, but with no result.

The guard held on, but Peace's boot did not. He fell on the track in the snow. The train was halted a minute later, and the guards and others, running back, found Peace where he'd fallen, insensible and bleeding from a wound in his head. He revived shortly and, wrapped in some rugs, was taken on to Sheffield.

There he was confined in a cell of the police station in Water Lane where he spent the night complaining of the cold, whining and moaning. He was attended by the police surgeon, the warders keeping strict watch on him. He was given brandy and milk, and in the morning, he announced that he wished he were dead.

Peace recovered so well from the railway misadventure that the doctor pronounced him fit to appear for his second examination January 30th. The proceedings took place in the Town Hall, and Peace, who was seated in an armchair, still complained of the cold. At other times, he moaned and groaned and protested against the injustice with which he was being treated, but the absence of any audience rather dashed the effects of his laments.

His counsel, Mr. Clegg, made a very ingenious attempt to prove that Peace had shot Dyson in self-defense. After a short hearing the court committed the prisoner to trial on the charge of wilful murder at the Leeds Assizes. Peace was immediately removed to Armley Prison. He would be tried the following week.

The apprehension with which this daring criminal was regarded by the authorities is shown by the secret hearing of his case in a cold corridor, and the rapidity with which his trial followed.

While he was in jail he wrote letters continually—to his wife, his mistress, his lawyer. Here is a revealing letter he sent to "Mrs. Thompson":

"My dear Sue, this is a fearful affair which has befallen me, but I hope you will not forsake me, as you have been my bosom friend, and you have ofttimes said that you loved me, that you would die for me. What I hope and trust you will do is to sell the goods I left with you to raise money to engage a barrister for me to save me from the villainous woman, Mrs. Dyson. It will have to be done at once, and the money sent to Clegg and Sons, 57 Bank Street, Sheffield. I hope you will not forget the love we have for each other. Do your best for me. I should like you to write and come and see me if you could. I am very ill from the effects of the jump from the train. . . . I remain your ever true lover till death, John Thompson (Charles Peace)."

But his mistress had already deserted him.

On February 4th, 1879, Peace entered the dock for the last time. He was pale and haggard and seemed to have aged a great deal. He appeared a small, crouching figure, with bloodshot eyes, his head covered with bandages and his body all a-quiver. Here was the finish of a life of crime.

Only two months passed between Peace's trial and sentence at the Old Bailey for the burglary at Blackheath and the trial for the attempted murder of the constable. Perhaps his experience was unique. To few men has it been given to undergo two criminal trials within the space of such a short period. And no criminal case in the

London of those years had created such excitement as that of Peace.

Lord Stuart, of Peace's counsel, said, "So far as I remember, he made no scenes; but I heard him muttering imprecations when certain witnesses spoke, to his having given utterance to vindictive sentiments towards the murdered man, Dyson."

After the summing up of Mr. Justice Lopes, it was evident that the jury had few doubts concerning the facts, for they were absent from court for only a few minutes. They retired at 7:15 P.M. and returned at 7:25 P.M.

Peace, who had been taken below during the interval, was brought back into the dock. His small figure appeared more shrunken than before, his eyes blazing with excitement, his hands shook.

In answer to the question of the official, the foreman of the jury replied almost in a whisper: "We find him guilty."

Peace at once became calm. All the excitement faded from his eyes; he seemed completely resigned. He watched the judge, with an expression which was aloof and almost contemptuous, deliver the death sentence. At the end of it, Peace shrugged his narrow shoulders, waved his hand to some people in the court, and went down the steps of the dock, passing as he went from the eyes of the living world.

It may be said that nothing could have been more deeply religious and sincerely repentant, to all appearances, than Peace's conduct and demeanor in the last weeks of his life. He threw himself into the work of atonement with the same uncompromising zeal and energy that he had displayed as a burglar. However powerless as a controlling force his belief in God and the devil may have been in the past, that belief was nevertheless strong, and in the presence of death it proclaimed itself with vigor, not in words merely, but in deeds.

Peace had one act of atonement to discharge more urgent than displaying Christian forbearance towards ignoble associates. That was the clearing of William Habron who was now serving the third year of his life sentence for the murder of Constable Cock. Peace drew an obviously authentic plan of the place where he had shot Constable Cock, and giving a detailed account of the crime, made a full confession of his own guilt.

William Habron, after certain formalities, was set free.

"Now that I am going to forfeit my own life and feel that I have nothing to gain by further secrecy," said Peace, "I think it is right in the sight of God and man to clear this innocent young man."

It would have been more right in the sight of God and man to have done it before, but then Peace admitted that during his entire career he had allowed neither God nor man to influence his actions. There was nothing of the hero in him, granted Peace, though he was fond of repeating doggerel that indicated his self-evaluation, or self-delusion:

> Lion-hearted I've lived,
> And when my time comes
> Lion-hearted I'll die.

Though Peace was bold in his pursuit of women, he does not seem to have implanted lasting affection in the hearts of the women with whom he associated. It is true that his wife was loyal enough, but her love seems to have been a very milk-and-water affair. And as for his mistress, "Mrs. Thompson," she was businesslike enough to apply to the authorities for the hundred-pound reward they had offered for the apprehension of Peace. She pointed out that the information she had given the police had enabled them to arrest their man. But there was some dispute on the subject, and whether she received the reward is not certain.

And yet, despite her commercial attitude towards her lover, she apparently still held some kind of affection for him. She made several attempts to see Peace during his last weeks in prison, but the authorities, for reasons best known to themselves, opposed the visit. These two—Peace and Sue Thompson—did not meet again.

As for Mrs. Dyson, whatever her relations with Peace may have been in the early days, she now hated him with real hatred. In speaking of him to a detective, she vilified her old admirer in violent terms. "Peace is not a man, he is a devil. Shakespeare himself was not adequate to describe his villainy!" She added that her life-long regret must be that she had ever known so despicable a creature.

February 25th, 1879, was the day fixed for the execution of Charles Peace. He now turned his thoughts to repentance. He encouraged the visits of the prison chaplain and was delighted when his old friend, Mr. Littlewood, Vicar of Darnall, came to see him. Mr. Littlewood was convinced of the genuineness of the man's repentance. Or was it remorse? There is a world of difference.

A few minutes before the vicar left the cell, Peace asked him to be kind enough to preach a special sermon on his fate as a warning to young people. One seems to perceive here the egotism of the criminal. Even after he is dead, he wishes to be spoken of, though his character be used as a symbol of evil.

Peace's health during the time of waiting was feeble, but his spirits were good. He wrote many letters to friends and relatives, all crowded with advice regarding conduct and morals. Apparently, he saw nothing ironical in his new attitude of preacher and moralist.

The last visit of his wife and daughter took place on the afternoon previous to the day of execution. He begged them to be calm, for he wished to keep his mind undisturbed. Then the three knelt and prayed.

William Marwood was the public executioner. He had achieved something of a reputation by his invention of the "long drop," the merciful method of hanging which was then in vogue. Previous to the coming of Marwood, the executions had been long-drawn affairs and had caused great suffering.

Peace advised his family to sell or exhibit for money certain works of art that he had designed. Among them was a sketch for a monument to be placed over his grave. The design is elaborate but well and ingeniously executed. In the opinion of Frith, the painter, it showed "the true feeling of an artist."

Peace awakened after his last sleep, which was calm, at six o'clock of a cold and frosty morning. He wrote more letters, all breathing Christian resignation and morality. He ate a hearty breakfast, but complained about the quality of the bacon. He said to a warder: "I wonder if Marwood could cure this cough of mine."

Remaining overlong in the lavatory, he answered to the knocking of the warder: "You're in a hell of a hurry; are you going to be hanged or am I?"

Then, when the time came, firmly and fearlessly Peace submitted himself to the necessary preparations. The procession to the scaffold was formed. For one moment Peace faltered as the gallows came in sight, but he recovered himself quickly.

As Marwood was about to cover his face, Peace stopped him with a gesture of irritation. He had no intention of being hurried out of life without further speech-making. He asked if he might address the gentlemen of the press, who had been admitted to the ceremony. No one refused him and he turned to the reporters.

"You gentlemen reporters know what my life has been. It has been base; but I wish you to notice, for the sake of others, how a man can die, as I am about to die, in fear of the Lord. Gentlemen, my heart says that I feel assured that my sins are forgiven me, that I am going to the Kingdom of Heaven." He asked a blessing on the officials of the prison and, in conclusion, sent his last wishes and respects to his dear children and their mother. "I hope no one will disgrace them by taunting them or jeering them on my account, but to have mercy upon them. God bless you, my dear children. Good-bye, and Heaven bless you. Amen! Oh my Lord God, have mercy upon me!"

After the cap had been placed over his head, Peace asked twice, very sharply, as a man who expected to be obeyed, for a drink of water. But this time his request was not complied with.

He died instantaneously and was buried in Armsley Jail.

Peace had brought the art of burglary to a degree of perfection it had perhaps never attained before. The amount of plunder he had realized during his years of crime was enormous.

He was a born fighter. A detective who knew him and on one occasion had almost captured him, said that he was a fair fighter—he always gave fair warning to those on whom he fired.

And so we must accept Charles Peace as a remarkable rogue whose unquestioned gifts as a man of action were squandered on a criminal career. In intellectual capacity he was undoubtedly above the average criminal.

If he had drawn the proper moral from his own life, it would be the very simple one that crime is no career for a man of brains.

XIII

JEANNE BRÉCOURT

Vɪᴛʀɪᴏʟ has played so frequent a part in what are sometimes called *crimes passionels* that the case of Jeanne Amenaide Brécourt would hardly call for more than a passing interest but for the amazing circumstances that surrounded the blinding of her victim.

In many crimes of passion a certain sympathy can be felt for a deserted woman who, in a moment of madness, commits a terrible act of vengeance. For Jeanne Brécourt, however, there can be no sympathy. She planned her diabolical deed coolly; she carried it out with careful calculation and premeditation.

Jeanne Brécourt was born in Paris in 1837. Her father was a printer, her mother sold vegetables. Both parents neglected the child, and she showed herself from her earliest moments as erratic, mischievous and vain to the point of absurdity. When little more than a babe, she stamped her foot with rage because a certain dress did not appeal to her. Forced to wear it, she soon cut it to threads.

Jeanne did not remain long with her family. A lady of title took pity on her and when she was five years old adopted her. Even as a little girl, she was haughty and imperious. At the age of eight, she refused to play with another child on the ground of her companion's social inferiority. "The daughter of a baroness," she said, "cannot play with the daughter of a wine merchant."

When she was eleven years old, her parents took her back and sent her into the streets to sell gingerbread— a dangerous experience for a child of her years, especially after the instability of living in separate households. After six years of street life, Jeanne sought out her former benefactress and begged her to take her back. The baroness consented, and found employment for Jeanne in a silk factory.

But work after she had seen what it was like to live with the baroness, was not included in Jeanne's scheme of life. She hated it with an almost maniacal hate. Very soon she found a way of escape. It came in the shape of marriage.

One day Jeanne, now eighteen years old, attended the wedding of one of her companions in the factory. She returned home after the ceremony, thoughtful. She said that she wanted to get married. The baroness did not take her statement seriously, and one day, when the grocer called to make his delivery, she said in jest to Jeanne: "You want a husband? There's one." But Jeanne was in earnest. She accepted the suggestion and, to the surprise of the baroness, insisted on marrying the man. Reluctantly the baroness gave her consent and, in 1855, Jeanne became the wife of the grocer, Gras.

A union so hastily and thoughtlessly entered into was not likely to be of long duration, even though the baroness came to their aid by helping them start a grocery business. But the marriage was founded on too rocky a foundation. Quarrels ensued, and there were blows, re-criminations. In a spirit of unamiable prophecy, husband and wife foretold each other's future.

"You will die in a hospital," said the wife.

"You will land your carcass in prison," retorted the husband.

In both instances, they were correct.

One day the husband disappeared. For a short time Jeanne returned to her long-suffering protectress and then she, too, disappeared, seeking fresh fields of adventure.

It is said that during the time which elapsed between Jeanne's exit from Paris and her return, she did many queer things. Perhaps the most respectable of them was an attempt to earn a living by writing. However, this effort failed and she returned to Paris a full-blown courtesan. She had dropped the name of Brécourt and called herself Jeanne de la Cour, adding to it the title of "Baroness."

Her experiences had doubtless been of the sort that does not tend to place men on a pedestal. Jeanne was now filled not merely with a dislike of men, but with an all-pervading contempt. She confessed that she now regarded the masculine animal as a thing to be exploited without mercy. Her philosophy of life is summed up in her own words: "Everything in this world is lies and dust. So much the worse for the men who get in my path. Men are mere stepping stones to me. As soon as they fail me, or are played out in regard to what they can spend upon me, I have no further for them. Society is a vast chessboard, men the pawns; I move them as I please."

Although Jeanne was ready to bleed her male friends to the last drop, the process does not seem to have been profitable. She was always more or less in money difficulties.

True to her philosophy, she had driven one lover, a German, to suicide, and brought another to his death by overdoses of cantharides. On learning of the death of the first, she reflected patriotically, "One German less in Paris!" That of the second elicited the matter-of-fact comment, "It was bound to happen; he had no moderation." A third admirer, who died in a hospital, was dismissed as "a fool who, in spite of all, still respects women."

Among Jeanne's other accomplisments was a gift for

blackmail. She exercised this gift with extreme callousness. No man was safe. She would fawn upon some half-drunken fool during a night of erotic passion—she was sensual to an inordinate degree—and in the morning she would proceed to blackmail him. One man, rendered a nervous wreck through her demands, died in an asylum. Wherever Jeanne moved, she brought ruin to health, to peace of mind and, of course, to the purses of her victims.

However, in ruining her lovers, Jeanne had also ruined her own health. She had to spend a brief period in a private asylum. There she was described as "dark in complexion, with dark expressive eyes, very pale, of a nervous temperament, agreeable and pretty." She was suffering at the time of her admission from hysterical seizures, accompanied by insane exaltation, convulsions and loss of speech. In speaking of her humble parents, she said, "I don't know such people." Her manner was bombastic and she was fond of posing as a lady.

After a few months Jeanne de la Cour was discharged from the asylum as cured, and on the advice of her doctor she went to Vittel. There she assumed the title of baroness and began her career again, but this time in a more businesslike manner. Her comments on her fellow guests at the hotel are caustic. She ridiculed some respectable married women who tried to convert her to Catholicism. To others, who refused her recognition, she made herself so objectionable that in self-defence they were frightened into acknowledging her. But she had many admirers among the men, including ex-ministers and prefects.

While she was staying at Vittel, an incident took place that reveals an interesting sidelight on her nature. There had been some pigeon-shooting, and one of the wounded birds flew into her room. She took pity on it, tended it, taught it not to be afraid of her and to stay in her room. So touching was her conduct considered by those who heard about it that she was nicknamed "the charmer." But she was well aware, she wrote to her sister, that with the true ingratitude of the male, the pigeon would leave her as soon as it no longer needed her help. However, for the moment, she loved it.

"Don't forget," she wrote, "that a woman who is practical and foreseeing, may also enjoy her pigeon-shooting, but the birds are her lovers."

Then something occurred which made Jeanne feel she could at last attain a settled, secure position which would assure her future. Her husband, Gras, the grocer, died, as she had foretold, in the Charity Hospital. Jeanne was free!

If she could bring down her bird, it was now in her power to make it hers for life. Henceforth all her efforts were directed to that end.

She was now nearing her fortieth year, her hair was turning gray, her charms were waning. Before her beckoned poverty, degradation, a miserable old age, a return to the wretched surroundings of her childhood—such as she knew to be the fate of many of her kind. There was nothing to be hoped for from the generosity of men. Her lovers were leaving her. She couldn't try blackmail without lovers on whom to work this devious trickery. Speculation on the Bourse, even the desperate expedient of claiming one of her lovers fathered a fictitious child—all these she tried as a means of acquiring money. Now she was really desperate. She must bring down her bird quickly. There was need for despatch.

It was at this critical point in the widow's career, in the year 1873, that she met, at a public ball, Georges de Saint Pierre.

Georges de Saint Pierre, twenty years old, became violently in love with Jeanne, almost twice his age. He came from an excellent family, had independent means, and considerable "expectations." He was of a simple, confiding and affectionate disposition. Very soon they became friends, and eventually there followed a liaison that lasted for three years without a break.

Saint Pierre idolized his middle-aged mistress of whose character he was, of course, entirely innocent. She represented herself as a widow who had met many vicissitudes, through all of which she had come out "unspotted." Saint Pierre looked upon her as a saint to whom the world had been harsh and even merciless. He told her he would try to make her life so happy that she would forget all that had gone before. His confidence in her was complete. Whatever her faults, he was blind to them.

Jeanne must have been a remarkable actress to eliminate so completely all traces of the primrose path and pose as a heroine of the "more sinned against than sinning" type. She realized that Saint Pierre loved and pitied her sufficiently to want to offer her protection more permanent than the protection offered by a mere lover. He was ready and anxious to make Jeanne his wife.

Jeanne's conquest, to all appearances, was complete. There can be no doubt that during the three years she was his mistress, Jeanne had succeeded in enslaving him completely. However, Saint Pierre was very young, and his family was deeply concerned over his future. They knew of his liaison. They hoped, no doubt, of breaking it off someday and of marrying him to some desirable young woman of position.

Like most young Frenchmen, Saint Pierre was very much under the influence of his family. He wrote to Jeanne from his home in the country that he was perfectly well and moderately happy, but deeply troubled by certain difficulties that had arisen between "myself and my dear parents."

Jeanne immediately guessed the cause of these "difficulties." She realized how strong was the opposition with which she was now faced. There was the possibility that she might lose not only a husband but even a lover.

She must have puzzled a great deal in those days, asking herself how to overcome this possible disaster. Then, quite suddenly, the solution came.

One day Jeanne happened to be at the house of a friend, a ballet dancer. She saw this friend lead into the room a young man. He was blind, and her friend, with tender care, guided him to a seat on the sofa. When, later, she was alone with her friend, she asked the reason for her unusual solicitude for the young man.

"I love this victim of nature," the ballet dancer replied, "and look after him with every care. He is young, rich, without family, and is going to marry me. Like you, I am nearly forty; my youth is vanishing. I shall soon be cast adrift, a wreck. This boy is my hope, my safety."

"You mean, then," said Jeanne, "that you will soon be in a position where you will no longer have to worry?"

"Yes," answered the friend. "I needn't worry any more about the future."

"I congratulate you," said Jeanne, "and what is more, your lover will never see you grow old."

"You see," said this practical-minded friend, "I need have no anxiety about him. He can never leave me, for he knows that no one else would put up with him in his helpless state."

Jeanne showed a great deal of interest, but no emotion. The incident of the blind man, as dependent on her friend as a baby on its mother, fired her blood. She began to turn over the picture in her brain. It fascinated her. Gradually there was born in her mind a scheme which she could put into action.

Years ago, in her childhood, Jeanne had had for a playmate a boy called Nathalis Gaudry. After serving in the army and wandering through the world, Gaudry had returned to Paris and found employment in an oil refinery where he was a good and honest workman, with an excellent record and character. He had been married, but his wife had died, leaving him with two children. Some chance brought Jeanne and her old friend together again, and the man immediately fell in love with her with an intensely strong and deep passion.

But Jeanne was now Jeanne de la Cour, living in refinement and some luxury, moving in a sphere altogether remote from that of a humble workman of an oil refinery. He could do no more than worship from afar this strange being, to him wonderfully seductive in her charm and distinction.

On her side, Jeanne was quite friendly towards her homely admirer. She refused to marry him, as he would have wished. But she made use of him.

On Sundays he helped her in her apartment, carried coals, bottled wine, and made himself generally useful. He was considered by any who saw him to be her brother. Occasionally, in the absence of a maid, Jeanne allowed him to attend her personally, even to assist her in her toilette. His passion for her, excited but not gratified, enslaved and consumed him.

Such was the state of Gaudry, emotionally, when in November, 1876, he received a letter from Jeanne in which she wrote: "Come at once. I want you on a matter of business. Tell your employer it is a family affair; I will make up your wages." In obedience to this message, Gaudry was absent from the refinery from the 17th to the 23rd of November.

The "matter of business" about which Jeanne wished to consult Gaudry turned out to be a scheme of revenge. She told him she had been cheated and defrauded by a man to whom she had entrusted money. The man had "ruined" her life. He had not only deceived her with callous brutality, he had also beaten her, robbed her and caused her inconceivable humiliation, and she could think of no better way to revenge herself on this man than by striking at his dearest object—by seriously injuring his son. She would then be satisfied—and would be ready to give herself to Gaudry when the punishment was complete.

The punishment she had in mind was to be performed with the help of a knuckle-duster, which she produced and gave to Gaudry. Armed with this formidable weapon, Gaudry was to strike her enemy's son so forcibly in the pit of the stomach as to disable him for life. Jeanne, of course, offered to point out to Gaudry the young man he was to attack. She took Gaudry outside the young man's club and showed him his victim. He was Georges de Saint Pierre.

For some reason—perhaps the reluctance of Gaudry, saying that "a soldier could not bring himself to strike a treacherous blow"—the idea of maiming Saint Pierre was abandoned. Perhaps Jeanne decided that blindness would prove a more effective means of retaining Saint Pierre's presence and affection.

Since talking with her friend, the ballet dancer, the idea of keeping Georges permanently attached had become an obsession with Jeanne. What use was a lover, however generous and faithful, who was free to take her up and put her aside at will? But that was her position as regards Georges de Saint Pierre. She remembered the wounded pigeon that, once recovered, had flown away. Only a pigeon, maimed beyond hope of recovery, could belong to her permanently. And so, in accordance with her philosophy of life, Jeanne was to bring down her bird, which henceforth would be tended and cared for by "the charmer" to her own satisfaction and the admiration of all beholders.

Jeanne knew the character of Saint Pierre. It was not strong; sooner or later, he might yield to the importunities of his family. So in January, she asked her nephew, who worked as a gilder, to get her some vitriol for cleaning her copper, and he complied with her request.

During Jeanne's brief and unsuccessful appearance as an actress, she had taken part in a play with the rather

cumbrous title, *Who Puts Out the Eyes Must Pay for
Them.* She may have forgotten this event. Its occurrence
so many years before may have been merely a sinister
coincidence. But the incident of the ballet dancer and
her sightless lover was fresh in her mind.

A little later, Jeanne again met Gaudry by appointment
and detailed her plan: vitriol was to be used to blind
the young man. On a certain night, still to be arranged,
Gaudry was to hide himself in the shadow of a small
pavilion that adjoined her house. She would prevail
upon Saint Pierre to take her to a theater or concert. On
their return, she would find a pretext for sending him
ahead of her to open the gate. The instant he aproached,
Gaudry, from his place of concealment, was to fling the
contents of the bottle in the young man's face. No detail
was left unconsidered by this callous monster. Nor did
the cruelty of the contemplated crime disturb her in the
slightest.

Gaudry hesitated, but a few kisses made him yield.
He was completely unable to resist Jeanne in any way.

Saint Pierre had returned from his country home.
Jeanne noticed a decided change in the young man. He
was listless, gloomy, absent-minded. He spoke of disagreements which had arisen between his family and
himself. It was clear to her that he was wavering; it was
clear, moreover, that although he still cared for her to
some extent, his passion was no longer of that intensity
that would survive heavy attacks from outside.

This knowledge stiffened her determination. She told
herself there could be no holding back. Making a pretense of cheering him, Jeanne said gaily: "The country
has depressed you. You need amusement, music, enjoyment. Tomorrow evening we shall go to the Opera.
We both love music and it will make us forget the sordid
realities of life."

On the following afternoon, when Saint Pierre was
away, Gaudry called at the house and received his final

instructions. At the same time, Jeanne handed him the
vitriol. Having repeated the instructions so that there
might be no misunderstanding, she hurried to keep her
appointment with Saint Pierre. Throughout the afternoon preceeding the visit to the opera, Jeanne had
chatted, coaxed and made love—all with a light heart.

Meanwhile, Gaudry sat and waited in the apartment.
From the window he could look out at the thoroughfare
on which the revellers would return home. The hours
passed slowly. He tried to read, to sleep. Between two
and three o'clock in the morning he was wakened by the
noise of wheels. They had returned. He hurried downstairs and took up his position in the shadow of one of
the pavilions.

As Georges de Saint Pierre walked up the drive alone—
for Jeanne stayed behind to fasten the gate—he thought
he saw the figure of a man in the darkness. The next
moment he was blinded by the burning liquid flung in
his face. Jeanne had brought down her pigeon.

Meantime, Gaudry had slipped from his hiding place
and contrived to get away without being seen by anyone.

Jeanne played her part well. She shouted for help and,
weeping hysterically, helped the police carry the wretched young man to her rooms, where she at once fell upon
his breast, sobbing, moaning, screaming.

Jeanne seemed to have succeeded in her plan. Saint
Pierre was injured for life—the sight of one eye gone,
that of the other threatened, his face badly disfigured.
Neither he nor anyone else suspected the real author of
the crime. It was believed that the unfortunate Saint
Pierre had been mistaken for some other person and by
accident made the victim of an act of vengeance.

Saint Pierre was indeed all Jeanne's now, lodged in
her own house to nurse and care for. She undertook the
task with every appearance of affectionate devotion. The
unhappy patient was consumed with gratitude for her

untiring solicitude—thirty nights she spent by his bedside. His belief in her was absolute. It was his own
wish that she alone should nurse him. His family was
kept away; any attempts his relatives or friends made
to see or communicate with him were frustrated by the
zealous Jeanne.

Throughout his convalescence, Saint Pierre would
hold Jeanne's hand by the hour, telling her that she was
his guardian angel, that no other woman would have
stood by him as she had done. Jeanne was satisfied. She
had gained, as she believed, a husband who would rely
upon her for every movement of his existence; whom
she could fondle or ill-treat as she chose.

Gaudry, however, was the one thorn in her thoughts.
She was not sure of the man. She knew him to be an
emotional, stupid fellow who might do some desperate
thing that would shatter her scheme. She therefore set
about tightening her hold on the man. She met him
more than once in obscure places. On one occasion the
meeting took place in a cemetery. That rendezvous was
observed by a police agent, but he then lost track of
Gaudry. At a later time, this meeting formed a link in
the chain of evidence that led to Jeanne's arrest.

The police had not been altogether satisfied with
Jeanne's story of the attack. At the time, M. Macé, who
afterwards became one of the most celebrated of the
Sûreté, was a mere Commissary, but his acute brain
had begun to tear apart holes in the official version. He
asked himself why the woman had allowed her lover to
go on in front of her on the night of the vitriol attack.
Two people, sweethearts, returning from an evening of
pleasure, usually enter a house together, reasoned Macé.
But a woman who *knew* that an attack was contemplated
would naturally take care to remain well in the background. A slender clue, but he proceeded to work on it.

A rigid watch was kept upon Jeanne's movements.
After the meeting in the cemetery, she was closely shad-

owed. Also, the authorities were encouraged in their
investigations by the family of the injured man. More
than one member had, intuitively perhaps, formed a
theory that the vitriol-throwing had been instigated by
the woman herself. Macé, evidently impressed by this
theory and still suspicious of the secret meeting with
Gaudry, decided to pay a visit to Jeanne's apartment in
the company of an examining magistrate.

His reception was not cordial. When he asked to see
the ill man, Jeanne replied it was impossible. He told
her that her attitude was not seemly. From that moment
there was a silent tug of war between the widow and
himself. But he insisted on seeing the patient and he
did. While he sat at Saint Pierre's bedside, the convales-
cent said he was sure he had been the victim of some
mistake and that he did not wish his misfortune to be
made public. He wished to be left alone with his brave
and devoted nurse and he intended to leave Paris shortly
for a change of scene and air.

Jeanne now cut the interview short on the ground
that her patient was tired. The magistrate asked her
where she intended taking her patient. She replied, "To
Italy." That, said the magistrate, would be impossible
until his inquiry was closed. In the meantime, she might
take him to any place within the Department of the
Seine, and she must be prepared to have M. Macé enter her house whenever he thought it expedient. With
this guarded warning, Macé and the magistrate left.

Macé now began to feel that the family's suspicions
were well-founded, and he continued to keep a more
rigid watch over Jeanne's movements. She was seen to
go to the bachelor apartment of Saint Pierre and take
away a portable desk which contained money and correspondence. Shortly after Jeanne left Paris with her
lover for the suburb of Courbevoie. By this time the
original diagnosis was confirmed. One eye was completely gone and there was only partial use of the other.

Macé learned, from the porter at Jeanne's house and other witnesses, about the disappearance of the man who called himself her brother, and he decided it was necessary to separate Jeanne from her lover. So the examining magistrate ordered Jeanne to be sent back to Paris, and the family of Saint Pierre now took her place. The change was made on March 6th.

On leaving Courbevoie, Jeanne was taken to the office of Macé where she was informed that she must consider herself under provisional arrest. "But who," she asked indignantly, "is to look after my George?"

"His family," was the curt reply.

Jeanne, walking up and down the room like a panther, stormed and threatened.

When she had in some degree recovered herself, Macé questioned her. How was it that her lover's assailant had got away so quickly by the open gate? She did not know. What was the name and address of her reputed brother? She was not going to deliver an honest father of a family into the clutches of the police. What was the meaning of her visit to the Charonne Cemetery? She went there to pray, not to keep an assignation.

"And if you want to know," she exclaimed, "I have had typhoid fever, which makes me often forget things. So I shall say nothing more. Nothing—nothing!"

Taken before the examining magistrate, Jeanne's attitude continued to be defiant and arrogant. "Your cleverest policeman," she told the magistrate, "will never find any evidence against me. Think well before you send me to prison. I am not the woman to live long among thieves and prostitutes."

Before deciding whether Jeanne should be thrown into such uncongenial society, the magistrate ordered Macé to search her apartment. On entering the rooms, Jeanne asked that all the windows should be opened. "Let in the air," she said. "The police are coming in; they make a nasty smell."

The search brought to light many strange things: letters from all sorts and conditions of men; letters denouncing her as the vilest thing in France; letters containing obscenities which shocked even the officers. A half-burned package of letters from Saint Pierre was also found. Soon after the vitriol episode, Saint Pierre had begged Jeanne to burn these letters, because they held certain confessions which he dreaded being revealed at some later time when both he and Jeanne might be dead. She had thrown the package in the fire to satisfy him, but had retrieved it immediately afterwards. Why? The answer was obvious. The letters would form an excellent weapon for blackmail if Jeanne's power over Saint Pierre in the future waned.

Macé, without delay, left for Courbevoie, there to enlighten Jeanne's victim as to the real character of his enchantress. The interview was a painful one. Saint Pierre refused to hear a word against her. It was only when Macé placed in his hands the bundle of burnt letters that he might feel what he could not see, and read to him some passages from them, that the unhappy man realized the full extent of Jeanne's treachery. Now the long catalogue of wickedness was unfolded to Saint Pierre and he realized the truth. His saint, his beloved, was a callous and shameless courtesan who, from her earliest years, had victimized men and wrung them dry, robbing them not only of money, but of life itself.

Saint Pierre's dream was shattered. He fell into an agony of despair. "To blind me," he exclaimed, "to torture me, and then profit by my condition . . . to lie to me, to betray me—it's infamous—infamous!" His disenchantment was complete.

That night the fastidious Jeanne joined the thieves and the prostitutes in the St. Lazare prison.

It was all very well to put her in custody, but her participation in the outrage on Saint Pierre was by no means established. The reputed brother still eluded the searches of the police. Jeanne's only hope of baffling her enemies now lay in keeping complete silence.

In prison, however, she became anxious, excited. Her very ignorance of what was going on around her, together with her lover's silence, made her aprehensive. She began to fear the worst. She determined to communicate at all costs with Gaudry and invoke his aid. Thus she herself broke the silence she had vowed.

Jeanne wrote Gaudry, appealing to him to come forward and admit that he was the man the police were seeking; and because she was shielding him, she told him, she had been thrown into prison. She drew a harrowing picture of her sufferings in jail. She had refused and had been forcibly fed; she would like to dash her head against the walls. If any misfortune might overtake Gaudry, she promised to adopt his children and leave a third of her property to him and his family. She persuaded a fellow prisoner, who was being released, to take the letter and deliver it to Gaudry at Saint Denis.

But the released woman did not deliver it to Gaudry. She showed the note to her lover who, scenting a reward, at once brought it to the police. Gaudry was immediately arrested and his identity as the mysterious person who had met Jeanne in the cemetery was proved beyond all question.

Gaudry made a full confession. It was his passion for Jeanne Brécourt, and a promise on her part to marry him which, he said, had induced him to perpetrate so abominable a crime. He was sent to Mazas Prison.

In the meantime, Jeanne was getting more and more desperate. Her complete ignorance of what was going on tormented her. At last she gave up all hope and twice attempted suicide with powdered glass and verdigris.

On May 12, 1877, Jeanne was brought face to face with her accomplice who again told his story of the crime. She repudiated the accusation with furious rage, calling Gaudry by the vilest names in her lengthy list of invectives. He refused to withdraw a syllable of the confession, saying over and over again that he was the victim of a temptation which he had found irresistible.

"What would you have?" he repeated. "A man who is violently in love with a woman is as a child in her hands. If she had told me to kill myself, I would have done it instantly."

The trial of the sordid pair was scheduled for July 23, 1877, at the Paris Assize Court. It dragged along for three days, during which time the court was filled with sensation hunters of all classes, several famous novelists being among the spectators.

The *Figaro* described Jeanne thus: "She looks more than her age, of moderate height, well-made, neither blatant nor ill at ease, with nothing of the air of a woman of the town. Her hands are small. Her bust is flat and her back round, her hair quite white. Beneath her brow glitter two jet-black eyes—the eyes of a tigress, that seem to breathe hatred and revenge."

Throughout the trial sympathy was shown the man Gaudry. Evidently the Court and the spectators held that he was the victim rather than the "villain of the piece." There is no doubt that Gaudry at the beginning of his association with Jeanne was a decent fellow. His tragedy lay in the fact that being in love made him subservient to the point of removing all self-will and all moral values. But now, whether for his own self-interest or because of his disillusion with her, not for a moment did he attempt to shield Jeanne. The fault, he said again, was entirely hers; he had merely been a tool in a stronger hand.

Throughout his testimony, Gaudry was interrupted from time to time by Jeanne: "Lies! All lies!" she screamed, clenching her fists, darting at him glances of hate. "Beast! Pig! Coward!" These were some of the epithets hurled at Gaudry.

Each counsel—both famous criminal advocates of France—worked well for his client. Each endeavored to shift the responsibility for the crime.

M. Demange represented Gaudry as acting under the influence of his passion for Jeanne. Lachaud, on the other hand, attributed the crime solely to Gaudry's jealousy of Jeanne's lover, Saint Pierre, and contended that he was the sole author of the outrage.

The jury found both prisoners guilty. By their verdict, they assigned to Jeanne the greater share of the responsibility. She was found guilty in the maximum degree. But in Gaudry's case certain extenuating circumstances were admitted. Jeanne was condemned to fifteen years' penal servitude, her accomplice to five years' imprisonment.

It is dreadful to think how very near Jeanne came to accomplishing successfully her diabolical crime. Had she not, torn by anxiety, written the fatal letter, she might have secured the fruits of her cruelty. Her undoubted powers of fascination, in spite of the fiendishness of her real character, are doubly proved by the devotion of her lover and the guilt of her accomplice.

The extent of the sentence on Jeanne indicates the degree of horror with which France viewed her crime. The Frenchman—ardent, passionate, with fiery Latin temperament—can readily understand, and regard with mercy, a lover going mad in a fit of jealousy or anger. But a calculating lover, coldly premeditating a crime for purposes of greed, is a figure of revulsion to him. This is a debasement of love and a crime of the lowest order. This, the worldly Frenchman will not forgive.

This, also, is why he will not forget the crime of Jeanne Amenaide Brécourt.

XIV

JEAN BAPTISTE TROPPMANN

MANY MEN, especially in their youth, have burned with ambition to make a big splash in the world—in art or science or industry. Few succeed. And almost none channel these drives in the demonic direction chosen by the strange youth, Troppmann.

"I will do something that shall astonish the world." This juvenile promise Jean Baptiste Troppmann made good in the year 1869, when he astonished the civilized world by one of the most cruel and diabolical murders ever perpetrated by a sane man. No crime of the nineteenth century had created a sensation comparable with that caused by the wholesale assassination of the Kinck family by their young friend, Jean Baptiste Troppmann.

The crime was then, and has been since, made the foundation for the most extravagant charges and suspicions. Some asserted at the time that the murders had been organized by the tottering government of Napoleon III in order to distract public attention from its own rotten condition. After the disastrous war with Germany, the French hatred of Bismarck found vent in the story that Kinck had been a Prussian spy; that he had become dangerous to the great Chancellor, and that Bismarck had procured, at the hands of his agent Troppmann, the destruction of the family. As a matter of fact, however, the crime of Troppmann is well capable of a less sensational explanation than that of political expediency.

Between seven and eight o'clock on the morning of

217

September 20, 1869, a farmer by the name of Langlois was on his way to work in the vicinity of Pantin, a suburb a mile and a half northeast of Paris, when he was suddenly stopped by observing on the path some stains of blood, dotted here and there with what appeared to be portions of brain. Following up these gruesome indications, the farmer found that they led him to a neighboring field, the soil of which bore traces of being recently disturbed. At the edge of the field, he noticed a handkerchief, projecting from the ground. On lightly moving the earth about this spot, Langlois came on a human head.

Without taking time to check further into the area, Langlois immediately went to inform the police, who arrived upon the scene and began to dig up the field in the part indicated by the farmer. In a short time six human corpses, still warm, were dug out from a ditch in which they had been interred. They were the bodies of a woman and five children—four boys and a girl—who had evidently only a few hours before met with a violent death in the deserted spot. The bodies seemed to have been trodden down into their shallow grave and an attempt made to give the soil above the same appearance that it had shown before it had been disturbed.

There were no marks of a struggle, death must have come on its victims unawares, for the ground was but little marked up; they had obviously offered little resistance to their assassin. Only on the hand of one of the children was there any trace of an attempt to block the impact of a weapon.

Medical examination showed that the woman had been first stabbed in the neck with a long knife and that, though this stab had been enough to cause immediate death, the murderer had inflicted thirty other wounds with the same weapon on the body of his victim. The two youngest children had been put to death in a similar manner. The other three had been battered to death by a heavy, pointed instrument, and two of them were strangled as well. Their faces, horribly smashed and disfigured, betrayed the ferocity of their murderer. In another part of the field were found a knife that had broken off at the handle, and a shovel and pick.

The general excitement caused by these horrible discoveries quickly gave the authorities a clue to the identity of the victims. On the evening preceeding the discovery of the crime, a woman with five children, giving the name of Kinck, had called at the Railway Hotel of the Northern Terminus. She said that she had come from Roubaix, a town in the Nord department, not far from Lille, and asked for her husband, whom she believed to be staying at the hotel. On being told that he was not there, she had gone away and had never returned.

The hotel servants, however, were able to identify these fugitive visitors with the bodies at the morgue, and further evidence from Roubaix proved beyond a doubt that these bodies were those of Madame Kinck and her five children, and that she had left that town on the 19th to go to Paris and there rejoin her husband Jean Kinck, and her eldest son, Gustave. The Kinck family numbered eight in all—the father, mother, and six children, ranging in age from the eldest Gustave, who was nineteen, to the little girl Marie-Hortense, only two and a half years old. At the time of her murder, Madame Kinck was about to become a mother again.

Such evidence as could be collected showed that Jean Kinck, some time before the murder, had left home for Alsace to transact some important business, that his eldest son had soon followed him there, that they had gone together to Paris, and that from Paris Kinck had summoned his wife and children to join him. It was further proved that a man, giving the name of Jean Kinck, had registered at the Railway Hotel at which Madame Kinck had called. But this man had disappeared since the discovery of the crime. Of Gustave Kinck, the son, no trace could be found.

Was the father the author of this awful multiple murder? Had the eldest son been his victim or his accomplice? For three days the mystery seemed wrapped in darkness. On the 23rd, however, light was shed on the affair by an accidental occurrence at the port of Le Havre.

On the evening of the 20th, a man, giving the name of Fisch of Roubaix, had arrived in Le Havre and put up at a hotel. He had attracted the attention of the police by trying to procure passage to America without the proper papers, and then endeavoring to buy fraudulently such papers. A gendarme, who met him three days later and asked him some questions as to his identity, was so dissatisfied with his replies and attempts to conceal a recent wound on his hand that he decided to take him before a magistrate. As they were passing the edge of the harbor, the man suddenly jumped into the water. But a courageous seaman, who had witnessed the scene, jumped in after him and, in spite of the ferocious efforts of the man to drown both himself and his rescuer, succeeded in bringing him to land. Thus the sailor frustrated what was obviously a determined attempt on the part of the mysterious man to escape further interrogation by suicide.

The man, who was in a state of shock, was taken to a hospital. There he was searched, and concealed in different parts of his person were found a number of deeds, bills, receipts, and other legal documents bearing the name of Jean Kinck. He had, besides, two hundred and ten francs in five-franc pieces, two watches—one gold, the other silver—and various articles afterwards identified as having been the property of the Kinck family.

When the mysterious patient came to, he at first declined to answer the questions that were put to him, pretending he was still in a half-conscious condition. But as soon as he discovered that he was suspected of being responsible for the murders at Pantin, he admitted that the papers found on him had come into his possession by the murder of the Kinck family, and he gave his name as Jean Baptiste Troppmann.

Troppmann declared that Jean Kinck and his eldest son, Gustave, were the actual killers of the rest of the family, that he had merely acted as the passive agent of his two friends in the commission of the crime, and that he had not seen the Kincks since the night of the murder, nor did he know anything their whereabouts.

The arrest of Troppmann created a sensation throughout France. Monsieur Claude, the celebrated Head of the Detective Police during the Second Empire, left Paris immediately for Le Havre to take personal charge over the prisoner's journey to the capital. He and his prisoner arrived at the Gare de Lyon.

Troppmann, who had been thrown into a state of tension and irritability by the large crowds that gathered at every station to catch a glimpse of him, had managed to hide his face behind a bandana handkerchief. At the Paris terminus the police cleverly eluded the mob, and Troppmann was driven with amazing speed to the morgue. The authorities had decided that before the prisoner should have had time to grasp the situation thoroughly, he should be suddenly confronted with the six bodies discovered at Pantin.

With that object in view, Troppmann was met at the morgue by the *Judge d'Instruction*, who had been entrusted with the case, and two of the prosecuting magistrates of the Imperial Court.

"Troppmann," said the judge, pointing to the marble slabs on which lay the bodies of Madame Kinck and her children, "do you recognize any of these dead persons?"

Without a tremor of emotion in voice or figure, and without taking off his cap or showing the least trace of pity or surprise, the prisoner, pointing to each corpse with his finger, replied, "That one there, that's Madame Kinck, that's Emile, that's Henri, that's Alfred, that's Achille, and that's little Marie."

After some further interrogation, Troppmann was taken to the Mazas Prison where he was booked as Jean Baptiste Troppmann, age twenty-one, a native of Cernay in Alsace, and a machinist by profession.

In appearance Troppmann was about five feet tall, and slightly built; except for his eyes, which were shifty and restless, there was nothing about his face that was in any way unusual, or indicative of cruelty or ferocity. His hair was brown, his complexion sunburnt. The most remarkable feature about him were his thumbs. They were remarkably long, reaching almost to the ends of the first finger, and disproportionately powerful as compared with the rest of his hand. There was about his whole bearing a youthfulness, almost a boyishness, that seemed strangely inconsistent with the horrible crime of which he was suspected.

The day following Troppmann's arrival in Paris, Sunday, September 25th, a butcher's dog, running about the field at Pantin, where the bodies of Madame Kinck and her children had been unearthed, was instrumental in the discovery of a seventh body—that of Gustave Kinck, the eldest son, who Troppmann had asserted was his father's accomplice in the murder of the family.

This new discovery was kept from Troppmann all day Sunday, which he spent in assiduously reading different issues of the Picturesque Magazine. But on Monday morning he was again taken to the morgue and confronted with the corpse of Gustave. On this occasion he seemed for a moment startled, and he covered his face with his handkerchief. "Ah, the poor fellow," he exclaimed.

"Take down that handkerchief," said the judge, "you

needn't pretend to cry. Look at this body. Do you recognize it?"

"Yes, it is Gustave."

"And you killed him?"

"No, it was his father, who was afraid he would reveal the crime."

"Come," pursued the magistrate, "you'll have to tell us something more convincing than that. It is too easy to lay the blame on one who is not here to defend himself"

"Ah!" replied Troppmann, "I wish I was in Gustave's place."

During the rest of the interview, Troppmann was perfectly self-possessed.

A careful examination of the body of Gustave established the fact—fatal to Troppmann's story—that Gustave had been killed and buried before his mother and the little children.

The fate of Jean Kinck, the father, still remained a mystery.

The career of Troppmann up to the date of the murders and his relations with the Kinck family were now made the subject of an official investigation.

It appeared that Troppmann's father was an Alsatian artisan, skilled in the setting up of machinery, and also something of an inventor. Jean Baptiste Troppmann was born at Cernay in 1848. He showed himself, as he grew to manhood, to be gifted with a superior intelligence and a profoundly vicious disposition. His education had been neglected, but he was a greedy reader of sensational novels and fabulous stories of famous criminals.

"From perpetually living in this imaginary world," writes the Abbé Crozes, who attended him to the scaffold, "he had lost all sense of right and wrong, and became filled with a burning desire to emulate those heroic criminals who rehabilitate their characters by giving the fruits of their crimes to the poor and suffering, and end their days by devoting to charitable objects an income that has been derived from the exercise of dagger and poison."

The Abbé even goes so far as to suggest that Jean Valjean was the model that had most probably served as an example to the distorted imagination of Troppmann. In the light of modern psychiatric knowledge, this is of course a naive interpretation of motives, but the good Abbé nevertheless sensed that Troppmann's towering ego made him feel he was endowed for the commission of deeds generally confined to the pages of fiction.

This intelligent young Alsatian of twenty-one, with his boy's face and pleasing voice, knew how to make himself pleasant and ingratiating, while inwardly he seethed with a sombre and brooding temper, capable of violent and ferocious outbursts, in one of which he had tried to kill his brother with a mallet. He had been favored by his mother, who had spoiled him, letting him have his own way in everything. His father had taken him into the business, but found him an indifferent and uninterested worker. Even before Troppmann was sixteen, he had molested girls, threatening them with savage treatment if they avoided his attentions.

In December, 1868, Troppmann had been sent by his father to Pantin, there to set up some machinery that he had sold to a Paris manufacturer. Young Troppmann remained there some six months, living near the place afterwards selected for the extermination of the Kinck family. The few persons who met the young man at that time were strongly impressed by his obsessive desire to become very wealthy. Shortly after Troppmann left Pantin, his father sent him on a similar errand to Roubaix, a prosperous manufacturing town near Lille. It was during his visit to this town that he made the acquaintance of Jean Kinck. Kinck was a compatriot of Troppmann's, a hard-working, industrious man, who had risen to be the owner of a prosperous business as a manufacturer of spindles for looms. He was devoted to his wife and children.

Troppmann, as soon as he had insinuated himself into the good graces of this happy family, exerted all his powers of persuasion to stimulate Kinck's desire to return to his original home in his native Alsace. Though Troppmann was only twenty-one and Kinck about fifty, the two became very friendly and held long conversations devoted to schemes for acquiring further property in Alsace. Perhaps Troppmann felt that through Kinck he might get rich.

It was about this time that Troppmann uttered the prophecy that he would one day astonish the world. He declared openly his obsession with wealth, and expressed the thought that any means were justified in acquiring it, provided that its owners afterwards made a beneficent use of it in America or some other distant country.

As a result of their frequent talks, Kinck and Troppmann had planned a journey to Alsace. On August 18th Troppmann left Roubaix, carrying in his pocket an itinerary drawn up by Kinck. On the 21st, he arrived at his parents' house at Cernay. The same day he wrote to Kinck, telling him to meet him at the railway station of Bollwiller, a small Alsatian town a few miles northeast of Cernay. Kinck accordingly left Roubaix on the 24th and arrived at Bollwiller about eleven in the morning of the following day. He carried with him a small sum of money and a number of blank checks on a banking firm at Roubaix.

Troppmann met him at the station and the two men got into an omnibus which took them to the neighboring village of Soultz, and the travelers walked off quickly in the direction of the village of Wattwiller. From that moment no trace could be found of Jean Kinck, except such as was furnished by the doubtful statements of Troppmann.

On the 25th Troppmann had returned alone to Cernay.

He appeared to be highly excited. He spoke of a man with whom he was involved in an important enterprise, and he spent a good deal of money having good times, including several trips to racetracks.

In the meantime, Madame Kinck was impatiently awaiting news of her husband. On the 27th she received a letter which, though purporting to come from him, was in the handwriting of Troppmann. In this letter Kinck explained that he had met with an accident to his hand that prevented him from holding a pen and was therefore using his friend, Troppmann, as an amanuensis. The letter enclosed a check for 5,500 francs, dated from Guebwiller, August 25th, and signed by Jean Kinck, who directed his wife to cash it at the bank. She was then to send the cash to her husband in a stamped and addressed envelope that was also enclosed. On the 28th Madame Kinck cashed the check and sent off the required sum.

On the 31st Troppmann presented himself at the Guebwiller post office and asked for the envelope containing money, describing himself as Jean Kinck and producing papers to prove his identity. The postmaster distrusted his youthful appearance, whereupon Troppmann stated that he was Jean Kinck, Junior. The postmaster, still unconvinced, confronted Troppmann with one of the relatives of Kinck living at Guebwiller, who declared there was no such person as Jean Kinck, Junior. The postmaster then refused to give up the money. Troppmann, stumped, left the post office to figure out a new plan of operation.

On September 4th he suddenly presented himself at Roubaix, at the home of the Kincks. He informed the family of the refusal of the Guebwiller postmaster to pay out the money. Urgent affairs, he said, had called Jean Kinck to Paris, but he brought them a letter which the former had dictated. It read: "My dear family, the time has come when I must declare to you the business that is occupying me. I have sent Troppmann to receive your registered letter as I am detained in Paris. He will explain how it is I cannot write in my own hand. You must all of you prepare to come to Paris. Don't fear the expense, as Troppmann has given me half a million. I insist on your coming. You, Gustave, must go at once to Guebwiller to drawn out the money. I enclose a power of attorney which you must get signed by the mayor. I send you a check for 500 francs. I have given all the necessary directions to Troppmann which he will explain to you, and you must be sure to do all that he tells you."

The power of attorney and the check did not accompany the letter, but Troppmann said that they would arrive by the next mail. He made Madame Kinck and her eldest son promise to carry out his instructions and then he departed. The next day they received the power of attorney and the check, both dated from Paris and purporting to be in the handwriting of Kinck.

On leaving Roubaix, Troppmann had returned to Paris and taken a room at the Northern Railway Hotel, giving his name as Jean Kinck. On September 5th Madame Kinck received a letter from this address, purporting to be signed by her husband. In this letter the directions for her visit to Paris were repeated, and then it said: "Our business is going on very successfully." Madame Kinck did not conceal her uneasiness about her husband's unusual proceedings and his continued inability to use his hand. However, she had full confidence in Troppmann and did implicitly as she was directed.

In accordance with these directions, Gustave had left home for Guebwiller, where he arrived on the 7th and awaited the power of attorney which his mother was to forward him after she had fulfilled the necessary legal formalities.

In the meantime, Gustave was getting tired of waiting at Guebwiller. When at last he received the power of attorney and presented it at the post office, he found that it had not been properly drawn up. So he telegraphed to Paris September 16th to "Jean Kinck, Northern Railway Hotel. Arriving tomorrow." Troppmann met him at the station and took him to the hotel. There he told him to write immediately the following letter to his mother: "September 17th—Just arrived Paris. You must come too. Leave Roubaix 2 P.M. Sunday, and Lille at 4:10, second-class. Bring all papers. Gustave."

This letter sent, Troppmann and young Gustave hurriedly left the hotel. They did not return that night. His companion was never seen again. Previous to the arrival of Gustave, Troppmann had purchased at an ironmonger's a garden shovel and a small pick.

Madame Kinck received Gustave's letter and left Roubaix for Paris on January 19th, accompanied by her five little children, all in high spirits at the prospect of seeing their father again. She decided to take an earlier train, with the result that she arrived some hours before she was expected. She went straight to the Railway Hotel and was told that Monsieur Jean Kinck had gone out. She declined to stay, saying she preferred to wait at the station where her husband would be expecting to meet her. It seems that Troppmann met her instead.

Troppmann seemed to have considered the purchase of gardening implements an indispensable preliminary to welcoming the members of the Kinck family to Paris. On that Sunday he had called at a toolmaker's and bought a pick and shovel of a larger and stronger make than those with which he had greeted Gustave. Later in the evening, at ten minutes to eleven, accompanied by Mrs. Kinck and her five children, Troppmann hailed a cab in front of the Gare du Nord and told the driver to go to the Crossroads. They started and the cabman was struck by the high spirits of the party. Arriving at their destination—a lovely building at the side of the road— the cab stopped.

Troppmann got out with Madame Kinck and the two youngest children. He told the other three to await his return and, followed by the mother and her two little ones, went down a narrow path leading to the fields. During his absence the children prattled with the cabman.

It was a dark night and the wind was high. After about a half hour, Troppmann returned alone. "We have decided to stay the night here, children," he said. He then paid the cabman and, accompanied by the three children, he disappeared for the second time down the narrow pathway. The cabman drove back to Paris. He had heard no sound proceeding from the direction of the fields. But the watchman at a neighboring warehouse thought he could make out, somewhere about midnight, feeble cries of "Mamma! Mamma!" lasting only a short time.

Troppmann did not return to the Railway Hotel until Monday morning, when he hurried to his room, made a rapid change of clothing and left the hotel for good. Some clothes he left behind were found to be stained with blood. That same night he reached Le Havre, where he was arrested, not having the proper papers for passage to America.

There was only one fact needed to prove conclusively that Troppmann was the sole murderer of the entire Kinck family, namely, the discovery of the remains of Jean Kinck. There could now be little doubt that the latter had not disappeared after murdering his wife and children, as Troppmann had alleged, but had himself been the victim of a crime conceived and executed by his friend.

On November 13th, when preparations were already being made to send Troppmann before the Assize Court, the prisoner confessed that he alone had murdered Kinck, his wife and their six children.

"On the 25th of August, last," said Troppmann, "I met

Jean Kinck. After taking some refreshment, we walked to Wattwiller. There we bought a bottle of wine and started for the ruins of the Castle of Herinfluch. I was carrying in my pocket a phial of prussic acid, which I had myself distilled. Taking advantage of a moment when Kinck was looking the other way, I emptied the contents of the phial into the bottle of wine. When we got to the top of the hill, I offered Kinck the wine. He took some, and he dropped like a log. The place was deserted. I dragged the body a few yards away from the road, dug a ditch and burned the body. I had previously emptied the dead man's pockets and taken away all his papers, including two checks and two hundred-franc notes. I then returned to my own people."

After describing the events between the death of Jean Kinck and the arrival of Gustave at Paris, Troppmann continued: "I met Gustave at the station on the night of the 17th. I said I would take him to his father. We went by omnibus as far as La Villette, and then walked to Pantin. When we reached a lonely part of the fields and were walking side by side, I stabbed Gustave in the back with a knife I had bought the day before. Without a cry, Gustave fell on his back and lay absolutely motionless. I don't remember what I did with the knife, but I understand it was found in his neck." He buried Gustave with the help of the pick and shovel which he had purchased that afternoon.

Then followed the account of the murders of Madame Kinck and her children. This boy-monster first stabbed the mother in the back. She had fallen without a cry, and then he struck the two little ones who died no less rapidly. He had then fetched the other three children. But before reaching the place where he was to commit the murders, he made them stop and then took each one separately to join their mother. On some pretext or other, he slipped a kerchief round the neck of each child as they walked along, and as soon as they came to the spot where the mother lay dead, he strangled them.

"I murdered the father," said Troppmann, "to get possession of the money which he said he had in the bank and which would have been paid out to his order. That order I proposed to forge by copying his signature. Having murdered him, it was almost a matter of necessity to me to kill all the rest of the family, since they all knew that Kinck had gone with me to my home."

The truth of this statement was borne out by the discovery on November 25th of the remains of Jean Kinck in a forest near the ruins of Herinfluch. Later Troppmann declared that he had committed the murders in association with three mysterious accomplices. It seems that a letter from his father gave him the first suggestion of such a defense. Troppmann, probably from a desire to mitigate the horror of his crime, adopted the suggestion, but the story was entirely unsupported by any evidence.

Such was the crime of Troppmann—the cold-blooded, wholesale murder of an entire family who welcomed him and made him their friend.

The trial of Troppmann was a sensational event. Every class of Parisian society clamored for details or a glimpse of the young assassin—from the Prince Imperial, a boy of thirteen, one of whose juvenile sketches of Troppmann is reproduced in Dayot's illustrated Album of the Second Empire, down to the workman who bought the accounts of the crime sold in the streets.

So great was the public curiosity that the Minister of the Interior was obliged to issue a circular pointing out that though the Mazas Prison has been besieged by such celebrities as the English ambassador and the Members of the Institute, by doctors and men of science, no one had been allowed to see the archcriminal. But he added by way of consolation that by calling at the entrance to the prison, visitors could see a life-size portrait of Troppmann.

The trial began before the Paris Assize Court on December 28th. Its result was a foregone conclusion; its proceedings shed no new light on the crime. It ended on the 30th of December with the full conviction of the prisoner, and he was condemned to death.

Throughout the trial, Troppmann had obstinately stuck to his story of the accomplices and this, with a plea of insanity, had formed the basis of the eloquent defense that the famous advocate, Lachaud, made on his behalf. The interval between his sentence and his execution, was spent by Troppmann trying to persuade different officials of the prison to bring him the means of suicide; in sending letters to the Empress, begging that his case be reconsidered. When he finally realized that all hope was at an end, he became obstinately silent and morose.

The execution of Troppmann took place at seven o'clock on the morning of January 19, 1870, on the Place de la Roquette, and has been immortalized by the pen of the great Russian novelist, Turgenev. Maxine Du Camp had persuaded him to be present along with Sardou, Albert Wolff, and other celebrities.

The short boyish figure of Troppmann, his fine muscular development and soft baritone voice and dignfied politeness; the way in which he raced along the passage from his cell to the place of execution, taking four steps at a time, at a speed that resembled a flight rather than a procession; the executioner's assistant bungling with gouty fingers as he cut the hair and bound the legs of the prisoner; the momentary shudder of the victim at the sight of the guillotine, to be immediately conquered by self-possession—these and other features of the scene become strangely vivid and human when set down by one of the greatest masters of the analysis of human motive and character.

Turgenev was not alone in being impressed by the

self-possession and dignity of Troppmann. He quotes a remark made by one of his companions. "It seemed to me," said Turgenev's friend, "as though we were in 1794 instead of 1870, as though we were not ordinary citizens escorting to the scaffold a common assassin, but Jacobins hurrying to his execution a *ci-devant* marquis."

That a monstrous criminal should give such an impression of his own superiority over the spectators of his execution may not be an argument against capital punishment, but it is a very strong argument against the publicity of executions. The courteous boy with the dignified bearing proves once again that not the scowl or the sullen look, but the inside of a man's heart, is the barometer of the murderous impulse. If appearance and manner counted, Troppmann would be one of the angels instead of the fiendish destroyer of a family.

XV

LANDRU

OF ALL the criminal types which fascinate the world, it is the "Bluebeard," the mass murderer of women, which the public finds most hypnotically interesting; and of all those Bluebeards, it is Henri Désiré Landru, with his great brown beard—described as a black beard at the time of his arrest and trial—who caught the imagination more intensely than any other killer of this type.

Landru was born in 1869, the son of a stoker at an iron

works. Nothing much is known about his mother. Long before Landru took to murder, when he was still merely a petty and unsuccessful swindler, his father committed suicide because he was heartbroken at his son's conduct. This reveals an unstable element in his psychic make-up, which flamed out most horribly in his son.

Landru seems to have been a shy, undersized lad. He received his education in a religious order. Having a rather sweet voice, he frequently sang in the choir. His manners, even when little more than a child, were gentle, insinuating, subtle. At sixteen, he became a student of mechanical engineering, and showed great enthusiasm for his work. But in spite of this affection for mechanics, he lacked the determination to persist in his studies.

From 1892 to 1894, he did the usual military service, and rose to the rank of sergeant. After leaving the army, he married his mistress by whom he had already had a child. He then obtained a position as a clerk.

Until he was about thirty years old, Landru led a life that was entirely moral. It was not until that time that he committed his first crime, was first convicted in 1900 and sentenced to two years' imprisonment for fraud. From then until 1914 he spent most of his time in prison. He was not exactly fastidious about his thefts—he was not above stealing an old bicycle, and he also tried his luck with a fraudulent financial agency.

His chief line of business was one considered even by the majority of rogues as despicable—the swindling of unprotected middle-aged and elderly middle-class women, mainly widows, anxious to find husbands. Landru got in touch with them through matrimonial advertisements.

His work was painstaking and thorough. He baited his trap with brilliance and precision. Sometimes he posed as a merchant, sometimes as an engineer, sometimes as a chemist or a lawyer; but always as something solid and respectable. He never called himself actor, painter or writer, knowing well that the simple-minded women he wished to attract would in the main belong to a class that regards all artists with suspicion. He wanted to give an impression of permanence and reliability, and his advertisements achieved that result.

His records show that he attempted, usually successfully, to establish connection with 283 women, a formidable figure which roused a huge bellow of laughter when mentioned at the trial. He appealed to these women by impassioned offers of marriage, verbal and written.

During this time, Landru continued to visit his wife and family—he had four children—who regarded him as a good husband and father. He carefully lived a double life, alternately inhabiting the underworld of Paris and returning home to conduct family prayers and dawdle the children on his knee. Also, he was constantly changing their abode and constantly changing his name.

The problem of lonely women is one that the exploiter of women invariably finds fascinating. Their lives are so montonous, so futile, so gloomy that they will rush to the first way of escape, and the woman-victimizer knows that he has only to beckon and they will surely follow. Landru, having had too much experience of the perils of crimes against men, now decided that women would prove a simpler matter.

Coldly, deliberately, he set himself to gain their affections, then to rob and kill them. The whole business was done in good businesslike style, and Landru showed himself the perfect clerk in that he kept a ledger wherein he entered the addresses of his victims and every sou that had been spent in connection with the "courtship."

What was he like physically, this petty pilferer, this formidable assassin? His beard, nose and eyes were his outstanding and arresting features. He was immensely proud of that beard, so proud that at the end, the authorities spared it and it fell with his head into the sawdust. His beard gave its name to its type—a "Landru,"

all such beards came to be nicknamed. There was nothing romantic otherwise in the drab personality of this
frail, undersized baldhead with his unusually thin nose
and his deep-sunk, awesome, magnetic eyes staring far
out into the distance. A witness at the trial said she remembered him well by his "monkey eyes."

There is no doubt, however, that to a certain type of
woman Landru was almost irresistible. They fell for him
at once and violently. That type was the middle-aged
widow. Of his victims, eight were such. Towards them
he showed great psychological finesse. He knew just what
they wanted: they wanted one more romance. They
wanted to be violently stirred from their deathlike leth-
argy. They wanted passionate embraces once again. They
wanted to love, to be loved. They wanted a man, and
if possible a man of superior station to their own.

Landru played on their yearnings with considerable
virtuosity. He wanted domesticity with a charming woman and, turning his "monkey's eyes" on the selected victim: "You are that one." They, in turn, saw in him the
mate of their disconsolate daydreams. He was so gentle
and so generous. Landru could, indeed, bring himself to
spend money when he regarded it as an investment. So
there were gifts of flowers, chocolates, meals in restaurants, and all those little attentions which women appre-
ciate. And what a letter writer he was! His love letters
were full of caressing endearments. The prosecuting
counsel at the trial pointed out that Landru's notebook
recorded that he kept a "date with seven women on one
day."

This merchant of murder was a marvelous liar, and
not only did he lie himself into the hearts of bemused
widows, but he lied himself out of trouble again and
again. In several cases the suspicions of his victims' relatives were lulled by his glib tongue, but not always for
long. In the case of a half dozen of his "fiancées," he had

to employ all his ready assurance to keep their relatives and friends from extending their inquiries.

This most bestial and ruthless of criminals relied on two main themes to quiet suspicion. The first was that his "fiancée" had left him and had gone abroad to very distant parts (the United States or Guatemala, for example); the second, that she was perfectly happy, would be writing very soon and there was no need to worry. Then he disappeared. It is almost incredible that he got away with it for so long.

But he must have had many rebuffs. Certainly many women must have withstood all his blandishments. A French writer, M. Fleuriant-French, in his book, *Le Secret de Landru,* gives one such instance. Landru, it seems, got in touch with one of these *rescapées,* as they were called. She was a Mademoiselle F——, who, being matrimonially inclined, was acustomed to examine the advertisements in the newspapers. One attracted her particularly—it was a typical Landru advertisement—and soon she made the acquaintance of a "Monsieur Lucien Guillet." This was in September, 1918. He hurried her down to his villa in Gambais, and hurriedly asked for a loan of two thousand francs. His financial situation was slightly obscure at the time.

Now, Mademoiselle F—— was no lovelorn derelict, but an astute young woman, who had Landru figured from that moment. She asked for time to think it over and went home. Soon after, Landru appeared at her residence and was greeted as follows: "Am I speaking to Monsieur Guillet or Monsieur Dupot or Monsieur Fremyet?"

A less spontaneous liar than Landru might have been taken aback at this question, but he was equal to it. "Dupot," he explained, was merely the name the local people gave to his villa after a former occupant. "Fremyet" denoted the manager of his Rocroi factory.

"That's too complicated for me," replied Mademoiselle

F—— dryly. "I love simplicity." And "Monsieur Guillet" found himself facing a slammed door.

Landru's first two murders were committed on the person of Madame Cuchet, a middle-aged housekeeper of forty, and her invalid son of sixteen, whom Landru also despatched. In the case of mass murder, it is not always easy to ascertain rigid facts concerning the sequence of crimes.

There are two versions of how Madame Cuchet met Landru who at the time, the spring of 1914, was "Monsieur Diard, engineer." One version states that they met through his matrimonial advertisements. The other, that it was by accident: her son applied at Landru's Malakoff garage for a job. This was probably the correct one.

Madame Cuchet fell in love with her fascinating engineer, and soon announced her engagement and approaching marriage. But if she was a simpleton, her sister and brother-in-law were not. They discovered Landru to be a fraud and persuaded Madame Cuchet to break her engagement to him. But the infatuated woman eventually went back to him. He persuaded her to take a villa in Vernouillet, a village on the outskirts of Paris, and pay six months' rent on it in advance. The stupid creature and her son and Landru arrived at the villa on December 8th.

From that date, nothing more was ever heard of Madame Cuchet and her son.

Landru had robbed her of all her savings by a clever trick. After the murders, he sold part of the furniture in the villa and the episode was ended. Her brother-in-law estimated the value of her resources at thirty thousand francs, but this is probably an exaggeration.

Why did not her relatives persist in their inquiries about her? Chiefly, it seems, because she had broken with them completely. She and her son passed out of their lives when she returned to Landru and they washed their hands of her. However, they referred her disappearance to the police.

Encouraged by the success of his first murders, this Landru soon made the acquaintance—through advertisement—of other widows. He was easily satisfied with little fish. He did not go out of his way to secure big prizes.

His second victim was Madame Laborde-Line, a widow of about forty-six, living in Paris and possessed of a tiny fortune. Little is known of her. She appears to have been a bored simpleton of the Cuchet type, perhaps the most colorless nonentity of all the butcher's victims. With supreme audacity, Landru had adopted the alias "Cuchet." He took her to the villa at Vernouillet and she was never seen again. She had told her landlady that she was deeply in love. Landru secured her assets by forgery and hid her furniture in his garage.

On May 1st, Landru inserted an advertisement in the matrimonial section of the *Journal* which attracted the notice of a Madame Guillin. She was one of the less dreary of the butcher's victims, a widow of fifty-one and in possession of about twenty thousand francs. She replied to the advertisement and presently made the acquaintance of a "Monsieur Petit, a consul, about to take up his post in Australia.

Madame Guillin was a woman of some character, but discontented with her lot. She had ambition and, in all probability, it was the prospect of becoming "Madame Consul," practically the wife of an ambassador in her opinion, a respected and influential figure in some vague foreign place, which attracted her far more than the "consul's" charms. Here was a chance to see the world and be a "somebody."

The "consul" had a car, a charming villa and an appearance of affluence and dignity. How easy to pretend she was in love with him. Incidentally, it is astounding how these women could find Landru's villas attractive, for they were shabby, melancholy habitations, sparsely furnished, with unkempt, ghostly "gardens."

In any case, she stored her furniture and went with Landru to Vernouillet on August 4th. He most certainly killed her that day. He got possession of her furniture, even her false hair, sold her jewelry and, by a complicated and ingenious bit of forgery and manipulation, he secured about fifteen thousand francs from the Bank of France, though it was in Madame Guillin's name. Either Landru was a very expert forger or the bank was somewhat careless.

Within the space of six months, Landru had killed four persons and caused their bodies completely to disappear. And that from an exposed and overlooked little suburban house. But it was time for him to move, for the neighbors were beginning to take rather a curious interest in his activities, and the police were becoming a little inquisitive, also.

He engaged another villa at Gambais, sometimes called the Villa Tric, not far from Paris. It seemed to be the dwelling place of his dreams. Here he could pose as a well-to-do personage, possessing all the comforts of wealth, and at the same time, the loneliness of the village would enable him to dispose of his victims without arousing suspicions. To this villa came a succession of women—the middle-aged, the old, the drab, the disappointed in life.

This scoundrel had now really perfected himself in his art. He must have felt a superior being in a sense; one who had established a complete immunity from that swift transition from crime to punishment. Here he was a fugitive from justice who had got rid of four persons and gleaned a handsome financial reward in the process. He had perfected his method. The future looked full of promise.

Landru now looked about for another "prospect." He examined the possibilities of Madame Héon, a widow living at Ermont, who had replied to one of his advertisements. She was a typical Landru type—lonely, disconsolate, longing for a fresh start in life, a little excitement, a little affection. She was fifty-five. He was still "Monsieur Petit," and, this time, representative of a big Brazilian concern. He took Madame to Gambais on December 8th, and she was never seen again.

Hardly had Madame Héon been destroyed when Landru was paying attention to the widow Collomb, an attractive typist of forty-four. She had about eight thousand francs. She had been living with some man May 1st, 1915, when she read the famous advertisement and thus became acquainted with "Monsieur Fremyet," director of a Montmartre factory. Landru recognized that she was of a type superior to his usual contacts, and therefore required different treatment. He must be the grave, cultivated gentleman who showed women the greatest consideration. She must be delicately flattered. This approach was entirely successful and madame was attracted.

This was in the summer of 1916. She introduced him to her family as her fiancé. Her mother did not like the "prosperous businessman." He replied to her questions evasively, and she tried to break the engagement. It seems that persons of intelligence instinctively mistrusted Landru. But nothing her mother could say or do could lessen Madame Collomb's infatuation, and she became his mistress. He got her down to Gambais on December 27th, and nothing more was heard of her. Her relatives tried to get in touch with her, and when they failed, began that search for her which eventually helped to end the butcher's career. But in the meantime, he had secured her money and her furniture.

With the profits that had accrued from his enterprise in murder, Landru became comparatively well-to-do, and he hired an expensive flat in the Rue Rochechouart in Paris, where he lived on a fashionable scale.

The next case represents one of the great puzzles in *l'affaire* Landru. It concerns a certain Andrée Babelay, a servant girl in the employ of a palmist, Madame Vidal. Andrée was nineteen, stupid, but not unattractive. She hadn't a sou in the world apparently. Landru picked her up in January, 1917, made up to her, got "engaged" to her, and took her to Gambais on March 29th. He undoubtedly murdered her that night. Why?

There are three possibilities. In one French study of Landru, there is the following story: Andrée was a vain, unscrupulous little creature. It was her habit to borrow her mistress's jewels on special occasions and wear them. Some time after meeting Landru, she borrowed them for an evening out with him. They glittered and so did Landru's eyes when he saw them. There were a fine collar of pearls and some valuable rings. Soon after, she left the palmist and went to live with Landru. One day he expressed surprise that she no longer wore her jewels. Hoping to fool him, she bought a few cheap trinkets and showed them to him in a fancy case. He took her to Gambais, found out the deception, and in a frenzy of rage at having been fooled, he killed her.

There are certain weaknesses in this story. First, Landru knew Andrée's circumstances. Could he expect a little slavey to possess expensive jewelry? Again, Madame Vidal, the palmist, must have been very negligent to allow her jewels to be borrowed. Then, again, Andrée must have been incredibly naive to imagine that Landru could possibly be deceived into believing that some cheap imitation trinkets were the valuable jewels he had seen before. The tale does not ring true.

The accepted explanation is that Landru originally had no intention of killing Andrée; he wanted her as a young, attractive mistress. But one day at Gambais her curiosity led her to pry into the contents of a receptacle which contained papers and other things belonging to his earlier victims. Realizing the danger of this discovery, Landru killed her to safeguard himself. There is confirmation of this explanation in something which Landru said at his trial, one of his greatest gaffes.

Landru had been asked why he kept Andrée's birth certificate and identity papers. He replied: "If I kept these papers, it's because she would not want them seen by her friends."

"Then tell me, you have some papers of somebody else—papers she might have seen in a little casket?"

"I must admit there were some of my papers there also."

It is said that both the counsel for the defense and prosecution were stupefied by this appalling indiscretion. "Ah!" said the President of the Court. "You say Andrée Babelay discovered some compromising papers which must have upset you terribly. So it was for that reason you made her disappear!" Landru tried to stammer out some reply.

The third explanation was that Landru was a sadist and enjoyed killing. Most mass murderers have derived a certain sensual satisfaction, a feeling of power, from the mere act of slaying, especially women. Yet Landru killed two other women, from whom he got practically nothing. But apparently, he did get *something*.

And now it was Madame Buisson's turn. Hers was the usual story: a widow of forty-four with a few thousand francs, longing to remarry, a student of matrimonial columns. She fell in love with Landru. He kept her in tow for nearly two years. She became his mistress, handed over to him the administration of her small estate—and she evaporated on August 19, 1917.

Landru next turned his eyes on Madame Jaume, a devout Catholic, aged about thirty-eight and separated from her husband. Her religious scruples had so far prevented her from obtaining a divorce. She worked as a seamstress and was a quiet, most respectable woman. Then what did she see in Landru, one asks. It seems it was loneliness all over again. The accounts of her meeting and dealings with him are contradictory and confused. At any rate, it is indisputable that she met him May 11, 1917. He was "Monsieur Guillet, engineer," again. She possessed sixteen francs and some rather good furniture. One story goes that when she refused to become his mistress, he declared that he was also a devout believer and that through a friend of his, an immediate annulment of her marriage at Rome was to be obtained from the Archbishop of Paris.

On the strength of that, she paid her first visit to Gambais in September, was pleased with it, and soon after that she promised to marry "Monsieur Guillet," if the annulment was successful. Again they went together by train to Gambais, Landru taking one single and one return ticket. This also—to his eventual chagrin—he entered into his litle notebook. That was the last appearance on earth of Madame Jaume. He secured her money and sold the furniture.

There were other "fiancées," other murders, but Landru, meanwhile, in 1917, had set up house with one woman of his chance friends for whom he appears to have had a genuine affection. He had picked her up on the street with her companion to whom she was engaged. She was younger than the others and moderately good-looking. She combined the odd professions of third-rate cabaret singer and assistant in a furrier's shop. To this girl, Fernande Segret, Landru was apparently generous, spending money on her with an open-handedness that was a new experience for him.

Fernande was impressed by the evidences of wealth "Monsieur Guillet," the engineer, produced. He persuaded her to throw over her fiancé and she did. She was never really in love with Landru. But we have the charming spectacle of Landru in love.

Fernande describes an occasion at the home of her parents when Landru was the life and soul of the party.

According to her, he entranced the company with his interminable joviality; he made the most "wonderful puns." He had a certain gift of repartee. But his claim to wit evaporates as completely as the bodies of his "fiancées." He was ready-tongued up to a point, but nothing more.

At the trial, where Fernande gave evidence, after an appropriate but shortlived display of emotion, she settled down with demure delight in the limelight and regarded Landru with an intent and mocking smile. It is said he never once glanced in her direction.

Landru had had a very long run of luck, but the end was now at hand. Taking every sort of risk, disdaining disguises, going his way boldly in Paris and in the country, it is probable that Landru had come to the point reached by many murderers when they foolishly imagine that they are protected by some mystic power. It is this effrontery, this overconfidence, that has brought about the downfall of many criminals.

Had Landru been more careful—had he avoided the public places—all might have been well for him. But, wrapped in a heavy coat of egotistical confidence, he went wherever he chose. He might have anticipated that some day he must come in contact with friends or relatives of his victims—people who might recognize him —and demand of him what had happened to their mothers, sisters, friends.

And that is precisely what did happen on April 12, 1919. On that day, Landru was making a purchase of a tea set for Fernande Segret in a china shop in the Rue de Rivoli, when he was seen and recognized by a Mademoiselle Lacoste, whose sister, Madame Pascal, had disappeared after a short acquaintance with the murderer. By a remarkable coincidence, Mlle. Lacoste had a friend who was a sister of the Madame Collomba whose death was also brought about by Landru. When Mlle. Lacoste described the mysterious bearded person to her friend, the latter immediately recalled the facts concerning her sister's disappearance. The fact that two women had vanished thus, after making the acquaintance of the one man, seemed to both women sufficient grounds for a visit to the police.

The police records were consulted and very soon the identity of the little man in the china shop in the Rue de Rivoli was established. Here was the Henri Désiré Landru who, under a dozen false names, had long since been a person known to the police as a professional criminal, though until now he had not been wanted on a capital charge.

The police lost no time in getting to work. Very soon they had discovered the whereabouts of the scoundrel in the Rue Rochechouart, where he was now known as Monsieur Guillet. The flat was raided, Landru was arrested as he was sitting down to a meal, and the place was searched with the thoroughness which French officials invariably display. Hidden in drawers and desks were many documents, and the famous notebook was one of them.

It must be recognized that Landru was a model of method. The police found the names of 283 women among his papers, and it is said that they traced all but ten mentioned in his notebook. He is supposed to have entered even the hours of death.

It is said that many women used to visit Landru, and French writers hinted darkly at many things. It is certain that Landru had affairs with other women, but did he murder them? There is no particle of truth that he ever killed any but ten, and that he killed them is overwhelmingly certain.

Landru, on being arrested, made no resistance. The professional criminal is a fatalist and rarely shows fight. When his time has come, he is frequently resigned.

The police took both Landru and Fernande to the Bureau of the Garde Mobile. Fernande was released almost at once, for there was no evidence whatsoever against her.

The first remarks made by suspected persons on arrest are often highly significant. They nearly always betray themselves. In some cases they are altogether too phlegmatic, almost resigned. In others, their protestations are unconvincing and soon fizzle out. Sometimes they blurt out those preoccupations to which their crimes have given birth. It was so with Landru. He did not protest his innocence; he did not attempt to show surprise. But he made articulate what must have plagued his mind a thousand times—the horror of the guillotine.

"Oh!" cried Landru. "Fancy accusing me of being an assassin. That's too much. For it could mean a man's head!" A very revealing remark.

To him, in whom there was no pity, no remorse, who merely regarded the murder of one woman as the prelude to the murder of another, there must have always been the shadow of a horrid engine before his eye; and in his ears, the rattle of a falling knife. That one remark that his head was in peril, betrayed his guilt.

From that time till his execution, almost three years later, he never again gave himself impulsively away. Although he must have realized that he would have to fight desperately for his life, he had obviously given up the idea of putting up what may be called a positive defense. His dour policy of merely trying to refute, though irritating, was a confession of hopelessness and helplessness, for his was one of the cases where it could be legitimately claimed that the accused had to prove his innocence. He may have thought that if no body was discovered, he could not be convicted of murder, but he had stultified that defense by his refusal to destroy the petty relics of his victims.

Landru's attitude towards his wife and family was a puzzle. He seems to have had some sort of real, permanent affection for poor Madame Landru, and also to have given her enough money to carry on. He was sincerely furious when she was arrested. Whatever she had done, it had been entirely under her husband's domination. She was obviously merely a witless cat's-paw, and she was released after some months in prison. If it were conceivably possible to find a redeeming feature in Landru's character, it might be in his attitude towards his family. At the same time, they were useful to him, and he exploited them ruthlessly. He said, "When I give an order to my children, they obey it without question." Subsequently the family changed its name and were heard of no more. Mme. Landru was finally divorced from him.

Landru's preliminary examination was in May. "You know the charge against you," said the magistrate. "Various ladies all disappeared after telling their friends that they were going away with you."

Landru admitted that he knew the ladies, but declared, "I am a *galant homme,* and I cannot allow you to ask me questions concerning them. If they have disappeared, it has nothing to do with me. It is not for me to say what has become of them. It is for you to make the necessary search. I am innocent, I swear. When you furnish proofs, I will discuss the matter." To most of the questions, the murderer answered only, "I have nothing to say. . . . You charge me with crime. It is for you to prove the crime. I am an innocent man." When it was pointed out to him that all the women whose names appeared in his notebook had disappeared after visiting him, he replied, "This is pure coincidence."

At one time, the judge said to the prisoner, "You look as if a secret weighed heavily on your conscience. What is it? Confide in me."

"Monsieur le judge," replied Landru gravely, "I am heartbroken to think that, thanks to all this scandal, my wife knows that I have been unfaithful to her."

What was the reason, he was asked, that when he took

the ladies to his home, he always, according to his note-book, took one single and one return ticket? Was it not that he knew the return would not be needed because they would never come back? Landru protested in-dignantly. "These ladies were my guests. Return tickets are not available for more than one day. If I had taken return tickets for them, it would have been like saying that I expected them to go back the same night. Such a thing is not done." He met every point with either some mild explanation or with silence. He fought with amazing skill every issue that was raised and fought so cleverly when under magisterial examination and in the courts that his real trial was delayed until near the end of 1921, two and one-half years after he was arrested.

That the majority of the women were killed by Landru is as certain as anything resting on circumstantial evi-dence can be. But to this day it has been impossible to discover how the killing was done, or how the bodies were destroyed. The theory of the police was that the victims were either poisoned or suffocated—but prob-ably poisoned—and that the bodies were dismembered after death and burned in the small stove.

The many temporary residences of Landru—princi-pally the houses of Vernouillet and Gambais—were searched. Detectives dug, wrenched up flooring, but found only ashes and fragments of bones—bones that might have been male or female—with a few teeth. Cer-tain feminine articles such as dresshooks and hairpins were discovered amid the debris, but Landru swore that they formed part of rubbish that was already in the house when he arrived there.

From the moment of his arrest, Landru became the focus of world-wide attention. In Paris his name was on everyone's lips and passed into a phrase: "Bluebeard, the man with a hundred names and a hundred wives." They sang about him in the café chantants and the mu-sic halls, caricatured him in the theaters and made him

the hero of innumerable little droll stories in which the
Parisian delights. France became a battling ground over
his innocence or guilt. Most people were so convinced
that he was guilty that they refused even to argue the
question. A number of women, strangely, regarded him
as a hero, and innumerable love letters poured into his
cell at the Santé Prison.

The trial of Landru took place on November 7, 1921,
at the Palais de Justice in Versailles, where he was
charged with twenty-six crimes of fraud and theft, and
with the murder of ten women and one young man,
whose names were entered in his notebook. Maître Robert Godefroy, famous, gifted and powerful advocate-
general, led for the prosecution. Maître de Moro-Giafieri,
the most brilliant member of the French Criminal Bar,
led for the defense.

Moro-Giafieri had great eloquence, a magnetic personality and a mesmeric power over juries. Utterly fear-
less, he was always ready to undertake the defense of
the most unpopular clients. If anybody could have saved
Landru, it was Moro-Giafieri.

The trial was a great spectacle. Expensive cars blocked
the streets around the courthouse. All classes were there,
but nearly all of them were women—a duchess, famous
actresses, noted courtesans, and ordinary middle-class
housewives. There was not too much space in the court
for the public, for there were two hundred witnesses to
be accommodated, and an army of press reporters and
photographers. The attendants could not keep the
crowds in order. The spectators laughed and jeered and
joked, despite the judge's protests, as though this were
a spectacle for its entertainment. When Landru said that
one lady he was charged with killing loved him as a
mother, there was a roar of laughter. *"Quel type!"* said
the ladies one to another.

Landru, guarded in his dock in the court, seemed a
dignified and decent figure compared with these spec-

tators. He looked smaller, gentler, frailer than people had expected. He was carefully groomed, his beard smoothed, his face ivory-white; and his deep-set eyes, under heavy bushy eyebrows, looked now with wonder, now with disdain, at the crowd hungry for sensation that had come to bait him. The one overwhelming impression that the prisoner gave was a sort of calm contempt for all there, a contempt which soon revealed itself in his comments and speech.

It was clear from the beginning that the trial was to be conducted in anything but a calm, judicial atmosphere. Counsel on both sides were ready to attack one another on the slightest excuse with dramatic fury. Here was a great occasion, with the eyes of the world on them, an occasion to be used to the full.

In his opening statement, the advocate-general turned on the prisoner: "You are guilty, Landru!" Landru's opening statement was a demand for proofs. "For three years I have been in prison and for three years you have leveled odious accusations against me. But you have brought only words, and words are not enough. Show me your proofs. You cannot. I have always maintained my innocence. I still maintain it today." And a little later, he burst out again: "Produce your corpses!" When he was cross-examined, he gave back as good as he received.

He scored more than once with relevant and even witty replies. Asked if he had not had in his possession at one of the houses a book on poisons, he answered at once: "One does not kill people with a book!" "You are an habitual liar, are you not, Landru?" was hurled at him by the counsel, whereupon he answered with a smile: "I am not a lawyer, monsieur!" Sarcasm, humor, bitterness—all these weapons were ready to his lips. Sometimes, he assumed an air of gallantry. "I cannot answer that question," he would say with his hand upon his heart, "because it involves the honor of of a lady.

Do not probe too deeply, monsieur. There are certain secrets connected with women which every man must respect."

On the last morning of the trial, certain ladies being refused admission because the room was already crowded, Landru bowed and said with a smile: 'If any lady would like *my* place, she can have it."

Doctors were called in to give evidence as to the sanity or insanity of the prisoner. One medical witness, who had carefully examined Landru many years previously, when he was in prison, was of the opinion that at that time Landru was an abnormal person, wavering between madness and reason. He was convinced, however, that now Landru was an entirely sane person. His behavior, his control, and the extraordinarily lucid manner in which he defended himself left no room for doubt as to his being entirely sane in the legal sense; that is to say, his mental condition left him responsible for his actions. This view was confirmed by other medical experts.

In the early days of the trial, Landru was the most possessed man in the court. But as the days went on, spectators could not fail to notice how the trial was telling on him, how his face grew whiter, his eyes more sunken, how his voice took on a new note of pain and how, at times, it seemed as though he would collapse before the trial was finished. But the spectators had no pity for him, and at every opportunity they gibed and scoffed.

The advocate-general had a comparatively easy task, when all the evidence was in, to drive his charge home. He denounced Landru, expressed his absolute conviction of the guilt of the "brutal callous monster," and demanded the death sentence. But the work before the defense counsel, Moro-Giafieri, was more difficult because his task was as hopeless as his rival's had been simple. But he nevertheless waged his case with amazing skill. (We are told that by this time he was as much convinced of Landru's guilt as was the advocate-general.) He laughed at the absence of direct proof. They could not produce a corpse and without a corpse there could be no murder charge.

He was ready to admit that Landru had had dealings with women. But it was not murder, it was white-slave trafficking—that had been his means of livelihood. The women mentioned had been spirited away to the brothels of South America. "A very bad man, certainly," he said, "but not a murderer." This brought smiles from the jury and derisive laughter from the spectators in view of the fact that persons who export women for brothels do not select unattractive, middle-aged widows and retired courtesans.

Moro-Giafieri's eloquence failed to prevent a verdict of guilty. At 7:30 P.M., the jury retired. They returned after being absent an hour and a half. Landru was found guilty on all indictments except two, these two being in connection with minor frauds. Sentence of death was then passed on Landru.

Moro-Giafieri appealed the case. It came before the Supreme Court, February 1st, but was, of course, rejected. A final appeal to the President of the Republic at the end of that month was also set aside. Three years had now passed since the arrest of Landru and he still contiuned to avow his innocence.

But Landru was finished. From the time of sentence till his execution, he hardly slept and he had to be almost forcibly fed. A strange, sudden sensitivity for a man who could embrace a woman at one moment, and kill her coldly and most brutally while she was sleeping in his arms, the next.

Landru had nothing to do with men. He seems not to have had even one male acquaintance. It was women, women, women! And forever in his head a murderous scheme against them. And to go quietly to sleep at Gambais with a strangled woman's body in the cupboard by his side, and to have been prepared to do just that same thing over and over again till he died.

His last morning came February 25th. Thousands of Parisians and people from all over France were craving to witness the last horrible scene. But to the chagrin of these pleasure seekers, the authorities had determined that this execution should be private, though a certain number of reporters were permitted to view it. The area around the Versailles prison was closed and houses overlooking the scene were uncermoniously cleared of their occupants. Strong forces of troops and police kept everyone away.

At 5:30 Landru awoke for the last time. When the priest asked him to accept absolution, he waved him aside, saying that he had no use for such ceremonies. Beside him, in the procession to the guillotine, marched his faithful counsel, Moro-Giafieri, and a few seconds before his end, Landru thanked the barrister for what he had done on his behalf. All was done very quickly, very neatly. The body was guided forward on the plank, the knife crashed and fell.

The man who had led lonely, affection-starved women to their doom had come face to face with his own vast loneliness.